Manipulation

MANIPULATION

Theory and Practice

Edited by

CHRISTIAN COONS

MICHAEL WEBER

OXFORD
UNIVERSITY PRESS

Oxford University Press is a department of the University of
Oxford. It furthers the University's objective of excellence in research,
scholarship, and education by publishing worldwide.

Oxford   New York
Auckland   Cape Town   Dar es Salaam   Hong Kong   Karachi
Kuala Lumpur   Madrid   Melbourne   Mexico City   Nairobi
New Delhi   Shanghai   Taipei   Toronto

With offices in
Argentina   Austria   Brazil   Chile   Czech Republic   France   Greece
Guatemala   Hungary   Italy   Japan   Poland   Portugal   Singapore
South Korea   Switzerland   Thailand   Turkey   Ukraine   Vietnam

Oxford is a registered trademark of Oxford University Press
in the UK and certain other countries.

Published in the United States of America by
Oxford University Press
198 Madison Avenue, New York, NY 10016

© Oxford University Press 2014

Library of Congress Cataloging-in-Publication Data
Manipulation : theory and practice / edited by Christian Coons and Michael Weber.
pages cm
Includes bibliographical references and index.
ISBN 978-0-19-933821-4 (pbk. : alk paper) — ISBN 978-0-19-933820-7 (hardcover :
alk paper)   1. Authority.   2. Manipulative behavior.   3. Control (Psychology)   I. Coons,
Christian, editor of compilation.
BJ1458.5.M36 2014
177—dc23
2013046992

9 8 7 6 5 4 3 2 1
Printed in the United States of America
on acid-free paper

Contents

Contributors

Anne Barnhill is an Assistant Professor in the Department of Medical Ethics and Health Policy at the University of Pennsylvania. She is a philosopher and bioethicist. Her philosophical interests include the ethics of personal relationships, sexual ethics, and the ethics of food.

Marcia Baron is Rudy Professor of Philosophy at Indiana University and Professor of Moral Philosophy at the University of St. Andrews. Her publications include *Kantian Ethics Almost without Apology* (1995), *Three Methods of Ethics: A Debate*, co-authored with Philip Pettit and Michael Slote (1997), "The Ticking Bomb Hypothetical" (2013), "Rape, Seduction, Purity and Shame in *Tess of the d'Urbervilles*" (2013), "Gender Issues in the Criminal Law" (2011), and "Self-Defense: The Imminence Requirement" (2011).

J.S. Blumenthal-Barby is an Assistant Professor in the Center for Medical Ethics and Health Policy at Baylor College of Medicine, with an Adjunct Appointment in the Department of Philosophy at Rice University, and a Greenwall Faculty Scholar in Bioethics. Her publications focus on libertarian paternalism, choice architecture, and the ethics of influencing and shaping people's decisions and behaviors in various contexts.

Eric M. Cave is Professor of Philosophy at Arkansas State University, in Jonesboro, Arkansas. He has published a book on rationality and the sense of justice, *Preferring Justice*, as well as articles on religious belief, the sense of justice, preference change, expected utility theory, pluralism, marriage, manipulation, and cohabitation. At this time, he is at work trying to sort out the nature and moral status of sexual seduction.

Michael Cholbi is Professor of Philosophy at California State Polytechnic University, Pomona. He has written extensively on the ethics of suicide and is presently conducting research on Kantian ethics, paternalism, and the ethics of grief. He is the editor of *Teaching Philosophy*.

Moti Gorin is a Postdoctoral Fellow in Advanced Biomedical Ethics in the Department of Medical Ethics and Health Policy at the University of Pennsylvania. His primary interests lie at the intersection of ethical theory, bioethics, social and political philosophy, and moral psychology.

Todd R. Long is Associate Professor in the Philosophy Department at California Polytechnic State University. His work on epistemic justification, the epistemology of religious belief, and the metaphysics of free will and moral responsibility has been published in journals such as *Philosophical Studies* and *Religious Studies*, and in collections from MIT Press and Oxford University Press. He enjoys family outings, making wine with colleagues, and managing the world's greatest fantasy baseball team.

Kate Manne is an Assistant Professor of philosophy at Cornell University. She specializes in moral philosophy. She joined the Cornell department in 2013, having spent two years as a junior fellow at the Harvard Society of Fellows, after graduating from MIT.

Claudia Mills is Associate Professor of Philosophy at the University of Colorado at Boulder, specializing in ethics and social and political philosophy. She has published a number of articles about manipulation in various policy contexts, such as manipulation in politics and manipulative efforts to shape reproductive choices. Her recent work focuses on philosophical and ethical themes in children's literature, as she is also the author of fifty books for children.

Allen W. Wood is Ruth Norman Halls Professor at Indiana University, Bloomington, and Ward W. and Priscilla B. Woods Professor emeritus at Stanford University. His B.A. is from Reed College, and his Ph.D. is from Yale University. In addition to Indiana and Stanford, he has held professorships at Cornell University and Yale University, and visiting appointments at the University of Michigan, University of California at San Diego, and Oxford University, the latter where he was Isaiah Berlin Visiting Professor in 2005. He is author of eleven books and editor or translator of twelve others, mainly in the areas of Kant and German idealism, and moral and political philosophy.

Manipulation

INTRODUCTION

Manipulation

INVESTIGATING THE CORE CONCEPT AND ITS MORAL STATUS

Christian Coons and Michael Weber

WE ARE SOCIAL creatures, and, as such, we influence one another in a variety of ways. Some ways are clearly benign, such as when a friend takes our advice or customers respond to a sale, while others are clearly problematic, such as bribery and violence. The historic focus in moral and political philosophy has been on coercive influence—specifically, if, when, and why it is permissible. Far less attention, however, has been paid to a subtler but perhaps more pervasive type of influence, namely manipulation. Manipulation manifests itself in many aspects of life: in advertising, politics, and in both professional and intimate relations. Given this, a more careful look at manipulation and its moral status seems called for. Hence this collection of original essays by leading thinkers on the topic.

Indeed, the question of whether we ought to be concerned about manipulation may be more pressing now than ever before, as new forms of communication—social and mass media—vastly expand opportunities to influence in noncoercive ways, while the burgeoning heuristics and biases research in cognitive science, psychology, and behavioral economics has expanded our ability to influence so much more effectively. These developments surely heighten concerns many already have had. For instance, social critics have long worried about manipulation in advertising. Moderates have argued that the institution of advertising just needs to be "cleaned up"—to root out the most egregious instances of manipulation, such as subliminal advertising. More radical critics think that such tidying up is insufficient because the institution is rotten to the core. In his contribution to this volume, Allen Wood takes up the more radical view. Advertising, he says, is manipulation in its purest and worst possible form. And this applies, he thinks, not just to commercial and political advertising but equally to so-called public service messages that influence people to quit smoking, avoid drugs, stay in school, exercise more, and the like. Together, he says, these forms of advertising do not just lead us to buy products we don't need or to vote for candidates who don't support our true interests. Advertising "corrupts the root of rational communication...[and] precludes the possibility of any human freedom." As an institution, Wood says, it manipulates people into acting on impulses "arising from what is most contemptible in their nature."[1] The free market itself, Wood claims, similarly manipulates us into acting on our most immediate and self-interested preferences—discounting both our long-term interests and the interests of others. And insofar as it leads to inequalities in wealth and power, he adds, it also robs the freedom of those with less while deceptively preserving the appearance of freedom. On Wood's view, then, manipulation is front and center in some of the deepest and most challenging critiques of modern society.

In his contribution to this volume, Michael Cholbi similarly suggests that manipulation is at the heart of some of our deepest social problems. In particular, he argues that the persistence of poverty can be explained at least in part by the fact that the poor suffer "ego depletion," which makes them more vulnerable to manipulative victimization.

Whether advertising is as bad as Wood thinks or a more moderate position makes sense will depend on answering some basic questions about advertising and manipulation. Is all advertising manipulative? Is all manipulative advertising morally objectionable? In sum, can some advertising be benign? Similar questions arise in a different context: romantic relationships and seduction. In this context, people influence one another in a variety of ways. Some are clearly morally objectionable, such as cases of what Eric Cave, in his contribution to this volume, calls

---

1. This is part of Wood's argument that there can be manipulation without a manipulator, just as there can be coercion without a coercer. In her essay in this volume, Marcia Baron argues against Wood on this point.

"unsavory seduction." His example involves psychological manipulation that "anchors" the target's remembered feelings of sexual attraction to various gestures and touches that the manipulator then performs to link those feelings to himself. What makes seduction unsavory, on his view, is that it is manipulative.

But is all seduction manipulative? Is some manipulative seduction nonetheless benign? If so, why? Cave addresses these questions in detail, while other contributors to this volume discuss everyday examples of it, such as flirting and wearing perfume or cologne. These practices are widely accepted as morally unproblematic. But are they? If so, is it because they are not manipulative, or because they are benign instances of manipulation? In the context of sexual morality, considerable attention has been given to coercion—to rape and to the nature of consent. But as this brief discussion suggests, there are also important—perhaps more complicated—questions having to do with manipulation.

As noted above, recent developments have expanded the opportunities to effectively influence noncoercively en masse—not just in how many people we can reach and where but also in how effective the efforts can be. Social psychological research is revealing biases to exploit, while our recorded online activities permit special attempts to influence us—efforts tailored just for us.[2] But perhaps the news is not all bad—perhaps these recent developments are a boon as much as a threat. For if manipulation can be benign, or at least morally less problematic than coercion, then perhaps we can make things better by implementing broadly manipulative public policies or procedures—where otherwise coercion would be required—along the lines suggested in Richard Thaler and Cass Sunstein's influential best-seller *Nudge: Improving Decisions About Health, Wealth and Happiness*.[3] Whether this is true or not will depend on the moral status of manipulation.

---

2. Patrick Todd, "Manipulation," in *The International Encyclopedia of Ethics*, ed. H. LaFollette (Oxford: Blackwell, 2013), 3139–45, suggests that for influence to count as manipulative it must be tailored to the individual target.

3. Richard Thaler and Cass Sunstein, *Nudge: Improving Decisions About Health, Wealth, and Happiness* (New York: Penguin Books, 2008. Thaler and Sunstein, it seems, do not regard the nudges they advocate as manipulative, in which case the moral status of manipulation is not relevant to evaluation of the policies they recommend. Others, however, have made this charge, including D. M. Hausman and B. Welch, "Debate: To Nudge or Not to Nudge," *Journal of Political Philosophy* 18 (2010): 123–36. We briefly discuss the charge in our introduction to *Paternalism: Theory and Practice* (New York: Cambridge University Press, 2013).

So too with advertising: whether the more radical view is warranted will depend at least in part on the moral status of manipulation. A number of essays in this volume address directly the question of manipulation's moral status. They also address questions that are necessary to effectively approach the issue, the most obvious being: What, precisely, is manipulation? After all, one cannot effectively defend a general view of what—if anything—is wrong with manipulation without having an eye to what it is.

I

Even cursory reflection reveals that a wide variety of acts are regarded as manipulative. Speech can sometimes be manipulative, but so too can one's choice of attire. Moreover, manipulation admits of "borderline" cases, cases where we can reasonably disagree about whether an act is manipulative—for example, someone's laughing at another's joke to curry favor, a realtor's use of scented candles for the showing of a house, and even a person's use of perfume and cologne on a date. Manipulation—or, more specifically, manipulative acts—therefore apparently resists easy characterization. Consequently, the project of determining whether there is a morally relevant feature common to all cases of manipulation will be at least as difficult.

However, moral philosophy isn't usually easy, especially in an area in need of more attention. And the mere fact that manipulation's boundaries are "fuzzy" does not entail there are none—and notably, there seems to be some consensus at least about which cases are unclear and which are not. But before discussing the prospects for an analysis of manipulation to help morally assess it, it's worth mentioning two plausible views—two methodological concerns—that suggest this project would not merely be *difficult* but also outright *wrong-headed*.

Consider cases like flattering to get ahead, sulking to get one's way, or maybe even trying to cheer up a depressed friend by feigning delight upon seeing him. The first two seem to be borderline/controversial cases; we'll get a fair bit of disagreement about whether they are, in fact, really manipulation. And the third is in many ways very much like some noncontroversial cases of manipulation; nevertheless, it is something most wouldn't call manipulation. One very plausible diagnosis of what's going on here is that the term 'manipulation' fits only if the act has a particular moral status. More specifically, being manipulative may *entail* a certain kind of moral failure or infelicity rather than explaining or grounding it. So, for instance, in the case of wearing perfume or making small romantic gestures, whether such acts are manipulative depends on whether they are morally problematic. If not, then they are not manipulative. If this is right, then 'manipulation' is an evaluatively "loaded" or "thick" concept.

This view surely seems plausible insofar as calling an act, artifact, or agent manipulative may not be to simply describe it. Indeed, Claudia Mills, who draws on some insights about manipulative action in her fascinating contribution to this volume on *aesthetic manipulation* (what it is for an artwork to be manipulative), argues that artworks can be manipulative only to the extent that they already fail on some standard(s) of aesthetic evaluation. Analogously, one might claim that actions count as manipulation only if they already fail on some standard(s) of moral evaluation. Such views can be formulated more or less strongly, as both Allen Wood and Marcia Baron point out in their contributions to this volume: according to the strongest formulation, manipulative acts are wrong by definition; according to a weaker formulation, manipulation (merely) implies some moral reason to refrain. If manipulation is morally loaded in this way, trying to first identify what manipulation is in order to investigate its moral status makes no sense—there would be no way to independently identify instances of manipulation without begging the very moral questions one seeks to address.

Despite the fact that 'manipulation' clearly has moral connotations, it's much less clear that it has them as a conceptual matter. As Baron points out in her contribution to this volume, while we may use the term 'manipulative' pejoratively when referring to persons, the same is not true when referring to actions. Alan Wood offers an example that illustrates the point: a speaker at a public gathering might be nothing but admired for *skillfully manipulating* an obstreperous heckler into sitting down and listening respectfully. Wood also notes that we often cite being manipulative in our *explanations of why* an act is wrong (e.g., "It was wrong/objectionable *because* you manipulated me"). Whether these explanations are plausible or not, they certainly seem like reasonable things *to say*. But if they are reasonable, then being manipulative is presumably distinct from its moral status—for explanations need to be distinct from what they purport to explain.

Furthermore, while it is sometimes possible to wonder if no acts are really right or wrong, doing so seemingly does not involve wondering whether anyone has ever done something manipulative! Similarly, an act consequentialist seems able to judge whether an act is manipulative without knowing its effects; and, in general, deontologists and consequentialists would seem to largely agree about which acts are manipulative even when they radically diverge on these acts' moral status. If that's so, being manipulative appears to be conceptually distinct from any particular moral status—if manipulation is wrong or morally problematic, it is not so "by definition."

While none of this is proof that manipulation is not morally loaded, it is enough, we hope, to establish that it's not foolish to try to first identify what manipulation is in order to then inquire into its moral status. And, even if it does turn out to be a morally loaded concept or term, it may be useful to proceed as if it were not. Notice that even if manipulation is conceptually wrong or wrong-making, not every act that is wrong or morally problematic is an instance of manipulation—physical assault, for example, is not manipulation. So, loaded or not, it's restricted to a class of actions with a particular character, and it's worth discovering what this character is even if we always designate it morally problematic. Doing so puts us in a position to identify what we actually take to be morally relevant and critically examine whether we should. As Wood emphasizes, treating manipulation as purely descriptive allows us to identify objective facts about such situations or actions that give us good reason for condemning them, rather than relying on nothing but sentiment or intuition to ground our moral judgments.

The second methodological concern is that it is a mistake to think that manipulation has a core character. Traditionally, in developing accounts of manipulation, authors look for necessary and sufficient conditions—the features all and only manipulative acts share. But not all terms or concepts appear to have such features. Wittgenstein famously made this point about games. Perhaps manipulation works similarly—and there simply is no core characteristic(s) one can morally examine. On one view of this type, what's common to all cases of manipulation is not a shared property but, rather, they all bear a resemblance to paradigm cases of manipulation. On this view, borderline cases are those where the resemblance is not clearly adequate or inadequate.[4]

This alternative has a natural appeal. However, it may not be altogether different from the approach of identifying necessary and sufficient conditions. For it is still necessary to identify *in what ways* an act must resemble a paradigm case. Only certain types of resemblance are relevant: if a

---

4. Thanks to Michael McKenna for encouraging us to consider this view.

certain act resembles a paradigm in time and location of its occurrence, say, this is almost surely irrelevant to whether or not it is rightly regarded as a case of manipulation. Moreover, the type of resemblance that's relevant seems to depend on what type of act it is. For example, if we used the same strategy for the act of throwing a baseball, the standards of resemblance would almost exclusively involve overt features of the behavior; but for manipulation, overt features are apparently irrelevant—one in the same behavior can be manipulative in one case and not in another. So it seems that attempting to identify the relevant kinds of resemblance may be much like attempting to identify necessary and sufficient conditions. There still may be an important difference between the two methodologies. For on the alternative methodology, different cases may resemble a paradigm in very different ways such that there is no feature common to all instances (of manipulation). But even here, the proposal is not so different; though no single feature is necessary, a disjunction of features will be.

There is a more radical alternative that entirely rejects the idea that there are necessary and sufficient conditions for an act to count as manipulative. Some diseases are defined—or at least diagnosed—symptomatically: a patient is said to have a certain disease if, out of some number of symptoms he or she has some sufficient number (e.g., 7 of 10, or 5 of 9). On this approach, no symptom is a necessary condition for having the disease. But various subsets (of a certain size) are sufficient. It might be the same with manipulation: to count as a manipulative act, an instance must share a certain number of (relevant) characteristics of a paradigm case, none of which is necessary.

Of course, if manipulation has no distinctive necessary conditions, there is no single feature that could make, or tend to make, all instances of manipulation wrong. Furthermore, it becomes less plausible to claim there is a *basic* moral norm to avoid manipulation. After all, this would effectively be to claim there are fundamental moral rules of the form *Thou shalt not do anything that resembles [x, y, z]*. But the nontraditional models may also offer some *positive* insights here. If there are many ways to be manipulative—even with no overlapping "core"—we can shift our focus to each of these types, helping us to sort the benign, the problematic, and the impermissible types, and the features that make them so. Indeed, we may find, as Jennifer Blumenthal-Barby suggests in her contribution to this volume, that manipulation is associated with many morally problematic features, and all or only some of them may be present in individual cases. These results might cloud the prospects for any single verdict on manipulation's moral status, but provide the nuance required to tackle the specific questions it raises throughout our personal, social, and civic lives.

In her contribution to this volume, Anne Barnhill briefly raises some of these concerns—acknowledging the possibility that 'manipulation' might be a combinatorily vague concept. But she is not ready to abandon the search for a traditional specification of necessary and sufficient conditions. And there are pragmatic and theoretical reasons to share in her optimism. While it would be a mistake to stubbornly insist on the traditional approach, given the lack of attention paid to the concept over the years, there's little reason to declare it a failure yet. What's more, its failure would be the best evidence for the nontraditional alternatives.

With that in mind, what can we say in general about manipulation? Minimally, we can begin by noting that manipulation is a kind of *influence*, one that is characteristically distinct from *coercion*—either in kind or in degree. But, like coercion, manipulation is often, perhaps always, thought to be antithetical to autonomy: the extent to which one is effectively manipulated is an extent to which one can be called "a puppet on a string" or "putty in another's hands." Nevertheless, we miss an essential feature of manipulation if we take these characterizations too strictly, because being manipulated never entails being a fully passive victim or instrument. Rather, the manipulated person *does* something, and does it *voluntarily*—successful manipulation entails some behavior or mental act that is attributable to the manipulated. Todd Long's contribution to this volume is relevant here. Some have thought that manipulation (of information) undermines free will and moral responsibility.[5] Long builds on previous work, arguing that (information) manipulation does not preclude moral responsibility.

While manipulative acts may have these features in common, they don't yet distinguish it or directly speak to its moral status. Perhaps in trying to fill out the characterization, it might be useful to consider some

---

5. Derk Pereboom, *Living Without Free Will* (Cambridge: Cambridge University Press, 2001), makes the most detailed case for this. Here we ought to note an important omission in our volume. Manipulation also plays an important role in current debates about free will and moral responsibility; here we find many examples of manipulation that seem to rob an individual of free will or moral responsibility. Though the examples in that literature (here, Pereboom is probably the most important figure)—often involving direct neurological intervention—are certainly manipulation in some sense of the term, they seem more closely related to *assault* or *invasion* rather than *influence*. Whether there really is a sharp distinction between these types remains to be seen; but in any case, this is a very important and active area of philosophical research that involves manipulation, or something very close to it, that is not specifically addressed in this volume.

of the traditional views about *why* manipulation is supposed to be morally problematic—after all, views about what feature(s) make manipulation wrong will also be views about what it is.

II

In his contribution to this volume, Wood offers a simple answer as to why manipulation is problematic, or at least in need of justification—one that offers a tidy picture of how it is related to coercion. For Wood, coercion and manipulation are continuous, with coercion being more "heavy handed." Coercion "destroy[s] free choice" by rendering all but one option unacceptable, whereas manipulation merely influences choice without removing it. For Thaler and Sunstein, this marks an important moral distinction, for their influential defense of paternalistic nudges—including their famous example of strategically placing healthier items in the cafeteria line—rests crucially on the premise that such nudges are preferable to traditional paternalistic measures, even if sometimes somewhat manipulative, because they leave all options open.

Nevertheless, Wood's picture here, even if correct, raises questions. While non-coercive influence, for Wood and others, is a necessary condition for manipulation, it is not sufficient. Our car purchases, for example, may be influenced by a good price or our friendship with the seller, but barring offers "we cannot refuse," such influence surely is neither coercive nor manipulative. Accordingly, there are at least two questions that must be considered: What demarcates *manipulative* non-coercive influence? And are these features morally significant in a way that might entail that manipulation is sometimes worse than coercion, even though the latter involves a greater restriction on an individual's choice?

Finally, it might be worth taking a step back and asking whether manipulation does, in fact, involve less of a threat to choice. Threats of incarceration, assault, or fines all seem to be more clearly coercive. Yet, individuals sometimes find it rational to ignore this influence. Contrast these with subliminal advertisements and/or cult indoctrinations, as these seem to be paradigmatically manipulative, though they can be much harder to resist—even when one is aware of their influence.

There are a number of proposals about which morally problematic features demarcate manipulation from other kinds of non-coercive influence. But in their contributions to this volume, Moti Gorin and Anne Barnhill powerfully argue that these proposals are questionable. Gorin specifically denies that manipulative influence essentially involves either harm, undermining another's autonomy, deception, or nonrational influence. Gorin's position is provocative, for two general reasons. First, it suggests that either manipulation per se cannot be morally problematic—as the characteristics mentioned above cover the traditional features that make acts morally problematic—or that manipulation involves a unique wrong-making feature that we typically neglect. Second, his case challenges two predominant ways of characterizing manipulation: as a kind of *deceptive* non-coercive influence and as a kind of *nonrational* influence.[6] Because it's so natural to characterize manipulation in these ways, it's worth taking a closer look at the types of cases Gorin thinks reveal that these features are inessential.

Though no one claims manipulation always takes the form of a lie, initially it seems plausible to claim that it involves a kind of "plan" concocted by the manipulator (perhaps even "subconsciously") to get the target to do something, and the plan is hidden from the target; it relies on the manipulator making things seem different from how they are. But it appears that sometimes there is manipulation without any deception. For example, Gorin introduces a case he calls *Off the Wagon*:

Off the Wagon: Wilson and Adams are up for promotion, though only one of them will get the job. Wilson is a recovering alcoholic and Adams sets out to encourage a relapse, intending this to disqualify Wilson for the promotion. Adams consistently drinks alcohol in front of Wilson, offers her alcoholic beverages, vividly describes to her whatever benefits there are to drinking and to drunkenness, and so on, all the while making no secret of his intentions. During a moment of weakness brought on by a particularly difficult and stressful event Adams takes a drink, which leads to more drinks, missed days at work, and an overall decreased ability to meet the demands of her job. When the time comes to announce who will be promoted, Adams is told by her managers that her recent poor performance has made it impossible for them to give her the new job and that they have selected Wilson for the promotion.

---

6. One of the most important and influential accounts of manipulation, advanced by Sarah Buss, is a deception-based account; see "Valuing Autonomy and Respecting Persons: Manipulation, Seduction, and the Basis of Moral Constraints," *Ethics* 115 (January 2005). Thomas Scanlon also appears to hold a view of this sort; see *What We Owe to Each Other* (Cambridge, MA: Belknap, 1998), 298. For the most prominent versions of the nonrational influence approach, see Marcia Baron, "Manipulativeness," *Proceedings and Addresses of the American Philosophical Association* 77, no. 2 (November 2003): 37–54; Patricia Greenspan "The Problem with Manipulation," *American Philosophical Quarterly* 40, no. 2 (April 2003): 155–64; and Eric Cave, "What's Wrong with Motive Manipulation?" *Ethical Theory and Moral Practice* 10, no. 2 (2007): 129–44.

The same point emerges when we think of celebrity endorsements and filling a house with cozy fragrances during an open house.

One diagnosis of what's going on in these cases, and indeed what's going on in all cases of manipulation, is a kind of influence that bypasses or subverts the target's rational capacities. This view is widely held, as Gorin notes, and certainly fits many instances of manipulation. However, it also seems too narrow, because sometimes manipulation engages (only) the target's rational capacities. Gorin provides two plausible examples. In the first, which he calls *Election*, a candidate influences people to vote for him by committing himself to policies he knows voters favor, but does so not because he believes they are the best policies but, instead, because he simply wants to get elected and receive the public attention he desires. The second, which appears in a separate work, is a case Gorin calls *Lucrative Suicide*.[7] In this case, James uses powerful atheistic arguments to get his cousin Jacques, who believes life is not worth living if God doesn't exist, to commit suicide so that he, James, will receive an inheritance.

Robert Noggle's influential approach—defended with minor modification in Barnhill's contribution to this volume and largely endorsed by several of our authors—can avoid some of these counter-examples. On Noggle's view, manipulation is influence that attempts to get the target to stray from (the influencer's) ideals or rational standards for belief, desire, and emotion. In her contribution to this volume, Kate Manne suggests what might seem to be a counter-example to Noggle's view, a case in which a lonely aunt sends expensive gifts to relatives out of a subconscious motive to influence them to feel the guilt *they should feel* (from her point of view) for not visiting her since the death of her husband. The example seems problematic for Noggle's view, on two counts. First, the influence, if effective, will lead them to meet—not stray from—the aunt's ideals or rational standards (for emotions). But Barnhill, in her contribution to this volume, points out that the ideals or rational standards for belief, desire, and emotion apply not just to the belief, desire, or emotion induced but also to the process of acquisition: "Manipulation can make someone fall short of one ideal while causing her to meet another ideal"—in this case, the gifts might prompt the ideal response—guilt; but guilt should be prompted by a moral failing and not a gift. Indeed, Barnhill notes that *paternalistic* manipulation, as a kind, always makes a person's desires or

7. Moti Gorin, "Do Manipulators Always Threaten Rationality?," *American Philosophical Quarterly* 51, no. 1 (January 2014).

motives ideal through a process involving non-ideal emotions, desires, or deliberations. But there's a second way Manne's example is problematic for Noggle: surely the aunt, as one deluded about her own intentions, does not consciously *try* to influence, though Noggle's account requires it.

To discern what's to be learned from this example, it will be useful to return to another example: Gorin's *Lucrative Suicide*. As Gorin points out, James manipulates Jacques into committing suicide by engaging his rational capacities—by presenting rational arguments against theism. But James doesn't really care whether the arguments he presents are good arguments or not. He only cares that they are effective. It just so happens that engaging Jacques's rational capacities is an effective—perhaps the most effective— means of influencing Jacques to atheism and suicide. James, we might say, is indifferent to rationality: it doesn't matter to him whether his influence engages or bypasses his target's rational capacities. But of course he could be similarly indifferent to whether the resulting belief, desire, or emotion is rational—indifferent whether it meets ideals or rational standards. In *Lucrative Suicide*, Gorin doesn't say whether James (the manipulator) takes atheism or committing suicide because god doesn't exist to be reasonable or not. But whether he does or not seems to make no difference to whether or not this is an instance of manipulation. Surely the argument could be rational from James's point of view (and he hasn't committed suicide himself only because of weakness of will). What makes it manipulative is that it doesn't matter to James whether atheism is rational, or whether it is rational to commit suicide because life has no point if God doesn't exist. It might just so happen that the beliefs, desires, and emotions that James wants to induce in Jacques are rational, just as it just so happens to be the case that the best means for inducing them engage his (Jacques's) rational capacities.

So the problem with Noggle's definition is that it requires that manipulation involve an attempt to in some way make the target fail to meet rational standards (for belief, desire, or emotion). What Gorin's example of *Lucrative Suicide* really suggests is that there can be manipulation even if *both* the means of influence and the end—the desired resultant belief, desire, or emotion—meet rational standards; what is crucial is that the manipulator be indifferent to the rationality of both the means and the end.[8] Similarly,

---

8. In footnote 28, Gorin complains that, among other things, Noggle's view cannot account for paternalistic manipulation. As noted above, however, Barnhill shows that Noggle's view can account for paternalistic motivation. We obviously think that Gorin's most powerful objection to Noggle is elsewhere.

Manne's vivid depiction of the subconsciously manipulative aunt isn't a description of someone who adopts some conscious intention—a "manipulative" intention. Instead, the hallmark is in something *missing*—the influence she intends (consciously or not) is not sensitive to whether it would meet her own standards for belief, desire, or emotion.

What emerges from reflection on existing views and the criticisms leveled by authors in this volume, then, is that manipulation may be best understood as non-coercive influence wherein the influencer has no regard for whether the influence *makes sense* to the manipulator were he or she the person being influenced. This characterization is similar to Gorin's own; perhaps it is just a reformulation or natural extension of it. Whatever the case, it seems very promising insofar as it handles new and interesting cases raised by authors in this volume that make serious trouble for the traditionally most widely accepted theories of manipulation.

Nevertheless, this account probably deserves further reflection. Note that according to this view, if a person is globally and thoroughly manipulative—always being indifferent to the rationality of the influence he exerts—then any time he non-coercively influences he manipulates. While this seems implausible, the approach may be on the right track and, as such, reveals something interesting about the nature of manipulation; namely, that its nature isn't reflected in the intrinsic "parts" of the act (the relevant behaviors, intentions, means, or ends)—indeed, not even in conjunction with the effects or circumstances of its performance. Being an instance of manipulation depends on no *positive* feature of the act or the agent who performs it. Rather, it depends on what the agent does *not* consider or would not consider as relevant to her plans. Admittedly, one may think this is actually an embarrassment to the view. After all, not one of the examples mentioned above *ever* mentions these deeper facts about the relevant agents; rather, they usually advert merely to behaviors and motives. Consequently, it might seem the analysis has become too sophisticated—as manipulation can manifest from motive and behavior alone.

With this objection in mind, a crucial "test case" would be one in which we would ordinarily call it a case of manipulation, but the agent does possess the relevant sensitivity—that is, she is not indifferent to whether her influence would be reasonable were she the one being influenced. Would we then retract our judgment that it's manipulative? If so, then we're on the right track. Consider, then, the case of Bill, who has a policy of always flattering and giving gifts to prospective employers. Bill is aware that this is frowned upon, but he thinks this gives him an even greater edge because his competitors won't do the same. He does not believe his meager overtures function as a bribe, but that they cast him in a more favorable light, though they provide no evidence of his qualifications or skill. Is Bill's policy one of manipulation? It seems so.

But now let's fill out the case a bit more. Bill comes from a culture where prospective employees typically offer gifts and flattery to prospective employers. Bill never internalized this as a norm: he never thought he was *obligated* to do so. Nevertheless, he thinks the practice "makes sense" because flattery and gifts suggest that one will be a better employee—one willing to make sacrifices and treat authorities with honor. For Bill, these qualities are almost as important in an employee as qualifications and skills. And, importantly, if Bill did not sincerely believe these things he would not adopt the policy. So does it still seem that Bill's policy is manipulative? The proposal we've been considering predicts that it is not. And to us, at least, this seems like the right result.

This picture of manipulation—a close cousin of Noggle's account— also may shed some light on manipulation's moral status. For one thing, it may be relevant to Baron's observation that *manipulative* persons may be essentially morally problematic but that manipulative acts are not. After all, the act's being manipulative depends on features of the agent—her indifference to whether she influences in ways she could accept were she the person being influenced. And for this reason, it may be also unclear how manipulation itself could be wrong. Our analysis suggests that being an instance of manipulation does not depend merely on an act's end, means, intention, effects, or even a combination of these features in a given context. And yet we tend to presume that when an act is wrong, it is so in virtue of one or more of these features; given this presumption, actions cannot be wrong because they are manipulative.

On the other hand—though we already presume philosophers with broadly Kantian leanings will be troubled by manipulation—it is remarkable that, on the characterization above, manipulation *essentially* involves traditional Kantian wrong-making features. Notice that on Noggle's view, manipulation, as a kind, involves influencing in ways the influencers could not themselves accept. Thus, on Noggle's view, manipulative acts generally appear to both violate an important variant of the Golden Rule (Do unto others as you could rationally have them do unto you) and involve treating others as a mere means—as beings to be governed by the manipulator and not by norms of rationality. Our final proposal, inspired by Gorin, yields a similar result: manipulation will involve an indifference to whether one treats others these ways and an insensitivity to whether one can accept for oneself the manner in which one influences others. What's more, these features are often taken to be sufficient for an act's wrongness, not just *a reason* to avoid acting these ways.

A full discussion of whether these really are wrong-making features and whether the analysis better grounds an indictment of the manipulative *agent* and not her *acts* would not be appropriate here.[9] Nevertheless, one further point here deserves mention. As Baron notes, manipulation "involves a recklessness, a disregard for the other *qua* agent...a determination to bring about a particular result and a willingness to be very pushy to reach that result." While our analysis concurs here, this is not what's distinctive about manipulation. Someone could meet this description and exclusively use force or coercion. And while coercion also often involves indifference to what is rational for the coerced—when a gunman demands "your money or your life," it matters little to him that it *ex ante* makes no sense for you to hand over your wallet—crucially the instruments of coercion (threats, incarceration, and other penalties) are attempts to alter the context of choice, making it rational for you to comply. In this way, the coercer typically treats the coerced as rational. In fact, coercion depends on the target's being rational, as Thomas Schelling pointed out years ago, for otherwise the threats are of no use.[10] The coercer effectively takes responsibility for why you're to act as he's chosen—you're to do *x* because *he* has done or will do *y*. What's more, there's a sense in which he respects your viewpoint by attempting to fashion the world (forming his intentions, setting up enforcement mechanisms, etc.) such that seeing it accurately makes it rational to do what wants he wants—by the target's own lights. Manipulation generally operates in the opposite way: one tries to influence behavior by altering another's viewpoint (one's beliefs, desires, values, and the feelings that inform them) while being indifferent to whether the alterations reflect what is true or desirable. Perhaps this explains why it's so much more natural to describe the manipulator as "messing with our heads" or as a "puppeteer"

---

9. For careful and extended skepticism, see chapter 9 of Derek Parfit's *On What Matters*, vol. 1 (Oxford: Oxford University Press, 2011).

10. Thomas Schelling, *The Strategy of Conflict* (Cambridge, MA: Harvard University Press, 1980). The comedian Steve Martin (a philosophy major in college) made the same point in a joke, explaining that one can foil a mugger by wetting oneself, or otherwise acting crazy.

Here again, we cannot fully address whether this makes manipulation morally preferable to coercion, or vice versa. But it should at least make us pause when it's quickly assumed that manipulation is on the more benign end of a continuum with coercion. The unusually self-aware and eloquent thug can at least say some things in his own defense that the manipulative "con man" cannot. For example, he could say "I acknowledge and respect your right to your own mind, your right to make your own decisions; but you have no special entitlement to things in it—and certainly no right to prevent me from forming intentions and sharing them with my peers. So, thanks for the wallet; I've done what I can to ensure this was a good choice, even by your own lights." In the end, it seems that we could be ruled by coercion or propaganda, and it's not obvious the latter is the lesser of two evils. While it may be more frustrating and frightening to be ruled by a Genghis Khan (as typically characterized) or Josef Stalin than by a David Koresh or some other cult leader, there may be an important sense—one worth exploring further elsewhere—in which the latter involves a much more regrettable loss of dignity and, perhaps, our very selves.[11]

---

11. The point might be bolstered by comparing manipulation to torture, according to the analysis of David Sussman, "What's Wrong with Torture?" *Philosophy and Public Affairs* 33, no. 1 (2005): 1–33. According to Sussman, what is often most disturbing about torture is that it turns the victim against himself—his own body and mind being the source of his misery. Similarly, it might be thought, what is so disturbing about manipulation is that the target is nonetheless responsible for choosing to do what the manipulator intends him to do and, as such, is a party to his own victimization.

1

Coercion, Manipulation, Exploitation

Allen W. Wood

HUMAN BEINGS ARE social creatures. This means that people are dependent on other people for nearly everything they need in life. That entails, in turn, that they regularly need to get others to do things they need or want them to do—or to refrain from doing things they need them not to do or don't want them to do. (When, in the following, I speak of needing, wanting, and getting other people to do things, I understand also cases where we get them *not* to do something.)

People get others to do what they want in a variety of ways. Some of these are morally unproblematic, at least most of the time. We can get other people to do things, for instance, because these others have a legal obligation to do them. Or they may have (and respond to) a non-coercible moral obligation, or just do it for us out of moral decency. Or we can offer them some inducement sufficient to get them to do what we want: buying and selling, when the buyers and sellers are free and the market is considered fair, falls under this heading. Even if they owe us nothing, and we can offer them nothing in return, we can also ask favors of people and sometimes they freely agree to what we ask.

Other ways that people get others to do things according to their needs or wants are morally problematic. It is one of my theses—not one for which I will argue directly, but one that I believe will emerge in the course of this chapter—that when getting others to do what you want is morally problematic, this is not so much because you are making them worse off (less happy, less satisfied) but, instead, it is nearly always because you are messing with their *freedom*—whether by taking it away, limiting it, usurping it, or subverting it. By 'freedom,' I mean the capacity of a rational human adult to govern his or her life, rather than having it subject to the will of someone else. But now I am getting ahead of myself. So let's back up and start again.

We have a range of concepts to deal with cases in which getting people to do things you want them to do is morally problematic. Two of these concepts are 'coercion' and 'manipulation.' People can be wrongfully coerced to do something for others that they don't want to do, even something they shouldn't have to do (such as turning a purse or wallet over to an armed robber on a dark street). They can be deceived or misled into thinking they owe us something when they don't. We can put them in a position where they find it awkward or embarrassing not to agree to accept a proposal or to do us a favor. Or we may play upon their fears, desires, and weaknesses to get them to do things we want them to do. These are not cases in which they are forced or coerced to act as we want them to act, and we may not be violating any right they have against us (still less any law), but the way we have treated them may still seem morally wrong. My aim in the following discussion is to discuss, and I hope clarify, the concepts of 'coercion' and 'manipulation,' and also to relate them to a third concept belonging to the same family, the concept of 'exploitation.'

Moralized and Non-Moralized Concepts

I have just spoken of "the" concepts of 'coercion,' 'manipulation,' and 'exploitation,' but I should begin by admitting that people may have different concepts corresponding to these words, for which different philosophical accounts might be appropriate, depending on the problems or issues we want to address. My aim here is to explicate these concepts in a way that helps us think critically about cases where getting other people to do things is morally problematic.

One question that is bound to come up in connection with all three concepts is whether to employ what I'll call a 'moralized' version of them. By this I mean an understanding of the concept in which it is taken for granted, as part of the very meaning of the term, that what it refers to is immoral. This is the way 'murder' is understood, for instance, when the term is treated as equivalent to '*wrongful* homicide.' Some acts of homicide may be justifiable, but to call an act 'murder' (when 'murder' is a moralized concept) is to say already that it is wrong. It would be self-contradictory to call a homicide 'murder' unless you are taking it for granted that it is wrong; so that to show that an act is murder, you must first show that it is wrong. Likewise, a moralized version of 'coercion', 'manipulation,' or 'exploitation' would be one that took it to be true, just as part of the meaning of these words, that an act of coercion, manipulation, or exploitation is wrong or immoral.

It is certainly possible to understand these concepts in a moralized way. And some philosophers do. Alan Wertheimer, for example, uses a moralized concept of 'exploitation' in his book *Exploitation*.[1] This is all right if he wants to examine cases that we assume going in are immoral, and to explicate, under the term 'exploitation,' what it is that we consider immoral about them. This usage of 'exploitation' might even enable us to treat problematic or controversial cases—for example, capitalist wage labor—by trying to decide whether they are really cases of 'exploitation' at all (in the sense of the word in which exploitation is, by definition, wrongful or immoral). Kant tends to use moralized concepts—for example, of murder (as *homocidium dolosum*) or lying (as *falsiloquium dolosum*)—in thinking about duties and their application. Not all cases of homicide or false-speaking need be wrongful, but duties prohibiting certain kinds of actions can be thought of as falling under moralized concepts, which it is the agent's task to apply with good practical judgment to a particular set of circumstances. Thus all cases of murder or lying can be regarded as wrong, but whether this case of homicide is a murder, or this case of false-speaking is a lie, might be the point at issue. This is a perfectly defensible way of thinking about general duties and cases that might be exceptions to them. (And it would permit a philosopher to subscribe to unexceptionable moral rules without being guilty of the inflexibility with which Kant is often charged—sometimes *justly* charged, but only here and there, and not systematically or in principle.)

But we may want to look at morally questionable cases in a different way. We may want to begin by trying to argue that capitalist wage labor is exploitative, whatever our initial moral stance on it might be, and then consider arguments that we should come to consider capitalist wage labor as wrongful or objectionable *because* it is exploitative. If we think that moral argument should proceed not merely by invoking our pro- or con- sentiments, or appealing to our unargued intuitions, but instead by identifying objective facts about a situation that give us good reasons for

---

1. Alan Wertheimer, *Exploitation* (Princeton: Princeton University Press, 1999).

condemning or approving certain things, then we would usually do much better to use a non-moralized sense of words like 'coercion,' 'manipulation,' and 'exploitation'—a sense in which these words can be used to refer to such objective facts.

I also think that using all three terms in a moralized sense distorts their common usage in certain ways that may mislead us, since I believe all three are quite commonly applied to behavior we *do not* regard as wrongful or immoral. Thus, in my opinion, people can be *rightfully coerced* (under the law) not to violate the person or property of others; a speaker at a public gathering might be admired for *skillfully manipulating* an obstreperous heckler into sitting down and listening respectfully; and a baseball manager may be congratulated for having *exploited* the base-stealing abilities of his leadoff man. To use the words 'coercion,' 'manipulation,' and 'exploitation' in a non-moralized sense does not, however, commit us to regarding these (or any) actual cases of coercion, manipulation, or exploitation as morally justified. We might use these words in a non-moralized sense while still thinking that coercion, manipulation and exploitation are always wrong (even wrong in the cases just cited). Some people think that abortion is always wrong, but they don't think that this is true simply in virtue of the meaning of 'abortion.' They realize that they are using the word 'abortion' in the very same sense that it is used by people who think abortion is not wrong. This, in fact, is what enables us to use the word 'abortion' in articulating substantive disagreements over whether abortion is always wrong, or sometimes wrong, or never wrong. For the same reason, if we want to think critically about problematic cases of coercion, manipulation, or exploitation, we might do better to use the non-moralized concepts.

Specifically, we do better with non-moralized concepts if we are considering cases where we are quite sure these concepts apply, but unsure, even so, whether we think the behavior is morally objectionable, or if we want to argue that an act is morally objectionable *because* it has the property of being coercive, manipulative, or exploitative. If we use these terms in moralized senses, all we can make of the claim that an act is wrong *because* it is coercive, manipulative, or exploitative is to take that claim as serving to categorize the *kind* of wrong under which (according to our attitudes, intuitions, or independent arguments) we have already decided the act falls. But this is not the only, or the most interesting, meaning of such claims of the form "...wrong *because*...." The most interesting such claims involve saying that an act has the moral property of wrongness because it has the objective, non-moral property of being such-and-such, and that its being such-and-such gives us, under these circumstances, a *reason* for condemning it as wrong.

Coercion

There are a number of different philosophical accounts of what it is to coerce someone. A good survey and discussion of them is provided by Scott Anderson.[2] He points out the ways in which different analyses are designed to treat specific questions—for instance, about the agent's lack of responsibility for coerced actions, the assumed wrongfulness of acts of coercion, the way coercion deprives people of freedom or autonomy (in some relatively thick sense of these terms), or the way that coercion relates to political institutions and the law. Compared to most of these accounts, however, my approach may appear very simple and unsophisticated. It proceeds unashamedly from the standpoint of the person who is coerced, or feels coerced, and the account tries to say when, and why, such a feeling is correct. I should therefore say up front that my account of coercion does not serve very well to settle questions about when coercion releases the agent from responsibility. Nor does it always help us pin the blame on the person who coerces (since as I see it, you may be coerced even if no one coerced you). What this account does, however, is identify cases of coercion as those in which your free choices have been in some way or another restricted, removed, interfered with, usurped, or preempted. These are, in my opinion, the most basic and important issues there are in determining when someone has been coerced, and in what cases the person is being wronged by coercion. Such issues as responsibility for coerced actions, and who (if anybody) is the agent of coercion, can be considered in this framework, but they turn on matters it does not emphasize.

According to the account I develop here, I am coerced to do something when I either do not choose to do it or if, when I do choose to do it, I do it because I have *no acceptable alternative*. I will speak interchangeably of being *coerced, forced,* or *compelled,* taking these terms, whatever the subtle differences in their use, to relate to the same basic concept. (I consider constraint as close to coercion, but think your actions or choices can be

---

2. Scott Anderson, "Coercion," *Stanford Encyclopedia of Philosopy*, edited by Edward N. Zaita. Accessed at http://plato.stanford.edu/archives/win2011/entries/coercion.

constrained even when you still have a plurality of acceptable options.) Consider a few cases where someone is coerced (forced, or compelled). If I am locked in a room, I am coerced (forced, compelled) to remain there because I cannot choose to leave. If I give you my wallet because you point a gun at me and threaten to shoot me if I don't give it to you, then I am coerced (forced, compelled) to give it to you because letting myself be shot is not an acceptable alternative. A mountain climber may be forced (compelled) to attempt an arduous climb up the face of a rock because, owing to a sudden change in the weather or an unanticipated landslide, he correctly regards it as unacceptably risky to take any of the other routes available to him. If you offer me a dangerous, degrading job at very low wages, and my only other option is to see my family starve, then I am forced (compelled, coerced) to take it, because letting my family starve is not an acceptable option. I might be coerced (or forced) not to drive your car away, either because it is locked and I can't get in, or because I fear I will be arrested and prosecuted for the theft, or (even if I am confident I could get away with it) because I regard stealing as wrong, hence unacceptable. If a judge rules in favor of the defendant because he finds that the facts of the case leave him no alternative under the law, then he is forced (or coerced) by the law so to rule. He might say "I have no choice but to rule in favor of the defendant," meaning that to rule any other way would put his ruling at odds with the law, which is unacceptable.

It might be claimed that if all our actions are causally determined, then we have no choices at all, and if we lack free will, then every action of ours is coerced, constrained, or compelled. I am sympathetic to this claim, but prefer not to open that can of worms in this essay. Some people think that even if our actions are causally determined, we still can distinguish cases of coercion or being forced from cases in which we can be called 'free' (call this "compatibilistically free"). For the purposes of this essay, I don't want to take any position on the issues raised by such claims. This goes along with the fact that my account of coercion is not designed to help us decide when people who are forced or coerced to do something are to be held responsible for what they do and when they are not. Even those who think our actions are causally determined, and none of them is free, usually are willing to say that sometimes people are wronged because their *freedom* (in some sense of that word) is wrongfully restricted. My discussion of coercion should be relevant to anyone who is willing to entertain this possibility, whatever he or she may think about issues of free will and responsibility. If someone thinks that the very concepts of right and wrong are illusory, then that person won't be interested in these issues anyway.

What Is an *Acceptable* Alternative?

As these cases are meant to illustrate, the notion of coercion I am explicating here is no clearer than the notion of what is an *acceptable alternative*. I can imagine someone thinking that this makes it so unclear as to render the concept of coercion useless, or at least problematic, in making moral judgments. But we should have known already that the concept is problematic, and we should also accept the fact that even so, the judgment that someone has been coerced is often morally important or even crucial in determining whether some action is wrong or whether someone's rights have been violated. Someone who thinks such determinations can always avoid using problematic concepts, or that it is the task of philosophy to render all moral concepts totally unproblematic before using them to make important judgments, had better stop aspiring to the unattainable and start living in the real world.

Alternatives can be acceptable or unacceptable for a variety of reasons. Some alternatives might be unacceptable because they threaten an evil so extreme that I can't or won't consider them (being shot, letting my family starve), while others might be unacceptable for moral or legal reasons. The standard in all these cases, as I understand it, is not merely subjective. Someone's just feeling that an alternative is unacceptable is not enough to make it unacceptable. Rather, I am supposing there is sometimes an objective fact of the matter that certain alternatives are (or are not) acceptable to a given agent under specific circumstances. The application of the term 'coercion' usually depends on that fact. Agents can be wrong in thinking that an alternative is acceptable or unacceptable.

Kant distinguishes duties of 'right' (*Recht*) from those of 'ethics' (*Ethik*) by saying that the former admit of external coercion (*Zwang*), whereas the latter duties admit only of "inner" (or self-) coercion (or constraint), where agents force themselves to do what they ought through the thought of duty.[3] Ethical duties do sometimes exercise coercion on us, in the sense

---

3. Immanuel Kant, *The Metaphysics of Morals* [1798], in *Practical Philosophy*, edited and translated by Mary J. Gregor (Cambridge: Cambridge University Press, 1996), 6: 219–20, 379.

I mean here, even if there are no external authorities with the ability to punish us for violating them. In the case of Kantian narrow or perfect duties, these would be cases of self-coercion. In cases of wide or meritorious duties, there is also self-constraint—a choice, even where there are a plurality of acceptable options, to act on moral grounds (rational desires and feelings, respect, conscience, love of human beings), even in the face of conflicting inclinations or at least in the absence of any inclination that might motivate doing the meritorious thing. They are cases of 'acting from duty' in the sense Kant uses that term in his famous (and usually misunderstood) discussion.[4] (Kantian moral virtue is the strength of character to give priority to such moral grounds over others in your actions generally, so that even when self-constraint is not needed, they do not play a merely "backup" role in your choice of actions.) Even in the case of external coercion, where all alternatives but one have been rendered unacceptable by the threat of what will happen if the agent takes them, the coercion operates through the agent's choice of the only acceptable alternative over these others. Kant's distinction may correspond roughly (and ignoring some of the subtler features of Kant's theory of merit) to the distinction we make in ordinary life between "the (morally) *right* thing to do" and "a (morally) *good* thing to do." When we say some action is "the right thing to do," we imply that every other alternative is morally *unacceptable*, whereas if it is only "a good thing to do," there might be other actions equally good, some of them perhaps even better. In the first case, we need to *coerce* (or compel) ourselves to do the thing, at least if that is the only way it will get done. But in either case, we might *constrain* ourselves to do the action out of moral considerations (or, as Kant would say, "out of respect for the moral law").

Disputes over whether someone is coerced may turn on what we decide is or is not acceptable for the person under the circumstances. Someone robbing me in my home may say: "If you don't tell me the combination to your safe, then you will force me to kill your child. I will have no other alternative." Here the robber is claiming that my intransigence in the face of his outrageous demand is really a coercive act of mine perpetrated against him. This claim is, of course, outrageously false. A decent person would think that, of course, he has at least one altogether acceptable alternative to killing my child—namely that of leaving my house and

---

4. Immanuel Kant, *Groundwork for the Metaphysics of Morals* [1798], translated by Allen Wood (New Haven: Yale University Press, 2002), 4: 397–99.

abandoning his criminal project of robbing me. As this example shows, moral judgments may sometimes enter significantly into determinations of what is and is not acceptable for the purpose of deciding whether someone is coerced. But I see no reason to think they always do. To regard it as unacceptable to let yourself be killed, for instance, usually does not involve a moral judgment.

Judgments about what makes you worse off relative to some "baseline" (a criterion used in some accounts of coercion) do not seem to me to do a very good job of settling the real issues about when someone is or isn't coerced.[5] Not only is the baseline always up for grabs (for instance, whether it involves moral judgments or only normal expectations), but also, there is always the question: *How much* worse off than the baseline are you being made? If the agent is made worse off relative to the baseline, then that might result in the agent's having no acceptable alternative—but it also might not. Not every harm or disadvantage imposed on an agent—even imposed wrongly or unfairly—results in the agent's being *coerced* to do what would be needed to avoid it.

The basic problem with "worse off relative to a baseline" accounts of coercion is that 'worse off' is a concept relating to *welfare*, while coercion is about *freedom*. Maybe being worse off sometimes amounts to a deprivation of freedom, but not every case of being worse off is a case of being less free, and not every case of being less free is a case of being coerced.

I understand 'coerce' as a success verb: I don't think a person has been coerced, forced, or compelled to do something unless the person actually does it—and moreover had no choice but to do it, either because he had no alternatives or had only unacceptable alternatives. If you threaten me, for instance, with a frivolous lawsuit unless I meet some unjust demand of yours, it might be a quite acceptable alternative for me to contest your lawsuit (which may be irksome to do, but not all that difficult), and in that case you have not in fact coerced me to meet your demand. At most, you can be said to have exerted unfair *pressure* on me—even *coercive* pressure, in the sense that it can certainly be said that you *attempted* to coerce me. But you cannot have succeeded unless I succumb to your threat—and judge the other alternative to be unacceptable. Even then, someone else might correctly judge that I had not really been coerced, if the individual

5. For the best known such account, see Robert Nozick, "Coercion," in *Philosophy, Science, and Method: Essays in Honor of Ernest Nagel*, edited by Sidney Morgenbesser, Patrick Suppes, and Morton White (New York: St. Martin's, 1969).

correctly judges that the option of contesting your frivolous suit was also an acceptable one.

Having your alternatives narrowed does sometimes raise issues about freedom—when this involves having options removed or rendered unacceptable. But the issue there too is always the presence or absence of acceptable options, and not being well off or badly off relative to a baseline. And if you have a plurality of acceptable options left, it still does not constitute coercion. Having your alternatives adversely affected does raise issues about your rights in those cases where worsening the alternatives deprives you of something to which you have a right. But it does not by itself limit your freedom, much less constitute coercion. We will see later that rendering an option less attractive (without either removing it or rendering it unacceptable) is one of the ways of influencing another that falls under the heading of 'manipulation,' which is to be contrasted with coercion.

Agents sometimes—unwisely, even disastrously—choose an unacceptable alternative over an acceptable one. Some agents are also faced with choices (commonly referred to as "tragic" choices) in which no alternative is acceptable. The language of coercion may be used in describing these cases: We can speak of someone's having been "subjected to coercive pressure," even if the agent does not do what this coercion would have forced the agent to do; and we say that the person in a tragic situation was "forced to make an impossible choice." But talk of coercion is most appropriate when the agent has exactly one acceptable alternative and takes it. It is especially appropriate in cases where there are other imaginable alternatives that have been either removed or rendered unacceptable for the agent, whether through circumstances or human agency. This last feature of most coercive situations may be what people really have in mind when they describe coercion in terms of someone's having been "made worse off" relative to an imagined "baseline." But for reasons already given, I do not think that is the right way to think about it: I don't think it's really coercion unless all the alternatives but one have been rendered *unacceptable*.

There may be different *species* of coercion (moral coercion, physical coercion, coercion through bodily restraint, coercion through threats, etc.). But I take them all to be species of coercion in the sense that they limit, remove, or interfere with an agent's *freedom*. The freedom to make choices for yourself, rather than having them made for you, is what I take coercion to be most fundamentally about.

Coercion, Wrongfulness and Responsibility

Clearly, *acts* of coercion (acts that put a person in a position where he is forced, compelled, constrained, coerced) are often wrong. It is wrong for the robber to coerce me to tell him the combination of my safe by threatening to kill my child. But coercion, as I understand it, can also be justified, or even morally required. If a policeman becomes aware of the robbery taking place in my home, then he is forced or coerced (because it is his strict duty as an officer of the law) to apprehend the robber and then, further, to coerce him to desist from his criminal act; the policeman might do this by point-ing a gun at him and leaving him no choice—no acceptable alternative—except to get into the squad car and be taken to jail. We normally think the coercion under which the policeman acts, and the coercion under which the robber acts, are here entirely right and just. Under the circumstances, wrong would occur (the policeman would be acting wrongly, the robber would be permitted to act wrongly) if they were *not* coerced (compelled, forced) to act as they do.

Rousseauians may want to add that the judge and the policeman, in obeying the law and doing their duty, are really only following their own will, and that this kind of rational coercion or self-constraint is not ulti-mately a curtailment of their freedom. That may be correct, but I don't think the deeper Rousseauian point can be made without including the idea that they genuinely are, in a straightforward and literal sense of the terms, coerced or constrained. That's because the deeper point is that although coercion is always a curtailment of freedom, it may also be true that some kinds of freedom may not be possible without coercion. What Rousseau means, after all, is that there are important kinds of freedom available to you *only by way of your being forced*—to be free. I think this is a profound truth, which we reject or neglect at our peril.

Does coercion require a coercer? Marcia Baron has suggested to me in discussion that 'coercion' implies a coercer, and that in many of the cases I regard as falling under coercion, it would be more natural to say that I am forced than that I am coerced. She may be right about these matters of ordinary usage. But in that case, the more interesting concept is the broader one (being forced), and the narrower one (being coerced by someone) should not get as much attention as it does. My agency is lim-ited, preempted, or taken over just as much in cases where I am forced, as she would put it, as it is in cases where I am coerced by someone. For that reason, I am also going to speak (I admit perhaps a bit not idiomatically) of a person being 'coerced' by circumstances, meaning that the individual is forced (compelled) by circumstances.

Many cases where I am forced to make a choice, because no other acceptable choice is available to me, are also cases where someone else, as a result, is in a position to coerce me (in the sense Baron would prefer to use 'coerce'). This is conspicuously true, for instance, in the case where I am forced to take the job you offer me because my only alternative is to see my family starve. This puts you in a position to coerce me in various ways, simply by threatening to fire me. Baron thinks we should also use the term 'coerce' in a moralized way, either as implying wrongness or as implying a moralized "baseline" relative to which a person is or is not said to be coerced. I reject this, for the reasons already stated. I repeat that I do not think there is only one possible approach to notions like coercion. For certain purposes, a moralized concept involving a coercing agent may be superior to the one I am using. I have already stated why I think my approach is the right one to use if we are to raise the basic issues about coercion as the limitation on or pre-emption of free agency.

For these reasons, moreover, I consider it an important thesis, connected to the concept of coercion that I am developing here: that *you can be coerced to do something without there being anyone who coerces you*. The policeman might fear the displeasure of his superiors if he does not arrest the robber, and the judge might fear being reversed by the appeals court. But neither fear, nor the possible agent involved in it, would have to play a role in their correct determination that they have no choice but to do what the law requires. If I am forced to accept the low-paying, dangerous job you offer me, neither you nor anyone else need have made the case that if I do not accept it, then my family will starve. Of course, the terms of my employment will permit *you* (subsequently) to coerce me in various ways, such as by threatening to fire me if I do not comply with your demands. Or my global subjection to your coercion may be part of the labor contract, as in cases of bonded labor. But my choice to accept your initial offer may be a coerced choice simply because I have no acceptable alternative, even if no one coerces me to make that choice.

That there can be cases of coercion without a coercer seems to me important, if we think there are certain ways in which people have a *right* to be free of coercion. Perhaps the state has a *duty* to prevent anyone from being put in a position where he has no acceptable alternative to taking certain kinds of degrading, dangerous, or underpaid employment. In that case, it should not matter whether anyone put the individual in this position. Also, having your family face the prospect of starvation might be seen as an issue only about *their welfare*; but looking at things the way I am suggesting enables us to see that it is just as much an issue about *your freedom*. I think this way of looking at things is the right one. Assumptions about coercion and freedom that blind us to it are responsible for some common and pernicious errors—for instance, that you aren't coerced unless some assignable person coerces you.

Kant holds some doctrines, too seldom appreciated, that help at this point. He thinks that you can violate right (*Recht*), "the right of humanity," without violating the rights of any assignable individual. This is what is really going on in the notorious example of the "murderer at the door." Kant is there considering a category of statement (which he calls a 'declaration'), on whose truthfulness humanity in general is entitled to rely. If you make a lying declaration to the intended murderer, you do not violate his right (since by his wrongful intent he has forfeited it), but you might still be acting wrongfully.[6] Conversely, however, Kant also thinks that your rights can be violated even if no assignable individual violates them. This is the category of "general injustice"; the state may, for instance, have an obligation to tax the rich to support the poor when their poverty itself constitutes a wrong, even if no one has done anything wrongful to deprive them of what is rightfully theirs.[7] Circumstances can force desperately poor women into prostitution under conditions where they are likely to be forcibly raped, injured, or even murdered by pimps or johns; circumstances force desperately poor parents to subject their children to child labor under deplorable conditions; they also force people into labor contracts that submit them, and sometimes even their descendants, into lifelong bondage. I want to consider these to be cases of coercion, even if we can't locate anybody whose intentional agency resulted in people's being so desperately poor that they were forced to do these things. A vital truth, insufficiently appreciated, especially in American society, is that extremes of wealth and poverty raise issues not only of welfare or flourishing but, even more basically, of freedom and servitude.

---

6. I have discussed this issue at length in *Kantian Ethics* (New York: Cambridge University Press, 2008), chap. 14, section 2).

7. See Wood, *Kantian Ethics*, chap. 11, sections 1–2. To acquaint yourself with the kinds of cases that make me want to speak of coercion without an assignable human coercer, see also Debra Satz, *Why Some Things Should Not Be For Sale* (Oxford: Oxford University Press, 2010), chaps. 4–10.

The concept of coercion I am developing may appear to confuse freedom with power, and being coerced with lack of power. There are always going to be endlessly many actions not open to me as long as I am not omnipotent. Notoriously, even an omnipotent being cannot choose both to remain omnipotent and to create a rock it cannot lift. It might seem that the account of coercion I am developing would require us to say such things as that I am *coerced* not to jump to the moon, or square the circle, or be immortal. For here too there seems to be no coercer, but are many things I cannot choose to do. Do we really want to say that I am forced (or coerced) not to do all the endlessly many things that lie beyond my power to do? Or that I might be wronged by lacking the power to do them?

Of course not. But I *do* want to say the following things: that I *have no choice* in any of these matters, that my human condition forces mortality on me, that (leaving spaceships, airplanes, and hot-air balloons out of the story) the law of gravity *compels* me to remain pretty close to the ground, and that the laws of geometry put *constraints* on what figures we can construct and what geometrical operations we can perform. I would speak of these cases pretty much in the same way as I would speak of being forced to stay in the locked room. But let's keep in mind that talk of coercion, constraint, compulsion, or being forced is most natural when there are options open to me which, however, I cannot take because they are *unacceptable.* This is not true of things I merely lack the power to do—jumping to the moon, squaring the circle, or being immune to mortality. For these never were options, and therefore they aren't options I don't (or can't) choose because they are unacceptable. As for the omnipotent being, I think it is true that if this being regards it as unacceptable for it to cease being omnipotent, then it is forced (coerced, compelled) not to create a rock it cannot lift. But unless it does create this rock, it is still omnipotent, and its omnipotence is even constituted in part by the power (which it always has) to create the unliftable rock it chooses not to create.

Some coerced choices (e.g., the policeman's choice to apprehend the robber, the judge's choice to rule for the defendant, even my choice to take the job you offer me) are clearly choices for which the agent is responsible. But some forms of coercion that remove choice (e.g., being locked in the room, assuming I did not choose to be locked in), as well as some coerced choices (e.g., the choice under duress to divulge to the robber the combination to the safe—let's suppose this time that it was someone else's safe), are not anything for which we would hold the agent responsible. As

I have said, my treatment of coercion is not designed to deal with responsibility in cases of coercion. Issues about duress, for example, are very complicated, and far more would need to be said than I can say here in order to deal with the question of when people are, and are not, relieved of responsibility for an action because it was an action to which they had no acceptable alternative.

Manipulation

Being manipulated into doing something is different from being coerced into doing it. The two seem to me to form a kind of continuum, with manipulation occupying the subtler end and coercion occupying the more heavy-handed end. The cases where they might seem to coincide or overlap are really borderline cases, where we are not sure how most suitably to describe the kind of influence under which the agent does the thing. In general, I operate within the following parameters: I don't think you are manipulated into doing something if you do not choose to do it, and you are not coerced into doing it if you had some other acceptable choice. 'Manipulation' refers to a way of interfering with or usurping someone's free agency that does not limit or destroy free choice but, rather, influences it in certain ways that promote the outcome sought by the manipulator. The question is: Which ways of influencing choice constitute manipulation?

This is a difficult question, because manipulation seems to me extremely varied in the forms it takes, and perhaps even less of a natural kind than coercion is. It is one of the strengths of Marcia Baron's APA address "Manipulativeness" that it gives us a taste of the variety of kinds of manipulation there are, the subtly different forms they take, and the equally subtle interplay between the forms.[8]

I take Baron's article to distinguish three basic forms of manipulation:

1. *Deception.* This includes outright lying to those manipulated, including making false promises to them, but also misleading them without actually misrepresenting anything, such as by encouraging false assumptions, or fostering self-deception that is advantageous to the manipulator's

---

8. Marcia Baron, "Manipulativeness," *Proceedings and Addresses of the American Philosophical Association* 77, no. 2 (November 2003).

ends, or getting the manipulated person to "view things differently" or interpret the situation in a light favorable to the manipulator's purposes.[9]

2. *Pressure to acquiesce.* This can involve browbeating, wearing down the other's resistance, and making someone agree to something just to avoid further discomfort or embarrassment. I think that threats, when the harm they threaten falls short of being coercive, should be categorized as this kind of manipulation. Pressure can also take the form of offering inducements, when (as Baron puts it), they give the manipulated person "the wrong sort of reason" for opting in favor of the manipulator's proposals.[10]

3. *Playing upon emotions, emotional needs, or weaknesses of character.* This includes eliciting an emotion with the aim of making use of it. Typical emotions used to manipulate are fear, sympathy, a sense of gratitude toward the manipulator, and feelings of guilt if the manipulated person does not consent to what the manipulator wants. Typical weaknesses of character employed for manipulation are vanity and the need for approval—especially the need for the manipulator's approval.[11] Though Baron does not mention it, another common character flaw through which people can be manipulated is *greed*, which tends to make people exaggerate the value or the importance of some prospective benefit, and to make them willing to take excessive risks when subject to its allure.

Some manipulation makes use of traits or dispositions common to most people, not even necessarily weaknesses, together with situational factors in which these traits come to look like weaknesses. The well-known Milgram experiments, in which a subject is manipulated into administering to someone (what the subject believes are) severe electric shocks, make use of our apparently normal tendency to defer to people in authority, and our reluctance to incur their disapproval.[12] These traits are manipulated through techniques such as hurrying the subject along (offering no time or opportunity for reflection on what is happening) and also the tendency to go down a "slippery slope" (the shocks are increased gradually, so that it

---

9. Baron, "Manipulativeness," 40, 43–44.

10. Baron, "Manipulativeness," 40–43.

11. Baron, "Manipulativeness," 44–45.

12. Stanley Milgram, *Obedience to Authority: An Experimental View* (New York: Harper & Row, 1974).

is hard for the subject to see where things are leading until it is too late).[13] Another obvious situational factor here is *surprise*: I do not think we need to wait for more experimental results to know that the results would be very different if the subjects were told ahead of time that what was about to be tested is their willingness to violate their own moral principles or practice cruelty out of deference to authority.

What do all these tactics, maneuvers, appeals, and stratagems have in common that make us consider them various forms of *manipulation*? This is not a question Baron answers directly, but her characterization of manipulativeness as a vice (in the Aristotelian sense) may offer us a clue. She thinks that what this vice gets wrong is fundamentally:

> *how much to steer others*—and which others, and how, and when, and toward what ends; and more generally, how and when and to whom and for what sorts of ends—to seek to influence others' conduct.... The manipulative person is too ready to think it appropriate—or appropriate for him—to orchestrate things so as to lead others to act as he wants them to; and in those instances where it is not inappropriate to try to engineer such a change, the manipulative person is too ready to employ means that should not be employed.[14]

Manipulativeness, as Baron sees it, is a form of arrogance with regard to the kind and degree of control one seeks to exercise over the choices of others—and, I would add, to bring out the contrast with coercion— over the choices they make when they do have other acceptable alternatives. Manipulation may, however, operate by making these other options less attractive without absolutely removing them or making them unacceptable. This is the main reason why, given the inherently unclear and context-dependent character of questions about what is and is not acceptable, there may be borderline cases where we are not sure whether a person has been coerced or merely manipulated. I think that result is just right; we should draw the distinction between being coerced and merely being manipulated according to whether we regard the alternative as having been made unacceptable or merely made less attractive. The manipulative

---

13. John Sabini and Maury Silver, "Lack of character? Situationism Critiqued," *Ethics* 115 (2005).

14. Baron, "Manipulativeness," 48.

person "steers" the other as a driver steers an automobile. The automobile is already moving through its own internal combustion engine and momentum, but its direction is influenced by the one who steers it. An automobile, of course, does not make choices, and the manipulator steers the person by seeking to influence these choices—but (as Baron puts it) in the "wrong ways."

I think we should not misunderstand this last phrase in a way that would turn our concept of manipulation itself into a moralized concept. That is, we should consider the ways manipulation influences behavior as in some way distinctive—a way that perhaps makes us *tend* to regard them as morally dubious—yet still without treating these ways as by definition morally wrong or bad. For I think there can, even so, be cases of manipulation of which, all things considered, we morally approve. Baron does claim to be considering manipulativeness "in a moralized way."[15] But she at least entertains that alternative view, which holds that "we should be able to say: 'It was manipulative, but was it in any way morally objectionable?'" Despite her Aristotelian approach, which would seem to require a moralized concept of manipulativeness, she is also interested in the controversy generated by some (especially Sarah Buss) who have argued, in Baron's words, that "being manipulative is not as bad as it is made out to be."[16] That interest pulls her, and it should pull her, as I have argued, in the direction of a non-moralized conception of manipulation. But later Baron describes the features that tend to make this behavior acceptable as those "that make what would otherwise be manipulation not be manipulation."[17]

There are two separate issues here: whether certain kinds of behavior are open to objection, and whether 'manipulation' is a moralized notion. A person who approves, or at least condones, behavior Baron would find objectionable because it is manipulative could either say it is manipulative but use the concept in a non-moralized way, and then perhaps go on to argue that it is not objectionable even though it is manipulative; or accept the moralized use of 'manipulative' and deny that the controversial behavior should be called 'manipulative.' I've already given my reasons for preferring the former alternative, at least for my purposes here.

---

15. Since she treats it as a moral vice; see Baron, "Manipulativeness," 39–40.

16. Baron, "Manipulativeness," 39. See also Sarah Buss, "Valuing Autonomy and Respecting Persons: Manipulation, Seduction, and the Basis of Moral Constraints," *Ethics* 115 (January 2005).

17. Baron, "Manipulativeness," 45.

What is characteristic of manipulative behavior, I suggest, is that it influences people's choices in ways that circumvent or subvert their rational decision-making processes, and that undermine or disrupt the ways of choosing that they themselves would critically endorse if they considered the matter in a way that is lucid and free of error. Deception by *flat-out lying* does this in an obvious way. It feeds the person false information, on the basis of which he makes choices the person presumably might not have made if he had known the truth. Other, subtler forms of deception— misleading, encouraging false assumptions, fostering self-deception—do this in more devious ways.

Pressuring gets people to make choices they would not have made if they hadn't been pressured, choices they might later say they should not have made. (And even if they don't say this, they might say it was objectionable to have been pressured into it.) Here it is significant that the "inducements" considered under the heading of "pressuring" offer the person "the wrong sort of reason"—a sort of reason that the person would not endorse on reflection, if behaving rationally and operating with normal, healthy motivations intact.

Appeals to emotions, needs, or character flaws also count as manipulative because they, too, subvert the rational self-government of the person. Such an appeal, as Billie Holiday says of love, can, like a faucet, be turned off and on (by the manipulator), and it also "makes you do things that you know is wrong." "The virtuous person," Baron says, who gets right what the manipulative person gets wrong, "tries to reason with the other, not cajole or trick him into acting differently."[18] But we should not misunderstand this talk about reason, taking it in a too simplistic or one-sided way. We rationalists are nearly always careful to avoid this, but anti-rationalists often do it because it appears to help their (unjust) cause. Not all emotions offer the "wrong sort of reason": although there is a lot of truth in what Billie Holiday says about love, what is done out of love need not be the result of manipulation and is quite often what the person most fully and rationally chooses to do. (Love is a very heterogeneous and multi-faceted emotion.) The main reason we should avoid a moralistic concept of manipulation, in fact, is that people can also be manipulated into doing what is objectively rational, and just what they ought to do. At the same time, this can be manipulation that is as morally objectionable as any other, as

---

18. Baron, "Manipulativeness," 48.

when it is not the manipulator's business to see to it that the other person behaves rationally or does what he ought. Not all appeals to emotion, or even playing on a character defect, need involve manipulation—only those that result in behavior the manipulated agent has good reason to regret, and are encouraged and made use of by a manipulative person for the manipulator's ends.

What manipulation seems always to involve is the circumvention or subversion of a person's capacity for self-government. And this seems to go to the heart of what makes it morally objectionable when it is. But it also explains why manipulation may be morally acceptable in some cases. As Baron points out, manipulative behavior directed toward children is often used in parenting, and may even be an indispensable part of education, as well as of literary style and other forms of art.[19] Manipulation is acceptable in dealing with children because children are not yet fully self-governing beings, so there is less rationality there to circumvent or subvert. Manipulation may be acceptable, or even admirable, when it is used to train the child in good habits, or encourage emotional responses that are conducive to the acquisition of the rational and emotional capacities of a healthy adult. (*Reason* and *emotion* are *not* opposites: emotions—even irrational ones—always have some degree of rational content, and healthy emotions are indispensable vehicles of rationality. We rationalists have always known this; its tediously predictable denial is one of the sad errors of those who reject rationalism.) We object to manipulating people's emotions mainly when we think the manipulation is not being used in their interest, or when we think it is likely to pose an obstacle to their acquisition or exercise of capacities to govern themselves rationally. Even in the acceptable cases, however, we can see why the techniques of manipulation circumvent or subvert rational self-government. They offer people "reasons of the *wrong* sort" even when these reasons are used in the interest of leading them forward, or back, to governing themselves according to "reasons of the *right* sort."

I may not agree with Baron when she suggests that one factor that might justify manipulative behavior is "the worthiness of the end"—at least if her claim is that the worthiness of any end, taken by itself, is sufficient to justify manipulation as a means to it;[20] but I don't think what I am

19. Baron, "Manipulativeness," 45–46.

20. Baron, "Manipulativeness," 46.

objecting to is quite what Baron meant. That's because her example of the worthy end is one where manipulation gets someone to see things (grief over a personal loss) in a better—or at least healthier—light. The end is to benefit the person manipulated, and even to benefit him in the direction of helping him to regain his capacities to take control over his life and lead it in a healthy and happy way. A worthy end might justify manipulation if it steers a child in the direction of self-government, or helps an adult who has left the path of healthy self-government to find his way back. This is why it might be admirable for the public speaker to manipulate the obstreperous heckler into respectful silence. The heckler's behavior may already be less than rational; if it is ill-considered and even discreditable to himself, then the speaker's manipulation may steer him back to a course which a reflective and rationally self-governing person would have followed without needing to be steered.

I also don't think I agree with Baron that manipulation is necessarily made less objectionable if the end is not self-serving on the part of the manipulator.[21] (Again, I am pushing the envelope. Baron does not say it is *necessarily* made less objectionable. I suspect her view is that *sometimes* it could be made less objectionable, and I don't disagree with that.) People can be manipulated in very objectionable ways by arrogant manipulators for ends that do not benefit the manipulators personally at all. People can even be manipulated by officious moralists to do the morally right thing, and this arrogant use of manipulation might be far more reprehensible than any of the petty moral faults of which the same people would otherwise have been guilty. What matters most, I would say, is the way the manipulation undermines and demeans the person manipulated, by violating and disrespecting his rational capacities to choose for himself how to live.

Advertising—and Manipulation Without a Manipulator

Manipulation takes a pervasive form in modern society in the form of *advertising*.[22] Advertisements routinely use many of the techniques of

---

21. Baron, "Manipulativeness," 47.

22. Baron, "Manipulativeness," 44.

manipulation that Baron describes: they lie so blatantly that anyone who believes what they say, or who even entertains it, even against his will, is almost certain to be misled. (No one, on reflection, ever really credits what advertisements say.) But advertisements do not work on us by having what they say actually believed. Advertisements are geared to encourage various forms of self-deception; they frame people's perceptions in ways that are carefully crafted to benefit the interests of the advertiser. Advertisements use constant repetition to wear down our resistance, to reinforce associations at a subrational level, to offer us inducements that are illusory or otherwise "of the wrong sort." Advertisements notoriously appeal to our emotional needs, our vanity, our need for approval, our self-doubt. They infantilize us in order to have their way with us. Even advertisements that manipulate people for what we might think are good ends—to vote for the right candidates, or to give up smoking—do it in bad ways. Advertising never aims to *convince*, only to *persuade*. It corrupts the root of rational communication, precludes the possibility of any free human community.

Baron has suggested to me in discussion that advertisement is not as objectionable as manipulation by friends and acquaintances because, first, no one is really deceived by it, since we do not expect truth from advertisers; and second, because we have no relationship with advertisers, there is no betrayal of trust or destruction of a valuable relationship as may be present when we are manipulated by acquaintances, colleagues, friends, or loved ones.

Her first point would matter only if it meant that advertisement did not work. But of course it does work. It is one of the more notable features of advertising that it regularly succeeds in manipulating us even though we tell ourselves we do not believe it (and perhaps—who knows?—even when we are correct in telling ourselves this). Perhaps advertising manipulates us without relying on deception, but by using other methods (more like pressuring or playing on our weaknesses), or perhaps there is such a thing as being deceived, or acting as if you were (which is just as good from the advertiser's standpoint), even by something you don't consciously or intellectually believe. I find the fact that we are manipulated even without actually being deceived more appalling than reassuring.

As to the second point, it is true that advertising involves no betrayal of trust in a personal relationship, but I find it downright horrifying that our entire social life should be so pervaded by large-scale and entirely impersonal mass manipulation. This seems to me even worse than manipulation by friends or acquaintances. It is terrifying to realize that people routinely permit themselves to be manipulated in this way by complete strangers, without their putting up any organized resistance to it. Baron's reaction itself testifies that we have even come to take it for granted that people will exercise this kind of control over us without our feeling there is even anything (or at least not very much) wrong with it. That is probably the aspect of the situation I find most intolerable.

Advertisers have known for decades (if not for centuries) that people are more easily controlled if we discourage them from thinking for themselves—indeed, from thinking at all—and instead encourage them to act on ill-considered impulses arising from what is most contemptible in their nature. Advertising reckons on our vices and our weaknesses, encouraging and enhancing them. As I've said, I think it does this even when it manipulates us to do something we should do—such as vote for the best candidates or to quit smoking. With calculated precision, advertising makes worse people of us in order to take advantage of us. Advertising is manipulation in its purest (that is to say, its worst) possible form. A world entirely without advertisements, like a world without wars, would be an immeasurably better world than the existing one.

I have argued that coercion does not require a coercer. People can be coerced by circumstances for which no assignable person (or persons) is (are) responsible. It might be wondered whether such a thing can happen with manipulation as well. I think it can. Advertising is a case in point, because it is not merely a practice engaged in by specific advertisers but also a social institution that over time shapes people's habits and preferences in the deplorable ways I have just described.

Moreover, the so-called free market itself is such an institution. Decisions made in the marketplace often have important consequences for society as a whole and for other people (a phenomenon economists call 'externality'). But participants in the market typically lack knowledge of and control over these consequences, and the context in which they make decisions encourages them not to think about the issues raised by these consequences. Thus the market itself, as a social institution, encourages people to make decisions that focus only on their immediate preferences, often their whims and caprices rather than their long-term interests, much less on the good of society or that of of future generations. The market itself, I believe, like advertising, plays a systematic role in manipulating people, encouraging them to focus narrowly on their own lives, and even regarding their own lives, to focus only on the present and the immediate future. It encourages people in the idea that they owe nothing to other people except those (such as their family) with whose interests they are immediately engaged. Through the ways in which it enables and intensifies inequalities of wealth and power, the market affects not only the interests but also the freedom of others, while also making it difficult for individuals to see that it is doing this, and thus creating the appearance of freedom where there is none. I think the way it does all this amounts to a form of manipulation, for which no assignable individual or individuals bear the responsibility.

It was one of the great achievements of Adam Smith's theory of political economy that it showed how in modern society the market shapes individuals who understand themselves as independent agents, capable of the autonomous management of their own lives and who relate to other market actors on terms of formal equality and self-interest rather than personal dependency.[23] He thus helped us to see how what he called "commercial society" educates people for freedom. But the market also has its baleful effects on human freedom, which I fear have been less often appreciated, precisely because the market itself manipulates us so as to conceal them. When we consider this aspect of the way the market shapes us, the term "free market" should always be heard as an oxymoron, not as a pleonasm. Only a society based on markets, and manipulated by advertising, could be one in which so many people regard it as a pleasant and even worthwhile activity to "shop"—to expose themselves to commodities (in a store or online) that they know they do not need, but with the clear expectation that they will come to desire them and be willing to part with money in exchange for them. Is it only an idiosyncratic crotchet of mine that I find this sick and revolting? Or is it that the sickness has become so pervasive that a sane attitude now looks like merely some philosopher's idiosyncratic crotchet?

The ambivalent relation of the modern market economy to human freedom was well appreciated by Hegel.[24] He accepts from Smith and other political economists the idea that the market, and especially the discipline of labor involved in participating in a market economy, involves a uniquely valuable moment of liberation and education (*Bildung*) constituting the kind of subjective freedom that he sees as the greatest glory of modern civil society. But Hegel also sees how the transformation of needs

---

23. On this, see Satz, *Why Some Things,* chaps. 1–2.

24. G. W. F. Hegel, *Elements of the Philosophy of Right,* edited by Allen Wood, translated by H. B. Nisbet (Cambridge, UK: Cambridge University Press, 1991), §§ 189–98, 241–46.

and preferences by the market economy, and the kinds of labor pertaining to modern civil society, and the social inequalities created or reinforced by the market, tend to corrupt people's tastes, degrade their human capacities, and lead to the social wrong involved in extremes of wealth and poverty that is a threat to human freedom and even to the ethical values of civil society itself.

Freedom as Independence of the Will of Others

I hope we are now in a position to see that there is a common theme here, which joins coercion and manipulation and makes them different ends of a continuum. Both involve the way in which you might get others to do the things you want, or things you think good for the agent or for others, by taking advantage of the opportunity to usurp another person's rational self-government and substitute your own choices for it. From this point of view, the value in the name of which we should object to both is what we can call freedom as *non-domination*. This can be distinguished from freedom merely as *non-interference*—the absence of some obstacle (which need not be a humanly created obstacle) to some person or persons doing certain actions. Freedom as non-domination is what some recent writers—Philip Pettit and Quentin Skinner—have called 'republican' (or 'neo-republican') freedom.[25] This is a value highlighted in much of the modern tradition in moral and political philosophy, especially in Locke, Rousseau, Kant, and Fichte.

This is the idea that lies behind Locke's conception of human beings as having a natural right to liberty: "The freedom, then, of man and liberty of acting according to his own will, is grounded on his having reason which is able to instruct him in that law he is to govern himself by, and make him know how far he is left to the freedom of his own will."[26] It is the basis of Rousseau's insistence on equal liberty as basic to the social contract.[27]

---

25. Quentin Skinner, "The Republican Idea of Political Liberty," in *Machiavelli and Republicanism*, edited by Gisela Bock et al., 293–309 (Cambridge: Cambridge University Press, 1999); Philip Pettit, *A Theory of Freedom and Government* (Oxford: Oxford University Press, 1997).

26. John Locke, *Two Treatises of Government* [1689], in *The Works of John Locke, A New Edition Corrected* (London: Thomas Tegg, 1823), 5:6, §63.

27. Jean-Jacques Rousseau, *The Social Contract and Other Later Political Writings* [1762], edited and translated by V. Gourevitch (Cambridge: Cambridge University Press, 1997), 49–51.

Its clearest statement may be in Kant's claim that our sole innate right is the right to freedom: "[I]ndependence from being constrained by another's choice," together with his "universal principle of right"; "Any action is right if it can coexist with everyone's freedom in accordance with universal law, or if on its maxim the freedom of choice of each can coexist with everyone's freedom in accordance with universal law."[28] Another dramatic statement of it is found in Fichte's conception of the "relation of right" as involving reciprocal recognition between persons, and the summons directed by each of us to the other to leave us an external sphere of free action.[29] The basic idea behind this value is that, as rational agents, we have a reason to want our actions to serve our ends rather than ends chosen by others without our sharing them. The philosophers just mentioned think we even have a right to freedom as independence from control by others, at least within the constraints imposed by the fact that others have the same right to this freedom that we have.

Being coerced, as I have developed the notion, does not necessarily involve a loss of *this* kind of freedom, because having no acceptable option does not necessarily involve someone else's having the power to usurp your control over your own actions. This notion of coercion is far too general and capacious for that. But in the real world, being coerced often does put others in a position to control you, depriving you of the choices you need to be self-governing. The employer of a worker who must accept any terms of employment or watch his family starve is in a position to take control of that worker's life. More generally, those who are in a position to coerce others are also in a position to deprive them of the freedom of self-government.

Manipulation, too, more directly (though more subtly) threatens to deprive us of the same freedom. It does not remove our freedom to choose, but it does subvert it. And because it operates outside the sphere of coercion, leaving us formally free to make choices for ourselves, it escapes many remedies for it that we might try to implement through coercion. We can try to prevent advertisements, for instance, from lying too openly and too dangerously, and perhaps we can even prohibit those directed (for example) at promoting nicotine addiction among children. In some countries,

---

28. Kant, *Metaphysics of Morals*, 6: 237, 230.

29. J. G. Fichte, *Foundations of Natural Right* [1796], edited by F. Neuhouser, translated by Michael Baur (Cambridge: Cambridge University Press, 2000), 39–45.

television advertisements are restricted to certain fairly lengthy periods before or after programming, so that they do not require (as is true in the U.S.) the programming to be specifically designed (i.e., warped, disfigured) so as to facilitate regular commercial interruption.

Nevertheless, manipulation often operates through communicative behavior that is indispensable to the exercise of freedom, so that it would be disastrously counterproductive to try to promote free self-government by coercively preventing manipulation. There are fairly narrow limits on our capacity, even in principle, to prohibit or coercively prevent what is most deeply objectionable about advertising—namely its manipulative character—without at the same time prohibiting or interfering with communicative and self-governing behavior itself. Perhaps there may someday be devised a form of education that will teach people how to protect themselves from advertising, or from other forms of manipulation to which people are now hopeless victims. But the modern world does not seem to have made any real progress in that direction. It sometimes seems that modern society has made people even more vulnerable to calculated mass manipulation than they were in pre-modern social orders.

Exploitation

It remains to say something (briefly) about the third concept—*exploitation*—that I want to relate to those of *coercion* and *manipulation*.[30] To exploit something, in the most basic sense, is to *use* it. Exploitation differs from mere use, however, in that what is exploited is used as part of a plan by the exploiter to achieve some end, in which the exploiter exercises some kind of domination or control over what is exploited. In the case of human beings as exploiters and as the exploited, exploitation involves the use by the exploiter, for some end of the exploiter, of something about the exploited—typically, some ability of the exploited or resource in the exploited's possession. The exploiter gains control over this ability or resource through some vulnerability with which the exploited is afflicted, of which the exploiter also makes use in gaining control over that about

---

30. For a fuller version of this account, see Allen Wood, "Exploitation," *Social Philosophy and Policy* 12 (1995); "Exploitation," in *Exploitation*, edited by Kai Nielsen and Robert Ware, 1–25 (New York: Humanities Press, 1997); and *Karl Marx*, 2nd ed. (London: Taylor and Francis, 2004), chap. 16.

the exploited of which the exploiter makes use for the exploiter's ends. Thus there are two elements in "human on human" exploitation: (a) the vulnerability of the exploited of which the exploiter makes use in gaining control; and (b) the capacity or other benefit of which the exploiter makes use through exercising this control over the exploited.

Sometimes we speak not of this *capacity* or *benefit* as the object of exploitation but of the *person* (him- or herself) as being exploited. I think we do this when we judge that the control of the exploiter over the exploited is sufficiently global, or the object of the exploitation as intimately enough involved with the very personhood of the exploited, that we can regard the entire person of the exploited as being controlled and made use of by the exploiter. I doubt that there is any precise way to determine in which cases this occurs, though there are clear cases of it, and also a tendency on the part of anyone who objects to a form of human on human exploitation to depict it as exploitation of the whole person.

I also doubt that we can determine precise conditions for saying that one person is vulnerable to another—as distinct from saying, for instance, that the first person merely wants something from the second that makes the first person do, quite freely and voluntarily, what the second person asks of the first. By the nature of the case, the vulnerability of those who are exploited usually makes them more eager to be exploited, and the exploitation in that sense is more voluntary for them than for the exploiter. So voluntariness cannot be treated as a criterion of non-vulnerability.

But there are clear cases of vulnerability. The victim of a successful blackmailer is obviously vulnerable to the blackmailer who exploits him. Someone in dire need of some medication or other temporarily scarce resource is clearly vulnerable to the price-gouger who provides it at a wildly inflated cost. If accepting the dangerous, degrading, and low-paying job you offer me is the only way to prevent my family from starving, then I am clearly vulnerable to you, and you are in a position to exploit my labor. I take it to be a pervasive empirical fact about the capitalist system—a fact usually left wholly unrepresented in economists' formal representations of market relations between employers and employees—that the working class is vulnerable to the capitalist class in this way. And this is no accident: those who own make use of the fact of their ownership by exploiting those who do not own; that is the principal meaning of *property* in capitalist society. It is why Marx put his attack on capitalist exploitation in terms of an attack on private property. There are, however, exceptional instances of this relation—for instance, in cases of athletic superstars employed by sports teams—in which the employer is the vulnerable party and the employee is the exploiter. So the vulnerability of workers is not a formal property of the employer-employee relation as such; it is merely a systematic empirical necessity that conditions capitalist relations considered generally.

Such practices as blackmail and price-gouging are forms of exploitation that nearly everyone finds objectionable.[31] But clearly in other cases exploitation is not always bad. It is *good* to take advantage of some vulnerabilities (e.g., the weaknesses in a legal case that lacks merit and deserves to be lost). In a competitive game, we try to exploit our opponents' weaknesses, and we expect them to try to exploit ours. Good sportsmanship involves an acceptance of these facts; if you didn't expect, or even want, your opponents to exploit your mistakes or failings, you shouldn't have chosen to participate in the game in the first place. But exploitation, when it operates through coercion or manipulation, and when these also are bad, is often bad because it shares in (or rides piggyback on) the badness of the coercion or manipulation that makes possible the exploitation.

The worst thing about exploitation is that under most circumstances, it is shameful and reprehensible to make use of other people's vulnerabilities for your own ends, and it is degrading to have your abilities and resources, and especially to have you yourself, made use of in this way. This is especially the case where exploitation involves—as it usually does—the exploiter's exercising coercive power over the exploited, depriving the exploited of their *freedom*—their independence of constraint by another's will. Defenders of capitalism usually represent it as a system of freedom. But their conception of freedom is perversely one-sided. It was quite accurately described many years ago by Bertrand Russell: "Advocates of capitalism are very apt to appeal to the sacred principles of liberty, which are embodied in one maxim: *The fortunate must not be restrained in the exercise of tyranny over the unfortunate.*"[32] The truth is that employers, in purchasing the labor of their employees, purchase fundamentally an *authority* over the workers, the supposed right to exercise coercive power over them, to deprive them of their independence of being constrained by another's choice, which Kant called "the innate right to freedom belonging to every

---

31. Though even they have had their defenders—see Eric Mack, "In Defense of Blackmail," *Philosophical Studies* 41 (1982), 273–84; and Matt Zwolinski, "The Ethics of Price Gouging," *Business Ethics Quarterly* 18 (2008), 347–78.

32. Bertrand Russell, "Freedom in Society," *Harper's Magazine*, April 1926.

human being in virtue of his humanity."[33] They exercise this authority for the whole of the worker's working life—and often, as far as they can get away with it, outside work as well.

The most important reason that workers have formed labor unions has not been to increase their bargaining power over employers with the aim of gaining economic advantage (higher wages, purchasing power). It is, rather, the aim of protecting their freedom, limiting the employer's power over their lives. Karl Marx recognized this as the fundamental reason for workers to organize:

> Just as little as better clothing, food and treatment, and a larger peculium do away with the exploitation of the slave, so little do they set aside that of the wage-worker. A rise in the price of labour, as a consequence of accumulation of capital, only means, in fact, that the length and weight of the golden chain the wage-worker has already forged for himself, allow of a relaxation of the tension of it.[34]

The *Communist Manifesto* does not proclaim as the end of the working class merely its material betterment but, rather, its *emancipation*. Exploitation is degrading to the exploited because it deprives them of freedom, which is fundamental to their human dignity.

Instead of seeing the vulnerabilities of others as opportunities to be exploited, people should regard the vulnerabilities of others as occasions to help them. Sometimes this help would most naturally take the form of helping them to remove the vulnerability. People who are too vulnerable to others, or vulnerable in the wrong ways, lack the dignity we think people should have. When we see many people extremely vulnerable, through poverty or other forms of disadvantage (that often accompany, cause, or result from poverty), then if we respect humanity and the rights of humanity, we want to see this vulnerability abolished. Those who do not—who regard the vulnerability of others as none of their concern, or who even welcome it as something to take advantage of—are a disgrace to the human species.

Human vulnerability is not always a bad thing, however. Good and decent human beings often welcome certain kinds of vulnerability, both in

---

33. Kant, *Metaphysics of Morals*, 6: 237.

34. Karl Marx, *Capital*. Translated by B. Fowkes and D. Fernbach (New York: Vintage, 1977–81), 1: 618.

themselves and in others. The right response to some kinds of vulnerability in others is not to seek its removal but, rather, to make the vulnerable not regret being vulnerable. To love someone, for example, is to be vulnerable to them; if we truly love, we do not want this vulnerability removed; rather, we hope the beloved will see it as an opportunity to behave generously toward us and return our love, rather than as an opportunity to exploit us. The dynamic of human relations between those who wrong others, those who are wronged, and the reconciliation of those occupying these roles is a clear case where human vulnerability can be seen to be a good thing. If I wrong you, this shows how you are vulnerable to me. But I thereby open myself up to your blame and reproach, and that shows how my wrongdoing itself has made me vulnerable to you. But the repentance of the wrongdoer and the forgiveness of the wronged display these vulnerabilities in a way that, in the end, makes us value them rather than regret them. That is why the dynamic of wrongdoing, blame, guilt, repentance, compassion, mercy, and forgiveness is fundamental to the moral and emotional content of all great religions, and represents what is deepest and most appealing about them.

Once we identify a case where exploitation is occurring, it is always a separate and substantive question what should be done about it. Where exploitation is an almost inevitable result of vulnerability, and vulnerability is not the direct result of identifiable human choices, there may be no obvious way to end it. Our first reaction, especially when we begin to appreciate this last point, may be to direct blame at or resentment against the exploiter. But this is often not nearly as appropriate as it might seem, and sometimes it is not appropriate at all.

It is significant, I think, that Marx did not react this way to capitalist exploitation. For example, in the Preface to *Capital*, he writes:

> To prevent possible misunderstandings, let me say this. I do not by any means depict the capitalist and the landowner in rosy colors. But individuals are dealt with here only insofar as they are the personifications of economic categories, the bearers of particular class-relations and interests. My standpoint, from which the development of the economic formation of society is viewed as a process of natural history, can less than any other make the individual responsible for relations whose creature he remains, socially speaking, however much he may subjectively rise above them.[35]

---

35. Marx, *Capital*, 1: 92.

It would be a complete misreading of this passage to see in it any stance on the general problem of free will or moral responsibility. Marx's point is that, whatever the state of their free will or moral subjectivity, for capitalists and landowners, as long as they remain such (and Marx does not expect them to renounce their property and go live like ascetic saints in the wilderness), it may not be an acceptable option, in practical economic terms, to cease their exploitation. They are, in the terms we have been discussing above, forced or compelled to be exploiters, and it is for that reason that Marx finds it inappropriate to blame them.

Although exploiters have greater power than those they exploit, it is not always easy for them unilaterally to put a stop to the exploitation, as long as they cannot avoid interacting with those they exploit. It is not always reasonable to expect those who are in a position to take advantage of vulnerability to forgo the opportunity. If they simply sacrifice their resources for the purpose of benefiting the vulnerable (whether by removing the vulnerability or treating it with generosity), this might not only seem unrealistically saintly of them but might just as easily be experienced by the exploited as condescending; it might be just another way of lording it over the vulnerable, subjecting them to a different kind of humiliation, even as exploiting (taking advantage of) their vulnerability in a different way. At most, it may be reasonable to hope that exploiters will not exploit on such terms as to perpetuate or even intensify the vulnerability of their victims. But it may not be obvious to them how to do this; finding such a path may require a moral creativity for which their social role gives them neither the talent nor the incentive.

Contrary to what we might have thought, therefore, it might be a more effective way of combating exploitation if the task of doing so is left to the weaker party: the vulnerable, those who are exploited. This may be why Karl Marx's recipe for emancipating workers from capitalist exploitation took the form of advice and exhortation directed not at the capitalists but at the workers: "Workers of all countries, unite!"[36] Organize and strengthen yourselves, so that you will no longer be vulnerable. Taking that advice would not involve the exploiting class's condescending to the vulnerable. (Marx was, on these grounds, among the first socialists explicitly to favor the formation of labor unions. Others—Robert Owen, Pierre Proudhon, Ferdinand Lassalle—either opposed them or saw little value in them.) The only burden we might want to impose on the exploiters is that they not

---

36. Karl Marx, *Marx Engels Collected Works* (New York: International, 1975), 6: 539.

get in the way, that they not treat the organization and empowerment of the exploited as an illegitimate encroachment on their prerogatives. When Marx directed his exhortations at the capitalists, or their political representatives, this was usually the form they took: don't oppose the development of the working class. And he argued that this was even in the long-term self-interest of the exploiting classes.

> Disregarding higher motives, their own interest bids the presently ruling classes to remove all the legally controllable obstacles to the development of the working class. This is why I have made such a prominent place in this volume for, among other things, the history, content and result of the English factory legislation. For one nature should and can learn from another.[37]

But Marx was not hopeful that the ruling classes would listen, and he expected them to fear and resist worker empowerment. We know all too well that these pessimistic expectations were correct.

Marx's more distant hope was that the working-class movement would then change society so that the exploitation of one class by another is not built into the social relations that constitute its economic structure. The moral progress of the human species consists mainly in its efforts to remove some kinds human of vulnerability (the kinds that threaten people's dignity) and to cherish others (the kinds of vulnerability that make the vulnerable glad they are vulnerable). Both efforts are aimed at the abolition of exploitation. For these reasons, it is an important measure of the moral level of a society whether it tolerates or even encourages exploitation, or whether instead it declares total war on exploitation and strives to abolish all but the most marginal and harmless forms of it. By this measure, the society in which we live—modern capitalist society, and especially American society, insofar as it celebrates capitalist exploitation—is a highly objectionable social order.

The Connections

Clearly not all instances of exploitation involve either coercion or manipulation. People can be vulnerable to others, and their vulnerability taken advantage of, without the vulnerable having no acceptable alternative to

---

37. Marx, *Capital*, 1: 92.

being exploited. In many cases (if starvation is the only other option, and it is unacceptable), people are forced into being exploited. But in other cases, it may be merely that, given their vulnerability, being exploited is the least unattractive of the acceptable options. The exploitation is nonetheless real for that. Nor must exploitation come about through manipulation. Exploiters sometimes do deceive, exert pressure that subverts the rational choices of their victims, or play on weaknesses of character. Not all vulnerabilities follow these patterns, and people who simply have a decisive bargaining advantage over others may exploit this vulnerability over these others without needing to engage in any of the tricks of the manipulator. Most manipulation through deception involves no vulnerability—a skillful liar can create a situation where only a person deficient in epistemic virtues would not be deceived. Nevertheless, instances of coercion and manipulation overlap in clear and significant ways with instances of exploitation. People sometimes have no acceptable option but to be exploited. Fear, credulity, greed, or vanity are vulnerabilities manipulators can exploit.

A common theme in cases where these three concepts apply—though, once again, nothing invariably present in such cases—is the deprivation of *freedom as non-domination*: the removal, preemption, or subtle undermining by one person of another person's rational control over his or her own choices and actions. It is also true that coercion, manipulation, and exploitation can involve threats to human well-being or happiness. But I believe—and have tried to make a case for it here—that the most serious moral issues raised by coercion, manipulation, and exploitation are issues about *freedom*.

2

What Is Manipulation?

Anne Barnhill

I. Analyzing Manipulation

Manipulation is often not defined in work on the ethics of manipulation. Some philosophers have offered analyses of manipulation, but often these analyses are either under-inclusive or over-inclusive. Under-inclusive analyses of manipulation consider only one variety of manipulation—for example, manipulation that is covert—when in fact manipulation comes in many varieties. Over-inclusive analyses of manipulation classify too broadly a category of influence as manipulation—for example, classifying all influence besides rational persuasion as manipulation, when in fact there are many kinds of non-rational influence that are not manipulative. An account of manipulation must strike the right balance: defining manipulation broadly enough to include the many varieties of manipulation, while not so broadly that non-manipulative forms of influence come out as manipulation.

Another challenge for an account of manipulation is accommodating cases of paternalistic manipulation. Manipulation can be paternalistically motivated, and can advance the manipulated person's interests. At the same time, a distinctive feature of manipulation as a form of influence is that it typically subverts self-interested motivation. An account of manipulation will, ideally, capture both features of manipulation.

In this chapter, I develop an account of manipulation that attempts to meet these two challenges. In section II, I detail the many varieties of manipulation that must be accommodated. In section III, I consider several accounts of manipulation, illustrating with cases how these accounts are either under-inclusive or over-inclusive. The most promising candidate is Robert Noggle's account of manipulative action as the attempt to get someone's belief, emotion, or desire to fall short of the ideals that in the view of the influencer govern the target's beliefs, desires, and emotions; this is discussed in section IV. Though the central insight of Noggle's account is correct, I question whether manipulation must be intentional, and whether the manipulator's ideals are the relevant ideals for attributing manipulation. Another limitation is that Noggle does not grapple with the complicated relationship between manipulation and self-interest. Through a series of cases (presented in section V), I try to clarify this relationship. I conclude:

Manipulation is directly influencing someone's beliefs, desires, or emotions such that she falls short of ideals for belief, desire, or emotion in ways typically not in her self-interest or likely not in her self-interest in the present context.

It's not an elegant account of manipulation. But it does, I think, have intuitive plausibility. Certain ways of making someone fall short of ideals—certain ways of turning her psychological settings away from the ideal, as Robert Noggle puts it—are manipulative, but other ways aren't manipulative. Manipulation is moving someone's settings away from the ideal in ways that are typically *not* in her self-interest, or likely not in her self-interest in the present context.

Before I begin, a note: the methodology that I employ in this chapter—using cases to zero in on the correct analysis of manipulation—raises two issues. First, there are different kinds of behavior that we refer to as manipulation. We must get clear about which of these behaviors we're trying to analyze and which we are leaving for another day. In section II, I distinguish these distinct kinds of manipulation: (1) manipulation of an object as opposed to manipulation of a person; and (2) manipulation via a non-ideal response, as opposed to manipulation via an ideal response. Our topic in this chapter is the manipulation of people via non-ideal responses. This kind of manipulation comes in multiple varieties: intricate vs. blunt manipulation, paternalistic vs. non-paternalistic manipulation, manipulation targeting emotions vs. manipulation targeting beliefs; and so on.

Second, there is a problem with using cases to zero in on the correct analysis of manipulation. There exists significant disagreement about whether specific cases are cases of manipulation. We disagree in our daily lives, as we accuse each other of manipulation and dispute the charges. Philosophers theorizing manipulation also disagree about specific cases, as I've learned in the process of writing this chapter. I might assert that something is an instance of manipulation and get puzzlement or a confident "No, it's not" in reply. Alert to this problem, I endeavor to use only relatively clear-cut cases in much of this chapter. However, to put my cards on the table, I recognize that the cases I employ in section V, to tease out the relationship between self-interest and manipulation, are not clear-cut. Depending upon whether the reader considers these cases to be manipulation or not, she will be led to accept or reject the conclusions that I reach about self-interest and manipulation.

There is an upside to all this disagreement about manipulation. It gives us something to explain, and it gives us a desideratum for an account of manipulation: this account should explain in general terms why there is so much disagreement about specific cases of purported manipulation, and should help to illuminate the contours of our disagreement in specific instances.

II. Varieties of Manipulation
Manipulation of People vs. Manipulation of Objects

We manipulate people, and we also manipulate things other than people—for example, we might claim that the Chinese government manipulates its currency,[1] keeping it artificially weak so that Chinese products are relatively cheap compared with others, or we might claim that a violinist expertly manipulates her violin. Our focus here is the manipulation of people, not the manipulation of other things.

Manipulation of a Situation vs. Direct Manipulation of a Person

In some instances, manipulation changes the options available to a person or changes the situation she's in, and thereby changes her attitudes. In other instances, manipulation changes a person's attitudes directly without changing the options available to her or the surrounding situation.[2]

---

1. Paul Krugman. "The Chinese Disconnect," *New York Times*, October 22, 2009, http://www.nytimes.com/2009/10/23/opinion/23krugman.html?_r=1&hp.

2. Ruth Faden and Tom Beauchamp recognize a similar distinction. They define manipulation as "any intentional and successful influence of a person by noncoercively altering the actual choices available to the person or by nonpersuasively altering the other's perceptions of those choices." Ruth R. Faden and Tom L. Beauchamp, *A History and Theory of Informed Consent* (New York: Oxford University Press, 1986), 354. Marcia Baron identifies multiple types of manipulation, including applying pressure, browbeating, and wearing someone down, *and* manipulation of the situation so as to artificially limit the other person's options. Marcia Baron, "Manipulativeness," *Proceedings and Addresses of the American Philosophical Association* 77, no. 2 (2003): 37–54.

An example of manipulation that changes a person's attitudes directly is a manipulative guilt trip that lays on guilt in order to induce acquiescence to the manipulator's wishes. An example of manipulation that changes the options available to a person is this hypothetical case:

> *Camping Trip:* Your partner wants to go on a family camping trip, but you don't. While you're discussing it, your partner calls out to your children, "Hey, kids! Who wants to go on a camping trip?" The children cheer. You correctly judge that it's better to go on the camping trip (despite its drawbacks) than to disappoint your children. You agree to go on the camping trip.

In this case, your partner changes the options available to you: at the beginning of the conversation, you had the option of refusing the camping trip without disappointing your kids, but your partner eliminated that option by involving the kids.

Manipulation via a Non-Ideal Response vs. Manipulation via an Ideal Response

In some cases of manipulation, the manipulated person is caused to have a non-ideal response of some sort. Consider, as an example, a manipulative guilt trip that induces compliance with the manipulator's wishes. Rather than discussing reasons for and against a course of action, and rather than just expressing her emotions, a guilt-tripping manipulator performs her emotions—which might be sadness, fear, or a variety of other negative emotions—in a way that induces excessive guilt or acute guilt. The guilt trip makes it emotionally difficult not to comply with her wishes, and induces acquiescence.

In other cases, manipulation does not consist of causing the manipulated person to have a non-ideal response. The manipulation consists, instead, of changing the surrounding situation. For example, suppose that in *Camping Trip*, agreeing to go on the camping trip is the ideal response once your kids' disappointment is on the line. The way that your partner manipulated you into going camping is that he changed the situation (i.e., he got the kids excited about camping), such that the ideal response for you to have is his desired response (i.e., agreeing to the camping trip). We can distinguish:

- *Manipulation via a non-ideal response:* Making someone have a non-ideal response, either by influencing her directly (e.g., saying or doing something to her) or by changing the situation in a way that will cause her to have a non-ideal response to the new situation.

- *Manipulation via an ideal response:* Changing the situation so that the target's ideal response to the new situation is the manipulator's desired response.

The phenomenon we are analyzing in this chapter is manipulation via a non-ideal response. I suspect that this is the core notion of manipulating people, and this is why many analyses of manipulation identify, as definitive of manipulation, a specific kind of response considered non-ideal; for example, manipulation involves inducing inappropriate emotions, or manipulation involves tricking someone.

For the sake of brevity, manipulation via a non-ideal response will hereafter be referred to simply as "manipulation."

Manipulation that Targets Emotions vs. Manipulation that Targets Beliefs

Manipulation comes in multiple varieties. Some manipulation plays on our emotions. For example, manipulative guilt trips target our propensity to feel excessive guilt and acquiesce as a result.

But manipulation does not always target emotions. Bob Goodin notes that some kinds of manipulation take advantage of our cognitive limitations; an example is overloading people with information so that "they will be desperate for a scheme for integrating and making sense of it," and then giving them an interpretive framework that serves your purposes.[3]

Manipulative Emotional Appeals vs. Non-Manipulative Emotional Appeals

Some ways of targeting people's emotions are manipulative, but others are not. Consider this hypothetical case:

Embezzlement: Janice has embezzled money from the company she works for. Janice's father, Mike, finds out. Over the course of a weekend together, Mike repeatedly says things like, "I didn't raise you to

---

3. Robert Goodin, *Manipulatory Politics* (New Haven: Yale University Press, 1980), 58–61.

be a thief" and "You should return the money." This makes Janice
feel very guilty and a result, she returns the money.

To my mind, *Embezzlement* is not a case of manipulation. Even though
Mike is trying to make Janice feel guilty, he is not manipulating her. Mike is
targeting Janice's emotions—he is not providing her with arguments, he's
not trying to change her beliefs, he's just trying to change how she feels—but
not in a manipulative way.

An account of manipulation should be able to distinguish between
manipulative appeals to emotion and non-manipulative appeals to emotion,
and explain why the former are manipulative but the latter are not.

Paternalistic vs. Non-Paternalistic Manipulation

Manipulation is sometimes in the target's best interests. For example,
consider this hypothetical case:

Medicine: A patient is being stubborn and won't take his heart medicine
even though it will greatly reduce his chances of a repeat heart attack.
A nurse gets him to take his medicine by saying flirtatiously, "You're
not going to make me beg, are you?" He smiles and takes his medicine.

Though *Medicine* is manipulation in the target's best interests, often
manipulation is not in the target's best interests. Manipulators are often
unconcerned with their targets' interests, or knowingly act contrary to their
interests. To give an extreme example, the investor Bernie Madoff, whose
Ponzi scheme defrauded investors of $50 billion, lured new investors
with manipulative sales tactics.[4] Madoff presented his fund as an exclusive

---

4. As reported in the *New York Times*:

Then, he and his promoters set sights on Europe, again framing the investments as
memberships in a select club. A Swiss hedge fund manager, Michel Dominicé, still
remembers the pitch he got a few years ago from a salesman in Geneva. 'He told me
the fund was closed, that it was something I couldn't buy,' Mr. Dominicé said. 'But
he told me he might have a way to get me in. It was weird.' Dozens of now-outraged
Madoff investors recall that special lure—the sense that they were being allowed into
an inner circle, one that was not available to just anyone. A lawyer would call a client,
saying: 'I'm setting up a fund for Bernie Madoff. Do you want in?' Or an accountant
at a golf club might tell his partner for the day: 'I can make an introduction. Let me
know.' Deals were struck in steakhouses and at charity events, sometimes by Mr.
Madoff himself, but with increasing frequency by friends acting on his behalf.

opportunity open only to the elite and lucky investor. Falsely presenting a product or opportunity as open only to a limited group of people, or available only for a limited time, can motivate customers to act quickly (and perhaps act rashly), rather than lose the opportunity.

Manipulating Behavior vs. Manipulating Mental States

In some instances, manipulation aims to change what someone immediately decides or does. For example, in the case *Medicine*, the nurse aims to make the patient take his medicine right away. But in other instances, manipulation aims to change how someone thinks or feels, without aiming to change what she immediately decides or does. For example, Bob Goodin considers it manipulative that the United States federal government renamed the War Department the "Department of Defense." Goodin writes: "Of course, defense presupposes a threat—one can only defend *against* something. The implicit assertion is that someone is threatening the nation, but by being implicit, this assertion escapes the questioning it deserves."[5]

This manipulative use of language is meant to change how people think and feel about the War Department, but is not meant to immediately change what they decide or do.

Intricate Manipulation vs. Blunt Manipulation

Manipulation is sometimes intricate—it plays on the details of someone's personality. Consider, as an example, this hypothetical case loosely based on purported fact:[6]

Cowboy: President X is unsure about some of the Vice President's proposed policies— approving the torture of prisoners, wiretapping phones without court approval, and invading other countries. The

---

Diana Henriques, "Madoff Scheme Kept Rippling Outward, Across Borders." *New York Times*, December 19, 2008, http://www.nytimes.com/2008/12/20/business/20madoff.html?pagewanted=all&_r=0.

5. Goodin, *Manipulatory Politics*, 100.

6. The journalist Jane Mayer wrote a book, *The Dark Side*, detailing the Bush Administration's war on terror. The case Cowboy is inspired by this passage from Mayer's book:

> After losing the battle to uphold the Geneva Conventions, [Secretary of State Colin] Powell concluded that Bush was not stupid but was easily manipulated. A confidant

Vice President plays on President X's "cowboy self-image" in a flattering way, saying things like: "You're the kind of man who makes the tough decisions that other people—who are too concerned about being popular—aren't courageous enough to make." President X is insecure and needs to identify with being a tough guy. President is motivated by the Vice President's words to make decisions he sees as "tough" decisions—approving torture and illegal wiretapping, and invading Iraq.

In this case, the Vice President has a manipulative strategy that's fine-tuned to President X.

But manipulation is not always intricate and does not always play on the details of an individual's personality. For example:

Open House: Your house is for sale. Before holding an open house for prospective buyers, you bake cookies so that the house will smell like cookies, knowing that this will make the prospective buyers have more positive feelings about the house and make them more inclined to purchase the house.[7]

This case of manipulation does not play upon the details of an individual's personality, but it relies upon widely shared psychological dispositions.

Covert Manipulation vs. Overt Manipulation

A key feature of some manipulation is that the manipulated person does not realize the way in which she's being influenced. For example, we could imagine

---

said that Powell thought it was easy to play on Bush's wish to be seen as doing the tough thing and making the "hard" choice. "He has these cowboy characteristics, and when you know where to rub him, you can really get him to do some dumb things. You have to play on those swaggering bits of his self-image. Cheney knew exactly how to push all his buttons," Powell confided to a friend.

Jane Mayer, *The Dark Side: Inside the Story of How the War on Terror Turned Into a War on American Ideals* (New York: Doubleday, 2008).

7. A website for home sellers advises: "Welcoming scents can also create a good first impression. Bake a loaf of bread or some cookies before potential buyers arrive, and let the odor waft through the house. Or scatter some cinnamon on a cookie sheet and place it in a warm oven during the open house." Louisa Pavonne, "Ten Tips for a Seller's Open House," April 1, 2007, http://voices.yahoo.com/ten-tips-sellers-open-house-262866.html.

that President X, in the case *Cowboy*, is not aware that the Vice President is intentionally playing on his need to see himself as making "tough" decisions, and that the Vice President's tactic would not succeed were President X aware of it. Some instances of manipulation, like *Cowboy*, are covert.

In other cases, manipulation is entirely overt. For example, manipulative guilt trips can be obvious and still be very effective. We can be lucidly aware that we're being manipulated into feeling guilt, even as we feel guilt and act on it.

III. Accounts of Manipulation

An account of manipulation (that is, an account of manipulation via a non-ideal response) will, ideally, accommodate the varieties of manipulation identified above: covert and overt manipulation; intricate and blunt manipulation; manipulation of behavior and manipulation of mental states; paternalistic and non-paternalistic manipulation; and manipulation that targets emotion as well as manipulation that does not. An account of manipulation will also, ideally, allow us to distinguish between emotional appeals that are manipulative and those that are not.

Manipulation as Deceptive Influence or Covert Influence

Some theorists analyze manipulation as deceptive or covert influence of some sort.[8] Robert Goodin observes that manipulation carries "especially strong connotations of something sneaky" and that manipulation characteristically happens unbeknownst to its victim.[9] According to Goodin, manipulation is deceptively influencing someone against his putative will.[10] Alan Ware also defines manipulation as a kind of covert influence; one feature of manipulation, according to Ware, is that the manipulated person "either has no knowledge of, or does not understand, the ways in which [the manipulator] affects his choices."[11]

---

8. Goodin, *Manipulatory Politics*; Alan Ware, "The Concept of Manipulation: Its Relation to Democracy and Power," *British Journal of Political Science* 11 (1981): 163–181.

9. Goodin, *Manipulatory Politics*, 9.

10. Goodin, *Manipulatory Politics*, 7–23 .

11. Ware, "The Concept of Manipulation," 165.

Though covertness is a key feature of some cases of manipulation, manipulation is not always deceptive or covert. Manipulative guilt trips, for example, can be plain as day. Deceptiveness or covertness might be a favorite technique of manipulators—manipulation is more likely to succeed if its target doesn't realize what's happening—but manipulation needn't be deceptive or covert.[12]

Manipulation as Defective Persuasion

Rather than covert influence, some theorists analyze manipulation as defective persuasion of some sort. According to Claudia Mills, what's distinctive about manipulation is that it purports to be legitimate persuasion that offers good reasons, but in fact bad reasons are offered. Mills writes that "a manipulator tries to change another's beliefs and desires by offering her bad reasons, disguised as good, or faulty arguments, disguised as sound—where the manipulator himself knows these to be bad reasons and faulty arguments." Mills writes: "Manipulation may then be understood as a kind of persuasion manqué, as an attempt at internally directed and non-physically-based influence that deliberately falls short of the persuasive ideal."[13]

Manipulation as persuasion manqué is too narrow an account of manipulation. Though some cases of manipulation are cases of changing someone's beliefs and desires by offering bad reasons disguised as good reasons, in other cases the manipulation changes someone's beliefs or desires without offering reasons or arguments at all. Consider *Open House*, the case in which prospective home buyers are made to have more positive feelings about a house because it smells like cookies. This is not an instance of purporting to offer reasons or arguments; it's an instance of changing background conditions so as to have a predictable psychological effect. Even on a capacious understanding of offering reasons, this is not an instance of doing so.

---

12. In "Manipulation," Joel Rudinow notes that manipulation need not involve deception, as does Robert Noggle. Joel Rudinow, "Manipulation" *Ethics* 88, no. 4 (1978): 338–47. Robert Noggle, "Manipulative Actions: A Conceptual and Moral Analysis," *American Philosophical Quarterly* 33, no. 1 (1996): 43–55.

13. Claudia Mills, "Politics and Manipulation," *Social Theory and Practice* 21, no. 1 (Spring 1995): 97–112, esp. p. 100.

Manipulation as Non-Persuasive Influence

According to other theorists, what's distinctive about manipulation as a form of influence is not that it involves distinctive means (e.g., covert means of influence, or bad arguments disguised as good arguments) but that it has a distinctive effect on its target (e.g., it plays on the target's weaknesses, or it influences her without improving her understanding).[14]

Ruth Faden and Tom Beauchamp identify three distinct kinds of manipulation: the manipulation of options; the manipulation of information; and psychological manipulation, which is the notion of interest here. Psychological manipulation is "any intentional act that successfully influences a person to belief or behavior by causing changes in mental processes other than those involved in understanding."[15] For Faden and Beauchamp, psychological manipulation as a form of influence is contrasted with persuasion: persuasion improves someone's understanding of her situation, but manipulation does not.[16]

Faden and Beauchamp see psychological manipulation as "a broad heading" including "such diverse strategies as subliminal suggestion, flattery and other appeals to emotional weaknesses, and the inducing of guilt or feelings of obligation."[17] In my view, their understanding of psychological manipulation is *too* broad. It counts as manipulation all influence that does not change the target's understanding. But there are many types of influence that do not change someone's understanding yet are not manipulative influence. One may influence someone by instilling a desire, motive, or emotion in her; while some ways of instilling desires, motives, and emotions are manipulative, others are not. For example, in *Embezzlement*, Mike makes his daughter Janice feel guilty for embezzling

---

14. According to Joel Rudinow, "A attempts to manipulate S iff A attempts the complex motivation of S's behavior by means of deception or by playing on a supposed weakness of S." The complex motivation of behavior is motivation that one presumes will alter the person's projects/goals. Rudinow, "Manipulation," 346.

15. The three kinds of manipulation are identified by Faden and Beauchamp: manipulation of options, in which options in the environment are modified by increasing or decreasing available options, or by offering rewards or threatening punishments; manipulation of information, in which the person's perception of options is modified by non-persuasively affecting the person's understanding of the situation; and psychological manipulation, in which the person is influenced by causing changes in mental processes other than those involved in understanding; Faden and Beauchamp, *History and Theory*, 354–68.

16. Faden and Beauchamp, *History and Theory*, 259, 261, 354–68.

17. Faden and Beauchamp, *History and Theory*, 366.

money, but he does not manipulate her. To give another example, expressing your sadness to an empathetic person could cause her to feel sad on your behalf, and decide to help you; this needn't be manipulative.[18] Contra Faden and Beauchamp, there are ways of influencing people that do not persuade—that is, do not improve someone's understanding—yet are not manipulative.

IV. Manipulation as Making Someone Fall Short of Ideals

Mills's analysis of manipulation as defective persuasion is under-inclusive, since not all manipulation is persuasion, and Faden and Beauchamps's analysis of manipulation as non-persuasive influence is over-inclusive, since some instances of non-persuasive influence are not manipulation. In both cases, manipulation is analyzed as influence that fails to be rational persuasion: manipulation fails to be rational persuasion either because it is *non*-rational persuasion or because it is not *persuasion* at all.

In my view, manipulation is not best understood as influence that fails to be rational persuasion. What's definitive of manipulation as a form of influence, in my view, is that it induces a non-ideal response. However, the best way to characterize this non-ideal response is not in terms of rational persuasion. This is one of the central insights of Robert Noggle's analysis of manipulation.

Noggle analyzes manipulative action as the attempt to get someone's beliefs, desires, or emotions to fall short of the ideals that govern beliefs, desires, and emotions.[19] More specifically, according to Noggle, manipulative action is the attempt to get someone's beliefs, desires, or emotions to fall short of the ideals that *in the view of the influencer* govern the target's beliefs, desires, and emotions; see more about this below. In explaining this analysis of manipulation, Noggle uses the metaphor of "adjusting psychological

---

18. One might counter that these examples *are* instances of increasing someone's understanding of her situation—Janice now understands that she did something wrong, and the empathetic person now understands that you are sad—and thus are not instances of manipulation, on their account. However, we can describe such cases so that they are *not* instances of increasing someone's understanding. For example, Janice already understood that embezzling was wrong, she was just failing to feel appropriate guilt; and the empathetic person already understood that you were sad, and your expression of sadness changed her desires and motives not by increasing her understanding but just by causing an empathetic emotional response in her.

19. Noggle, "Manipulative Actions."

levers": manipulative action attempts to adjust psychological levers away from what the manipulator thinks are the ideal settings for the target.

Noggle gives us an account of *manipulative action* as the attempt to get someone's beliefs, desires, or emotions to fall short of ideals. We can slightly modify Noggle's account from an account of attempted manipulation into an account of manipulation:

Manipulation is intentionally making someone's beliefs, desires, or emotions fall short of the ideals that in the view of the influencer govern the target's beliefs, desires, and emotions.

Manipulation can make someone fall short of one ideal while causing her to meet another ideal—that is, manipulation can move one psychological lever away from an ideal setting, while moving another psychological lever toward an ideal setting. For instance, paternalistic manipulation often makes a manipulated person's resulting desires or motives more ideal, but does so through a process involving non-ideal emotions, desires, or decision making. As an example, the flirting nurse in *Medicine* makes the patient more ideal in one respect (he's now willing to take his medicine), but does so through a process involving non-ideal emotions and decision making.[20]

Noggle emphasizes that manipulation is *not* non-rational persuasion. Whereas manipulation intends to make its target fall short of ideals for beliefs, desires, and emotions, there are many instances of non-rational persuasion that are meant to make the target's beliefs, desires, and emotions more ideal. Noggle writes:

Suppose you remind me of starving children in Rwanda, and describe their plight in vivid detail in order to get me to feel sad enough to assign (what you take to be) the morally proper relevance to their suffering. Surely you have not manipulated me, though you may have engaged in non-rational moral persuasion....Or if a psychologist uses conditioning to instill desires that conform to the patient's beliefs about what there is reason to do, then she is engaged in therapy rather than manipulation. These examples show that trying to move someone toward that person's ideal conditions is not in itself manipulative, even when it takes place by "non-rational" means. Rather it is what we might call "non-rational counselling."[21]

---

20. Noggle acknowledges this sort of case in fn. 20 of "Manipulative Actions."

21. Noggle, "Manipulative Actions," 49.

According to Noggle, the category of manipulation is orthogonal to the category of non-rational persuasion. Whether influence is manipulation doesn't depend on whether the influence is non-rational persuasion. Rather, whether influence is manipulation depends on whether the influence is intended to make the person fall short of ideals for belief, desire, and emotion.

For example, in *Open House*, the smell of cookies is meant to make prospective buyers feel more favorably toward the house and be more motivated to buy the house. Being motivated to purchase a house because it smells good on the day you visit is non-ideal motivation. What's manipulative about *Open House* is that prospective buyers are made (by the smell of cookies) to fall short of ideals for desire, emotion, and motivation. But it need not be manipulative to use the smell of cookies to influence someone if this influence does not make her fall short of ideals for belief, desire, and emotion. For example, suppose that the smell of cookies is used to whet the appetite of a patient who ought to eat more but is disinclined to eat because her illness has ruined her appetite. Using the smell of cookies to instill a desire to eat cookies is not manipulative in this instance, and that is because it makes the patient's desires more ideal rather than less ideal.

A virtue of Noggle's account is that it can distinguish between manipulative appeals to emotion and non-manipulative appeals to emotion, and can explain why the former are manipulative but the latter are not. For example, manipulative guilt trips involve instilling excessive guilt or making someone feel guilty in a manner that causes inappropriate acquiescence, both of which are ways of making someone fall short of ideals for emotion. But other ways of making someone feel guilty can get her *closer* to ideals for emotion, and thus are not manipulative. For example, in *Embezzlement*, Mike causes Janice to feel what he believes to be appropriate guilt about embezzling money. Because he believes that he's making her emotions more ideal, he is not manipulating her.

Noggle's account must be modified to exclude certain non-manipulative ways of making people fall short of ideals for belief, desire, and emotion. Consider the following example:

> *Ecstasy:* A car salesman wants to convince a customer to buy an expensive car that the customer is ambivalent about. He covertly gives the customer the drug ecstasy, which makes her much more agreeable to buying the car. The customer agrees to buy the car.

In this case, the salesman intentionally makes the customer fall short of ideals for emotion, motivation, and deliberation, yet this does not seem like a case of manipulation. Drugging someone is undoubtedly a problematic form of influence but not a manipulative form of influence. Similarly, hitting someone over the head so that she can't think clearly is a problematic form of influence but not a manipulative form of influence. As Claudia Mills notes, manipulation involves changing someone's mental states by targeting her "beliefs and desires, her goals and plans, her values and preferences."[22] Manipulation changes beliefs, desires, and emotions by targeting emotions, beliefs, and desires. Drugging someone changes her beliefs, desires, and emotions by causing a global drug-induced psychological change, not by targeting her beliefs, desires, and emotions. Similarly, hitting someone over the head changes her beliefs, desires, and emotions by causing cognitive impairment, not by targeting her beliefs, desires, and emotions.

Let me suggest this modification to Noggle's account: manipulation is *directly influencing* someone's beliefs, desires, or emotions so that she falls short of the ideals that in the view of the influencer govern the target's beliefs, desires, and emotions.[23] The notion of "directly influencing" someone's beliefs, desires, or emotions should be understood to exclude influence such as drugging or brainwashing someone, but to include cases like baking cookies in order to make prospective buyers like a house.

Whose Ideals?

The core of Noggle's account of manipulation is correct: manipulation is making someone fall short of ideals for belief, desire, and emotion. However, I'm uncertain whether all the details of Noggle's account are correct. Specifically, is manipulation making someone fall short of the *manipulator's* ideals for belief, desire, and emotion? Or making someone fall short of objective ideals? And must manipulation be intentional, as Noggle thinks, or can there be unintentional manipulation?

---

22. Claudia Mills, "Politics and Manipulation," 99.

23. The beliefs, desires, or emotions that are directly influenced needn't be the ones that fall short of ideals. Manipulation *can* intentionally influence a belief, desire, or emotion without directly targeting that belief, desire, or emotion—e.g., in distracting people with soaring rhetoric, you're making someone fall short of ideals for belief not by targeting those beliefs, but by influencing her emotions

According to Noggle, manipulation is making someone's beliefs, desires, or emotions fall short of the ideals that in the view of the influencer govern the target's beliefs, desires, and emotions. Noggle identifies several such ideals, including the ideal of attending to all and only true and relevant beliefs; the ideal that desires conform to one's beliefs about what there is most reason to do; and the ideal that emotions make salient what is most important or most relevant to the situation at hand. These ideals include, according to Noggle, rational ideals and moral ideals. Since people dis‐ agree about which beliefs are true beliefs, which emotions are appropriate emotions, what's most relevant to the situation at hand, and so forth, people thereby disagree about which beliefs, desires, and emotions are ideal.

According to Noggle, the *influencer's* conception of which beliefs, desires, and emotions are ideal *for the influenced person* is what's pertinent to determin‐ ing when manipulation has occurred. [24] Manipulation occurs when the influ‐ encer intentionally makes the influenced person fall short of the ideals that the influencer believes hold for the influenced person. Thus, Noggle con‐ cludes, "a racist who attempts to incite racial fears may not intend to move the other person away from what *he*—mistakenly—takes to be the other person's ideal condition, and so we cannot accuse him of acting manipu‐ latively."[25] If a racist believes that holding racist fears is ideal, then he does not act manipulatively in trying to induce those fears in others.

According to Noggle, when making a determination of manipulation, the *objectively* correct ideals for beliefs, desires, or emotions are not relevant and the *influenced person's* ideals for belief, desires, and emotions are not relevant. I think our concept of manipulation is more complicated than Noggle allows. Though I agree with Noggle that the ideals of the influenced person are not pertinent, I disagree with Noggle that objective ideals are also irrelevant. On the contrary, our willingness to label influence "manip‐ ulation" depends upon both the influencer's conception of what's ideal

---

24. Noggle, "Manipulative Actions," writes: "What makes a form of influence manipulative is the *intent* of the person acting, in particular the direction in which she intends to move the other person's psychological levers" (49). "Even if the influencer has a culpably false view of what is our ideal, the influence is not a manipulative action so long as it is sincere, that is, in accordance with what the influencer takes to be true, relevant, and appropriate" (50). "Often children (and some adults as well) have an inflated sense of their own importance; they gen‐ uinely believe that their pains and projects are (or ought to be) more significance significant than those of other people, not only to themselves but to others as well. Such cases are some‐ what intricate morally. On my view such an agent does not in fact act manipulatively" (50).

25. Noggle, "Manipulative Actions," 50.

and our own conception of what's objectively ideal. We invariably consider influence to be manipulation when it intentionally causes someone to fall short of ideals that are *both* the objective ideals (in our opinion) *and* the ideals that (in our opinion) the influencer believes apply to the influenced person. However, when an influencer's ideals deviate from what we consider the objective ideals, then our usage of "manipulation" is inconstant, varying from case to case and from person to person. Consider this case:

> *Guilt Trip:* Janice has booked a vacation trip to New York City. Janice's father, Mike, doesn't want her to go because he thinks that New York City is too dangerous a place. Over the course of a weekend together, Mike repeatedly says things like, "If you go, your mother and I will be sick with fear!" knowing that this will make Janice feel extremely guilty. Mike thinks that it's appropriate for Janice to feel extremely guilty for making her parents worry so much. This makes Janice feel very guilty and as a result, she cancels the trip.

Is this a case of manipulation? People disagree. Some think that since Mike believes he's making Janice feel an appropriate amount of guilt (i.e., Mike thinks he's making Janice more ideal rather than less ideal), this is not manipulation, even though Mike is in fact making Janice feel an inappropriate amount of guilt. Though they might conclude that Mike has the wrong standards for what counts as appropriate emotion, they don't think that Mike has manipulated Janice. But other people are inclined to call Mike's behavior manipulation, since Mike makes Janice feel what they judge to be an inappropriate amount of guilt. For these people, Mike's ideals and intentions are not conclusive in determining whether Mike has manipulated Janice; it's also relevant whether Mike has in fact made Janice fall short of rational ideals. Consider another case:

> *Narcissist:* Maria is an extreme narcissist. She will do whatever it takes to get what she wants. She has no opinion about what is rationally and morally ideal for other people, because she doesn't conceive of other people as agents to whom rational and moral ideals apply. Maria regularly employs guilt, flattery, and deception to get other people to do what she wants.[26]

---

26. I thank Kate Manne for suggesting this kind of case.

Does Maria manipulate other people? According to Noggle's account of manipulation, Maria does not manipulate: she never intentionally makes people fall short of the ideals for belief, desire, and emotion that she thinks apply to them, since she lacks a conception of what ideal belief, desire, and emotion is for other people. Consistent with Noggle's view, we might be tempted to say Maria doesn't manipulate other people because she doesn't really understand what manipulation is. On the other hand, a very natural response to this case is to judge that Maria does manipulate others and, in fact, is a master manipulator. She treats other people like instruments rather than rational and moral agents. The fact that she acts with disregard for rational and moral standards does not seem to render her behavior non-manipulative; to the contrary, that's what's makes her a master manipulator.

Thus, contrary to Noggle's account, it is not clear that manipulation is making someone fall short of the ideals that the *manipulator* believes govern her beliefs, desires, and emotions, as opposed to making someone fall short of objective ideals for belief, desire, and emotion. There appears to be disagreement on this matter.

Must Manipulation Be Intentional?

Must manipulation be intentional? One reason for doubt is that we're willing to call influence "manipulation" even when we've little knowledge of the influencer's intentions. When we notice that a competent-seeming adult A is influencing someone B such that B falls short of the rational ideals that we think apply to B, we're un-self-conscious about calling this "manipulation" despite our ignorance of A's precise intentions. Does this suggest that manipulation need not be intentional?

An alternative explanation is that we attribute manipulation so liberally because we make certain presumptions about the purported manipulator A: we assume that A shares our rational ideals, that he is aware of his effect on B, and that he is acting intentionally. When we notice A influencing B in ways that make B fall short of the ideals that we think apply to B, we assume that A is intentionally making B fall short of the ideals that A thinks apply to B.

If our uninformed attributions of manipulation *are* based upon such presumptions, then this would explain why there is, not infrequently, disagreement about whether manipulation has occurred in specific cases.

The explanation of this disagreement is that we vary in our willingness to make these presumptions about purported manipulators.

In addition, if our uninformed attributions of manipulation are based upon presumptions about the purported manipulator, presumably we'd be willing to abandon a charge of manipulation when our presumptions proved false. This does sometimes happen. Upon examining a case of purported manipulation more closely, we sometimes conclude that the purported manipulator A was clueless (that is, unaware that he was making B fall short of the ideals that A thinks apply to B) or conclude that A has different ideals than us (and hence disagrees that his effect on B is to make her less ideal). Some people then conclude that A did *not* manipulate B after all. But others are still inclined to conclude that A manipulated B, albeit unintentionally. Our intuitions seem to vary somewhat, from person to person, on this point.

Another interesting observation is that some people are inclined to call clueless A (the person who unwittingly makes person B fall short of the rational ideals that we think apply to B) a manipulative person even if they are not willing to say that clueless A engaged in manipulation.[27] This use of language—referring to people as manipulative even though their behavior doesn't quite amount to manipulation—actually makes sense. Person A is making others fall short of rational ideals and hence is a social threat, even if he's doing so unwittingly. Referring to A as "manipulative" usefully identifies him as a social threat of that sort.

To return to the question that opened this section, must manipulation be intentional? That depends upon who you ask. Some people allow that there can be unintentional manipulation. Others think that manipulation must be intentional, but allow that a person who lacks the intention to manipulate might nonetheless be a manipulative person.

V. Manipulation and Self-Interest

Noggle's central insight about manipulation is correct: manipulation is making someone fall short of ideals for belief, desire, and emotion. But Noggle's account does not capture the complicated relationship between manipulation and self-interest.

---

27. As Benjamin Sachs expressed it (in conversation with me), manipulation is about intention but manipulativeness is about effect.

Consider the following hypothetical case:

Reelection: President X has moral qualms about some of the Vice President's proposed policies—approving the torture of prisoners, wiretapping phones without court approval, and invading other countries. His political advisor wants him to approve these policies because she believes that making decisions that appear to be "tough" decisions will increase his popularity and ensure his reelection. She tells the President, "If you make decisions that appear to be 'tough' decisions, this will increase your popularity and ensure your reelection," because she believes that he wants to be reelected and will therefore be motivated to make decisions he sees as "tough" decisions, despite his moral qualms about these decisions. Because he wants to be reelected, President X is motivated by his advisor's words to make decisions he sees as "tough" decisions (e.g., approving torture and illegal wiretapping, and invading other countries).

Does the advisor manipulate the President in this case? My intuition is that she does not. But this is a case of causing someone to fall short of ideals for belief, desire, or emotion. The advisor appeals to and stokes the President's self-interest, causing him to feel excessive self-interest. This excessive and inappropriate self-interest crowds out his moral qualms and crowds out other emotions that he ought feel, such as guilt or compassion for the victims of war or torture; the advisor's influence makes him fall short of ideals for emotion. Let's stipulate that the advisor recognizes these ideals and believes that they apply to the President. Thus the advisor intentionally causes him to fall short of ideals that she thinks apply to him and that are (very plausibly) objectively correct ideas, fulfilling our definition of manipulation. Yet this does not seem to me like a case of manipulation.

Notice that this case, *Reelection*, is the mirror image of a manipulative guilt trip. In a manipulative guilt trip, a manipulator causes someone to feel excessive guilt, and this excessive guilt dampens her self-interested motivation. In the case of *Reelection*, President X feels too little guilt and has an excessive amount of self-interested motivation. In both cases, someone is caused to fall short of ideals for guilt and self-interest. But the guilt trip (too much guilt, too little self-interest) seems like manipulation, whereas *Reelection* (too much self-interest, too little guilt) does not seem like manipulation. What explains this difference?

A tempting explanation is that *Reelection* is not manipulation because President X is made to act in his best interests. Perhaps manipulation is directly influencing someone's beliefs, desires, or emotions such that she falls short of ideals for belief, desire, or emotion, *and such that she does not act in her best interests.* The idea—to return to Robert Noggle's metaphor—would be that adjusting someone's psychological settings away from the ideal settings is manipulation, but only if this adjustment away from the ideal is not in her best interests. But this cannot be correct. Manipulation sometimes *is* in the manipulated person's best interests. Recall the case Medicine, in which a patient is manipulated into taking his medicine, which is in his best interests.

To complicate the picture further, consider another case:

Reelection II: The President's political advisor believes that it is in President X's best interests to be reelected, but is worried that he is not sufficiently motivated. She knows that, as a graduate of Yale University, he feels an intense competitive malice toward graduates of Princeton University. In order to motivate him to do what it takes to win reelection, she reminds him that his opponent is a graduate of Princeton University.

In this case, the President is falling short of various ideals. For example, in feeling intense competitive malice toward someone merely because of his alma mater, he is feeling an inappropriate emotion. Let's stipulate that his political advisor recognizes as much. Is it manipulative for her to stoke the President's intense competitive malice in this way? I'm of two minds. When I imagine his intense competitive malice as a settled part of his personality— as something that's under his control, and that doesn't prevent him from pursuing his other goals and acting on his settled decisions—then it doesn't seem manipulative for his advisor to stoke his intense competitive malice in order to motivate him. But when I imagine the intense competitive malice as a hot emotion—an emotion that's not fully under his control—then it does seem manipulative for his advisor to motivate him by appealing to his intense competitive malice. What could explain these intuitions?

Perhaps manipulation is adjusting someone's psychological settings away from the ideal settings in ways that are typically not in her self-interest. But adjusting someone's settings in ways that typically *promote* her self-interest is not manipulation. This would explain why the question of whether the advisor manipulates the President, in *Reelection II*, depends upon the kind of non-ideal malice she stokes. If she appeals to a cold, competitive malice that's under his control, then he does not manipulate him, because feeling controlled, competitive malice, and making decisions on the basis of it is likely to be in his self-interest. However if she stokes a hot competitive malice that's not tightly controlled, then she does manipulate him, since feeling and acting on not-tightly-controlled malice is typically not in one's self-interest. Similarly, when she stokes his excessive self-interest in the previous case, *Reelection*, she makes him fall short of ideals, but in a way that's likely to be in his self-interest. Thus she does not manipulate him in *Reelection*.

Consider one last case:

> *Reelection III:* The President's political advisor is a turncoat: she's secretly working for his opponent in the reelection campaign. She knows that if the President is motivated by competitive malice during a debate, this will turn off voters and they will stop supporting him. She knows that, as a graduate of Yale University, President X feels an intense competitive malice toward graduates of Princeton University. She reminds him that his likely opponent is a graduate of Princeton University, in order to make him manifest his intense competitive malice and thereby help his opponent win the election.

When the advisor motivates the President by appealing to cold competitive malice in this case, it seems like manipulation—even though motivating someone by appealing to cold competitive malice is typically in his self-interest. Why is it manipulative to appeal to his competitive malice in this case but not in the previous case? Perhaps because it is *not* in his interest, in this case, to be motivated by cold competitive malice. Thus our account needs one last modification:

Manipulation is directly influencing someone's beliefs, desires, or emotions such that she falls short of ideals for belief, desire, or emotion in ways typically not in her self-interest *or likely not in her self-interest in the present context.*

This final account of manipulation captures, I believe, the complex relationship between manipulation and self-interest. Certain ways of intentionally making someone fall short of ideals—certain ways of turning her psychological settings away from the ideal—are manipulative, but other ways aren't manipulative. Moving someone's settings away from the ideal in ways that typically are not in her self-interest, or not in her self-interest in the present context, is manipulation. But moving someone's settings away from the ideal in ways that typically *are* in her self-interest, and furthermore are in her self-interest in the present context, is not manipulation.

3

Towards a Theory of Interpersonal Manipulation

Moti Gorin

Introduction

People are complicated beings, exhibiting an extremely wide range of behaviors that are due to an equally wide variety of causes. Consequently, there are myriad means available to influence this behavior. We make claims, both true and false. We construct good arguments and bad ones. We make different sounds and facial expressions. We clothe, decorate, situate, and move our bodies in seemingly infinite ways. We make use of tools and other sorts of artifacts. We alter our environment and in so doing stimulate our perceptual, cognitive, and emotional faculties. Each of these means of interpersonal influence can be used manipulatively, though none of them is essentially manipulative.

In what follows, I begin to chart a novel account of interpersonal manipulation. Most of the arguments are negative, as the bulk of the essay is devoted to showing what manipulation is *not*. After criticizing several more or less plausible accounts of manipulation I sketch what I take to be a more promising view. I conclude with some very brief remarks on how the theory of manipulation I begin to develop here might help provide the basis for a new and interesting ethical analysis of manipulation.

Manipulation and Common Wrongs

Manipulation commonly involves ethically suspect behavior such as deceiving, harming, undermining autonomy, or bypassing or subverting the rational capacities. Hence, it is tempting to think there is some necessary connection between manipulation and these other things. There are also theoretical advantages to insisting on tight links between them, for though deception, harm, autonomy, and the rational capacities remain to varying degrees contested concepts it is at least fairly clear what the major competing normative ethical theories have to say about them. A necessary connection between one or more of these concepts and manipulation would allow for the derivation of conclusions regarding the nature of manipulation from claims about deception, harm, autonomy, or the bypassing or subverting of the rational capacities. The most interesting ethical questions about manipulation would turn out to be questions about other phenomena whose natures have been more frequently discussed and which are better understood. For example, if manipulation always involved deception, then answers to questions about the ethical status of deception would also serve as answers to questions about the ethical status of manipulation. This would leave us with a relatively tidy way to approach questions about the normative dimension of manipulation.

In the following four sections I examine the relationships between manipulation and deception, manipulation and harm, manipulation and autonomy, and manipulation and the rational capacities. I argue that although manipulation often does involve one or more of these, it does not always do so. An account of manipulation that reduces its normative significance to concerns raised by deception, harm, and threats to autonomy or the rational capacities will fail to capture much that is interesting and important about manipulation. Such an account will therefore remain incomplete. I will begin with a discussion of the relationship between manipulation and deception and then move on to discuss harm, autonomy, and the rational capacities. My strategy will be to motivate accounts of manipulation according to which these wrong-making features are necessary conditions of manipulation and then to provide counter-examples to these accounts. The central conclusion of this section is that manipulation does not essentially involve deception, harm, the undermining of autonomy, or the bypassing or subverting of the rational capacities. None of these can provide a necessary condition in the analysis of interpersonal manipulation.

Manipulation and Deception

The first account I will examine pays special attention to the epistemic features of manipulative interactions and in particular to the role of deception in these interactions. On this account, which I will call the Deception-Based View, manipulation always involves some element of deception. A defender of this view can correctly point out that many paradigmatic cases of manipulation involve deception and that deception may enter into a manipulative encounter in more than one way. First and most crudely, a manipulator may lie—that is, he may state something he knows to be false with the intention that it be believed to be true. Here is one example of this.

Not Credible: Henry wishes to undermine the credibility of his colleague Elizabeth. He lies to her about various matters on which she rightly takes him to be an authority. Later, when Elizabeth is having a conversation with other experts in Henry's field, she relies on the "information" Henry provided her. The specialists, who correctly judge that Elizabeth is advancing false claims, begin to doubt her competence. The experts' judgments that Elizabeth is an unreliable source of information or that she is incompetent are products of Henry's manipulation.

In this case of epistemic manipulation, Henry has manipulated Elizabeth as well as his peers, and his method of doing so included the telling of lies as its central component.

Less crudely, a manipulator may say something that is true but which he intends will lead his interlocutor to believe something false. Depending on the other beliefs an agent has and on the context of the exchange, the acceptance of a true belief may lead to her acceptance of a false belief. Here is one such case.

Synagogue: David is romantically interested in Susan and so is his friend Jack. David knows Jack is a committed Catholic who prefers to date other Catholics. David knows that Susan, too, is Catholic but he does not wish Jack to know this, as David would like to reduce the amount of competition he might face for Susan's affection. David recently saw Susan entering a synagogue. Though he knows Susan was there only to meet with the rabbi about an upcoming fundraiser for a nondenominational charity, the next time he has lunch with Jack he mentions that he saw Susan at the synagogue. David intends that this will lead Jack to believe that Susan is Jewish and, consequently, that Jack will come to believe that Susan is not a viable romantic option for him.

David states something he believes to be true and he intends that Jack accept the statement as being true. Nevertheless, David intends that Jack's acceptance of a true claim will lead to his holding a false belief and ultimately that this will lead to the behavior David is seeking from Jack. David's behavior is both manipulative and deceptive but it does not involve a lie.

The Deception-Based View of manipulation captures an important feature of manipulation, namely that it can "prevent [a manipulee] from governing herself with an *accurate understanding* of her situation."[1] In the cases discussed so far, manipulators do this by causing manipulees to have false beliefs whose content extends beyond the intentions of the manipulator, though of course the manipulators also deceive the manipulees about their intentions (otherwise it would not be easy to deceive them about anything else). But manipulators sometimes prevent manipulees from having an accurate understanding of their situation by causing them to have false beliefs or to fail to have salient true beliefs whose content is limited to the ends at which the manipulators' actions are aimed and the role the manipulees play in the achievement of those ends. In such cases, the manipulators' intentions are "masked" though the manipulees are not deceived about anything external to the intentions of the manipulators. Here is such a case.

Flattery: Carlos approaches his boss Lucinda at the company holiday party and tells her that her recent restructuring of the company's distribution system was altogether brilliant. Though Carlos happens to believe Lucinda's recent performance really was brilliant, he would have told her this even if he believed her efforts displayed rank incompetence. Carlos knows he is telling his boss something she has heard from many others and which she already believes, and he believes that due to his own limited business experience Lucinda probably will not take his opinion to carry much weight as an evaluation of her work. Carlos believes the only value of his expressing his opinion lies in its potentially causing Lucinda to be positively disposed towards him, and he wants badly for her to be so disposed in light of his recent performance review, during which Lucinda expressed serious concerns about Carlos's ability meet the requirements of his job. Carlos is motivated to appear to compliment Lucinda exclusively by the effect he thinks doing so may have on her attitudes towards him.

Carlos does not deceive Lucinda about his opinions of her work but he does act deceptively insofar as he wants it to appear to Lucinda that his comment was motivated by his beliefs regarding the features of Lucinda's behavior that really do justify a compliment, and not exclusively by his desire to get into her good graces. Carlos must rightly assume that if Lucinda believed he was merely trying to ingratiate himself to her, his action would be unlikely to elicit attitudes that would benefit him. By masking his intentions with

---

1. Sarah Buss, "Valuing Autonomy and Respecting Persons: Manipulation, Seduction, and the Basis of Moral Constraints," *Ethics* 115 (January 2005): 226.

respect to Lucinda's attitudes towards him Carlos attempts to mislead Lucinda about the purpose of his disclosing (what just happens to be) his opinion to Lucinda. The masking of his intentions is necessary for their satisfaction and is a central element in his plan. Carlos is attempting to "prevent [Lucinda] from governing herself with an accurate understanding of her situation" insofar as the success of his plan—that is, that Lucinda have certain attitudes about him—depends on her misconstruing the purpose of their interaction. Carlos acts deceptively and manipulatively, though the scope of his deception is limited to the content of his intentions.

In all cases of successful deception the intentions of the deceiver will to some extent remain hidden. In most cases of deception the masking of the intentions is of derivative, instrumental importance from the point of view of the deceiver, as the more central aim of the deceiver is the acceptance by the deceived of false beliefs about some state of affairs that is independent of the intentions that lie behind the act of deception. But in other cases of deception the object of the deception just is the content of the deceiver's intentions. The victim of the deception comes to have false beliefs only about what the deceiver is doing in interacting with her. As the case of Carlos and Lucinda illustrates, it is possible for an agent to speak the truth while nevertheless dissembling, as the content of the propositions asserted (e.g., that Lucinda's performance was brilliant) is independent of the content of the intentions that underlie their assertion (e.g., that Lucinda come to view Carlos in a more favorable light.)

When one agent interacts with another agent the latter typically will have expectations about the intentions of the former and the role she (the latter) plays in those intentions. Generally these expectations are not the product of any explicit statement or agreement but are, rather, assumed to underlie the interaction. In typical cases of communication an agent expects that her communicative partner adheres to certain norms of discourse—for example, that she be neither more nor less informative than necessary, that she speaks with the intention to convey what she believes to be true, that she says only what is relevant, and that she is reasonably careful to avoid saying things that may lead to misconceptions or confusion.[2]

---

2. These expectations correlate roughly to the four maxims constituting Grice's Cooperative Principle (quantity, quality, relation, and manner). Grice was attempting to provide a theory of meaning in formulating the Cooperative Principle and in examining various failures to abide by the Principle. I do not mean to endorse Grice's semantic theory. I appeal to Grice's categories here because they are helpful in articulating the kind of expectations that are generated in a wide range of social interactions. For Grice's discussion of the Cooperative Principle, see H. P. Grice, "Logic and Conversation," in *Studies in the Way of Words* (Cambridge, MA: Harvard University Press, 1989), 22–40.

I propose to add to this list a Transparency Norm, which requires that an interactive partner not hide her intentions in interacting when these intentions are relevant to the intentions or interests of the person with whom she is interacting. Unlike the truth-telling norm, which is quite general and has application in most (if not all) contexts, the Transparency Norm may have a more limited applicability, the criteria for which will vary with context. For current purposes, I hope only to have shown how deceptive manipulation may involve a particularly nuanced kind of deception, one in which a manipulee is deceived not about the truth value of what the manipulator is claiming but, rather, about what both manipulator and (as a consequence) manipulee are doing. Indeed, in all cases of deceptive manipulation, whether the content of the deception is limited to the intentions of the manipulator or extends beyond them, a central aim of the manipulator is to deceive the manipulee about the role the latter plays in the plans of the former. Unlike in non-manipulative deception, where the point of the interaction is to cause false beliefs with content extending beyond the intentions of the manipulator, in cases of manipulative deception such beliefs, if they are at all present, are of derivative value to the manipulator, whose central concern is to mask her intentions and the role the manipulee plays in these intentions. The Transparency Norm would rule out deceptive manipulation as well as most standard cases of deception such as lying and is thus more general than a standard truth-telling norm. It is by playing on the expectations of manipulees, expectations generated by adherence to the Transparency Norm, that manipulators prevent manipulees from governing themselves with an accurate understanding of their situation.

In *What We Owe to Each Other*, Thomas Scanlon discusses how our causing others to have expectations about our behavior can generate moral obligations. In this context, he articulates a principle meant to rule out unjustified manipulation. He calls this principle "Principle M," and it requires that (in certain circumstances) agents not hide their (relevant) intentions in interacting with others.

> *Principle M:* In the absence of special justification, it is not permissible for one person, A, in order to get another person, B, to do some act, X (which A wants B to do and which B is morally free to do or not do but would otherwise not do), to lead B to expect that if he or she does X then A will do Y(which B wants but believes that A will otherwise not do), when in fact A has no intention of doing Y if B does X, and A can reasonably foresee that B will suffer

significant loss if he or she does X and A does not reciprocate by doing Y.[3]

According to Scanlon, Principle M is a valid moral principle. This is because:

[c]onsidering the matter from the point of view of potential victims of manipulation, there is a strong generic reason to want to be able to direct one's efforts and resources toward aims one has chosen and not to have one's planning co-opted...whenever this suits someone else's purposes.[4]

Here Scanlon voices a concern similar to that expressed by Buss when she says that manipulation can "prevent [a manipulee] from governing herself with an *accurate understanding* of her situation."[5] The explanation for Principle M—that is, that people have strong reasons to want to be able to direct their energies towards aims they have chosen, and that hiding one's intentions when interacting with others can undermine this ability—may capture one ethically troubling element that is sometimes present when one agent manipulates another. The basic idea seems to be that when one's intentions impact the intentions of others, it can be wrong to mislead others about what one's intentions really are. Scanlon goes on to discuss other more general but related principles that he thinks account for the wrongness of promise-breaking and lying, and he claims that these principles are generalizations of Principle M.[6] On his

---

3. Thomas Scanlon, *What We Owe to Each Other* (Cambridge, MA: Belknap,, 1998), 298.

4. Scanlon, *What We Owe to Each Other*. I think it is plausible that Principle M is indeed a valid moral principle. However, the principle is formulated in such a way as to preclude more than one kind of morally questionable behavior, and thus it is not clear that it best accounts for the wrongness of manipulation rather than some other kind of wrong. First, as Scanlon points out, agent A makes it impossible for B to "direct [his or her] efforts and resources toward aims [B] has chosen." Second, A has intentionally sought to gain an advantage at B's expense, as we are told B will suffer significant loss. Third, A has deceived B about A's intentions, the content of which intentions form the basis of B's decision to behave as A wishes. None of these three things forms an essential component of the others—they are conceptually independent. One might commit one of these putative wrongs without committing the others.

5. Buss, "Valuing Autonomy and Respecting Persons," 226.

6. Scanlon, *What We Owe to Each Other,* 299–322.

view, unjustified manipulation is a special case of lying, and thus Scanlon seems committed to the Deception-Based View of manipulation.

In each of the cases discussed so far, a manipulator deceives a manipulee by making claims (whether true or false). However, a manipulator may avoid making claims and yet use deception to control the behavior of others. For example, advertisers frequently arrange non-propositional visual and auditory stimuli in ways that associate the products they are trying to sell (or the policies they are trying to promote) with the preferences of members of the target demographic, even when there is no rational or causal connection between the stimuli and the products (or policies) with which they are being associated. Many such cases will clearly count as manipulative. Or, a manipulator may make changes in the environment which are intended to lead to the manipulee's holding false beliefs and behaving on the basis of doing so. Carol Rovane provides a nice example of this kind of manipulation:

> [Y]ou are about to leave the house without your umbrella. And… I decide that it would be amusing to get you to take it.… I happen to know that you always take your umbrella on days when your housemates take theirs. I also happen to know that there is an umbrella stand near the door which is usually full of umbrellas, except on days when your housemates have taken them. So I remove all of the umbrellas but yours from the stand with the following aim: you will notice that the other umbrellas are gone, you will infer that your housemates have taken their umbrellas, and you will decide to follow suit by taking yours.[7]

Here the manipulator avoids making any claims at all and yet the manipulation is deceptive.

The cases presented above are representative of a large class of manipulative actions of the sort captured by the Deception-Based View. However, there are counterexamples to the Deception-Based View.

Off the Wagon: Wilson and Adams are up for promotion, though only one of them will get the job. Wilson is a recovering alcoholic and Adams sets out to encourage a relapse, intending this to disqualify Wilson for the promotion. Adams consistently drinks alcohol in front of Wilson, offers her alcoholic beverages, vividly describes to her whatever benefits there are to drinking and to drunkenness, and so on, all the while making no secret of his intentions. During

---

7. Carol Rovane, *The Bounds of Agency: An Essay in Revisionary Metaphysics* (Princeton, NJ: Princeton University Press, 1998), 78.

a moment of weakness brought on by a particularly difficult and stressful event Adams takes a drink, which leads to more drinks, missed days at work, and an overall decreased ability to meet the demands of her job. When the time comes to announce who will be promoted, Adams is told by her managers that her recent poor performance has made it impossible for them to give her the new job and that they have selected Wilson for the promotion.

Wilson has manipulated Adams by engaging her compulsion to drink alcohol. And Adams's awareness of Wilson's intentions does not undermine the intuition that this is a genuine case of manipulation. In this case the manipulator does not deceive the manipulee about anything. The manipulator's intentions are known to the manipulee and no false claims are advanced. Therefore, manipulation need not involve any deception. The Deception-Based View is false.

Manipulation and Harm

According to the next account of manipulation I will examine—the Harm-Based View—manipulation essentially involves harm, and this is what provides us with a reason to avoid engaging in it. The Harm-Based View accounts for the fact that often when we criticize an instance of manipulation one of the features we single out is the harm done to the manipulee. It also accounts for the fact that manipulators often do advance their own interests at the expense of those whom they manipulate. David in *Synagogue* seeks to increase the likelihood of his getting what he wants (a relationship with Susan) by decreasing the likelihood of Jack's getting what he wants (also a relationship with Susan), and Adams in *Off the Wagon* improves his situation by making Wilson significantly worse off. Scanlon's Principle M involves one agent deliberately gaining advantage at the expense of another agent who, as a result of their interaction, would suffer significant loss. Indeed, it might be thought that the motivation for the Deception-Based View is grounded at a deeper level in a concern about harm. Perhaps a defender of the Deception-Based View mistakes the importance of process (deception) with that of a salient consequence (harm) of that process. In any case, an account of manipulation that takes harm to be an essential normatively relevant feature will capture some cases of manipulation that are left out by the Deception-Based View— for example, *Off the Wagon*. It will also explain why manipulation often does involve deception, for people who are mistaken about their situation—for example, about the consequences of their behavior—are more likely to behave in ways that are detrimental to their own interests.

Typically, people resort to manipulating others when they believe other methods of influence will fail. Sometimes there simply are no good reasons that can be given to someone to motivate her to behave in some way—not because she is not amenable to reason but because she *is* amenable to reason and what is being asked of her is contrary to reason. When an agent believes some possible action of hers will be detrimental to her interests she probably will be strongly disposed to avoid doing that action. Moreover, if she has sufficient evidence for her belief and is rational there may be no good argument to convince her otherwise. In such cases, it may be necessary for the person seeking control to manipulate the agent into doing whatever it is she wants her to do. As an effective means of directing people to do voluntarily what is not in their best interest, at least according to their own considered judgment (which may or may not be consistent with their judgment at the time of the manipulated act), manipulation often does involve harm to the manipulated agent.

But the Harm-Based View does not stand up to much scrutiny. Perhaps the easiest way to see this is by reflecting on cases of manipulative paternalism. Though it is difficult non-manipulatively to direct people to act in ways that are inconsistent with their own considered judgments regarding their interests, people are prone to acting against their interests on their own, sometimes consciously. Manipulation can be used to *prevent* them from doing so. The "libertarian paternalist" policies proposed by Richard Thaler and Cass Sunstein are intended to cause people to behave in ways that benefit them and they do so in ways that exploit irrational (or, weaker, nonrational) tendencies.[8] For example, if a cafeteria manager gets people to eat healthful foods by carefully arranging the order in which the food choices are displayed in the cafeteria, it is plausible that he has manipulated his customers to act in ways that benefit them.[9] Here is a more straightforward example.

Dementia: Mildred, who suffers from dementia, appears to have an infection. Her son Nathaniel wants her to go to the hospital but is

---

8. Richard Thaler and Cass Sunstein, *Nudge: Improving Decisions About Health, Wealth, and Happiness* (New York: Penguin, 2008); Cass R. Sunstein and and Richard Thaler, "Libertarian Paternalism Is Not an Oxymoron," *University of Chicago Law Review* 70 (2003): 1159–1202.

9. Sunstein and Thaler, "Libertarian Paternalism," 1184.

unable to persuade her to do so by citing the reasons that support her doing so (e.g., that infections left untreated may be life-threatening, that the hospital is the best place to treat the infection, etc.). Nathan knows that his mother would go to the hospital if she were told to do so by his father. The problem is, his father has been dead for a number of years. However, due to her dementia, Mildred often mistakes her son for her husband. Nathaniel waits until his mother calls him by his father's name and then, pretending to be his father, tells her that he would like her to go to the hospital to have her infection treated. She agrees.

This case raises a number of difficult ethical questions. However, it should be clear that Nathaniel has manipulated his mother and also that he neither intended harm nor likely brought any about. His action was manipulative but beneficent. Unless we implausibly stipulate that to manipulate someone is *ipso facto* to harm her, the Harm-Based View will be subject to many similar counter-examples.

Manipulation and Autonomy

The third view I will examine is the Autonomy-Undermining View of manipulation. According to this account manipulation essentially involves the undermining of an agent's autonomy. The Autonomy-Undermining View is more difficult to assess than the previous two accounts. Theories of autonomy vary and thus an account of manipulation that makes autonomy-undermining central will need to specify which notion of autonomy is at issue. Broadly speaking, there are two approaches one may take in analyzing autonomy. The first is purely "internalist" in that it seeks to locate autonomy in the relations between an agent's propositional attitudes, irrespective of the source of those attitudes or the processes underlying their acquisition and development. The second is "externalist" in that it looks to the sources of an agent's motivational set and the manner in which members of that set were acquired and arranged—that is, their history. Externalist accounts may themselves differ significantly in how they distinguish between autonomy-conducive histories and autonomy-undermining histories. In this section, I briefly describe internalist and externalist accounts of autonomy and then argue that whichever of these provides the best theory of autonomy, each is consistent with manipulation. Manipulation does not entail the undermining of autonomy.

Internalist Theories of Autonomy

On one influential internalist account of autonomy all that matters is the degree of coherence between first-order and higher-order propositional attitudes.[10] An autonomy-undermining theory of manipulation that construes autonomy in this way must insist that manipulators intervene between their manipulees' first-order attitudes and their higher-order attitudes. To illustrate, suppose an agent has a second-order desire D_2 that some first-order desire D_1 of his not move him to action. According to the internalist, a manipulator may undermine this agent's autonomy by, say, altering the intensity of D_1 so that D_1 is now action-causing for the agent. If the agent acts on D_1 despite the presence of D_2, then the agent has not acted autonomously. Part of the explanation for this is that he was manipulated, since it is the manipulation that led to the misalignment between the relevant attitudes. According to the internalist theory an action is autonomous when higher-order and lower-order attitudes regarding that action cohere in a specific way, and thus for manipulation to be essentially autonomy-undermining is for it to be essentially coherence-undermining.

The problem with trying to explain manipulation by reference to an internalist theory of autonomy is that there are cases of manipulation that clearly do not threaten the coherence of the manipulated agent's attitudes. Drawing on the case provided in the last paragraph, a manipulator may leave D_1 alone, opting instead to alter D_2 so that it coheres with D_1. If the agent then acts on D_1 he will have done so autonomously according to the internalist. Similarly, a manipulator may alter attitudes on both higher and lower levels so that an autonomous decision not to do X becomes an autonomous decision to do X.

For example, as a result of being exposed to subliminal messages an agent who wants to avoid hurting her friend and also wants to want to avoid hurting her friend might form the desire to slap her friend as well as the desire to be the kind of person who desires to slap her friend. If as a result of this she does slap her friend, this would constitute a case of manipulation, though according to the internalist account of autonomy the agent acted autonomously. On this picture manipulation cannot be essentially autonomy undermining, for autonomy is preserved despite the manipulation or even as a result of it.

---

10. See, for example, Harry Frankfurt, "Freedom of the Will and the Concept of a Person," *Journal of Philosophy* 68, no. 1 (January 1971): 5–20.

I do not believe manipulation necessarily undermines autonomy. However, in order to vindicate this claim I will need to do more than merely rehearse some of the well-known objections to internalist theories of autonomy. I will need to show how manipulation is consistent with autonomy as the latter is construed by externalist theories as well.

Externalist Theories of Autonomy

Before discussing any particular externalist theories of autonomy it is important to note an ambiguity about what 'external' is supposed to denote in such theories. On the one hand, there are questions about the sources from which and the processes by which an agent came to hold the propositional attitudes or, more broadly, to be in the behavior-underlying states in question. On the other hand, there are questions about the agent's attitudes about those processes. I call theories that focus exclusively on the first class of questions *pure externalist* theories. Such theories seek to distinguish between autonomous and non-autonomous behavior (broadly construed to include the acquisition/holding of propositional attitudes, emotional fluctuations, etc.) by reference to the processes that lead up to the states of the agent that underlie the behavior. According to a pure externalist theory of autonomy, the truth of autonomy claims can be determined in the absence of any reference to the agent's attitudes about her own states or the processes that lead up to them.

The second class of externalist theories, which I label *mixed theories,* hold that in answering the question of whether or not some agent is autonomous with respect to some behavior we must look at the processes that lead to the behavior as well as at the content of the agent's propositional attitudes. With respect to the propositional attitudes, these theories focus in particular on the content that represents the sources and processes that lead to the development or alteration of the agent's behavior-underlying states. According to a mixed theory of autonomy an agent cannot be autonomous with respect to some bit of behavior if she does not have (*inter alia*) non-negative attitudes about the processes leading up to the states that underlie this behavior. In other words, the agent must approve of the processes.[11] This relation between an agent's attitudes and the processes that lead to her behavior plays the same role in the mixed account

---

11. I understand 'approve' rather weakly as a kind of (actual or perhaps even hypothetical) pro-attitude.

that the relation between lower-order and higher-order attitudes plays in the internalist account. That is, it is meant to ensure that in order to be autonomous an agent must in some sense authorize the forces that move her. But unlike internalist theories, mixed accounts require that the salient propositional attitudes have as their content the processes that lead to or underlie the relevant behavior.

Accounts of manipulation that appeal to an externalist conception of autonomy are difficult to assess because manipulation is itself a historical (i.e., external) process, one that is often construed as being antithetical to autonomy by definition. In order to defend my claim that the presence of manipulation is at least sometimes consistent with autonomous behavior I will have to pursue one of two courses. The first is to argue that externalist theories of autonomy fail and so it does not matter that according to these theories manipulation and autonomy are inconsistent. This would leave the internalist theory standing and (as sketched above) autonomy as the internalist construes it is consistent with manipulation. The alternative approach is to show that manipulation does not always threaten autonomy as understood by externalist theories. I will pursue the latter strategy for two reasons. The first is methodological. I do not want the plausibility of my account of manipulation to depend on the truth of a controversial theory of autonomy. Second, I happen to think history does matter when it comes to autonomy. Some of the standard objections to purely internalist theories are decisive in the absence of any appeal to externalist considerations (i.e., historical processes).[12] However, my claim that manipulation is consistent with autonomy does not require that externalist theories are true but only that, if they are true, it is not clear that they can easily rule out manipulation as an autonomy-respecting form of influence.[13]

I will take two routes toward supporting the claim that manipulation is consistent with externalist conceptions of autonomy. The first will be to provide a case of manipulation in which, intuitively, no one's autonomy is undermined. Next, I will argue in more general terms that the most plausible kind

---

12. Here I have in mind certain counterexamples to internalism. Mele provides some powerful ones in Alfred Mele, *Autonomous Agents: From Self Control to Autonomy* (Oxford University Press, 2001).

13. I thank George Sher for pointing out that my arguments regarding manipulation and autonomy can remain neutral on the question of which sort of theory of autonomy—internalist or externalist—is the one we ought ultimately to adopt.

of externalist theory of autonomy cannot exclude manipulation. Here is a case of manipulation in which intuitively no one's autonomy is undermined:

Cafeteria: Concerned about skyrocketing obesity rates, the manager of a cafeteria wants his customers to eat healthful food. One way to do this is by getting his customers to choose salads instead of french fries. Suppose people tend to choose the items they encounter first— that is, those placed at the front of the food line.[14] Knowing this, the manager places the salads at the front of the line and places the french fries farther down. Consequently, more people begin to choose the salads, just as the manager intended. In this case, at least some customers—those who would have selected the french fries had these been placed at the front of the line—are manipulated into choosing the healthful items. Yet, intuitively no one's autonomy is undermined.

Cafeteria shows that a person's autonomy can remain intact despite the presence of manipulation in the history of the behavior whose autonomy is in question.

There are general arguments to the conclusion that the most plausible theory of autonomy is a mixed theory and that such theories, like internalist theories and pure externalist theories, render autonomy consistent with manipulation. With respect to the first half of this claim, in order to accommodate some strong intuitions about autonomy, intuitions regarding the importance of the agent's attitudes about her own agential capacities, a defender of an externalist account of autonomy cannot appeal to just those processes that underlie the agent's behavior. This is because even if these processes are free from problematic external interference an agent who is alienated from these processes will lack a critical component of autonomous agency. She will not conceive of herself as an agent acting independently of problematic interferences.

In the absence of the satisfaction of an attitudinal condition an agent may meet pure externalist conditions for autonomy[15] and yet falsely believe she is being controlled by autonomy-undermining forces. Or she may be

---

14. Sunstein and Thaler, "Libertarian Paternalism," 1164. They discuss the same example in Thaler and Sunstein, *Nudge*, 1–4.

15. That is to say, the history of how she came to be in the states she is in and to have the attitudes she has may include no external interferences that obviously threaten autonomy (e.g., brainwashing).

free of any problematic external interferences and yet lack a coherent set of attitudes—that is, she may not identify with her lower-order attitudes. It may be a necessary condition for self-governance that an agent has a conception of herself as self-governing. It is plausible that an agent's attitudes about her own agency partly determine the extent to which she actually is an agent, and thus an analysis of autonomous agency must make some appeal to an agent's representations of and attitudes about her situation. If this is right, a defender of an externalist theory of autonomy is pushed towards a mixed theory, a theory that incorporates some attitudinal condition such as the condition requiring that an agent approve of the processes that lead up to her behavior.

Thus far I have tried to motivate externalism about autonomy and I have sketched some of the reasons why an externalist might be pushed towards a mixed theory. It still remains to be argued that mixed theories render manipulation consistent with autonomy. Here I will draw from the literature on autonomy and in particular from work that is critical of internalist theories. As already noted, one of the most powerful objections to internalist theories is that higher-order and lower-order attitudes can be brought to cohere in any number of ways, some of which are manipulative. My strategy will be to show that the attitudinal condition in mixed theories— that is, the condition requiring that an agent have the right sort of attitudes about the processes leading to her behavior—is vulnerable to the same problem. It will be easier to see this with an example. Take John Christman's analysis of autonomy:

(i) A person P is autonomous relative to some desire D if it is the case that P did not resist the development of D when attending to this process of development, or P would not have resisted that development had P attended to the process;

(ii) The lack of resistance to the development of D did not take place (or would not have) under the influence of factors that inhibit self-reflection; and

(iii) The self-reflection involved in condition (i) is (minimally) rational and involves no self-deception.[16]

---

16. John Christman, "Autonomy and Personal History," *Canadian Journal of Philosophy* 21, no. 1 (1991): 11.

Whether or not an agent resists the development of some propositional attitude (condition [i]) is going to be determined (at least partly) by her other propositional attitudes, so a question arises as to whether the agent resisted the development of these attitudes.[17] The same question then arises with respect to the attitudes that determined whether the agent resisted *those* attitudes. And so on. Condition (ii) may be meant to stop the regress but it can do so only with respect to methods that inhibit self-reflection (e.g., brainwashing). Other methods, such as presenting an agent with a circumscribed set of options, presenting those options in one order rather than another, or even creating a context in which an agent is *more* likely to be self-reflective are not ruled out by the condition specified in (ii).

As far as I can tell there is no way for an account of autonomy that incorporates an attitudinal condition to exclude manipulation. The only way to exclude manipulation is by jettisoning the attitudinal condition and sticking with a pure externalist view. However, as I have already suggested, I do not think pure externalist accounts of manipulation work. (And even if they do work *qua* theories of autonomy, cases like *Cafeteria* suggest that such theories may not be able to rule out manipulation). Therefore, the most plausible competing accounts of autonomy—the internalist account and the mixed externalist account—construe autonomy in manner that renders it consistent with the presence of manipulation.

Manipulation and the Rational Capacities

Perhaps the most popular account of manipulation is the one according to which manipulation essentially bypasses or subverts the rational capacities of the manipulated agent. I will refer to this account as the Bypass or Subvert View (BSV) of manipulation. I have argued elsewhere that BSV is false and do not have the space here to recite these arguments in any detail.[18] Thus, I will recapitulate only the main claims and

---

17. I ignore the hypothetical versions of Christman's analysis. First, I am not yet sure how to interpret them. Second, unless the hypothetical consent is the consent of a idealized agent, hypothetical consent seems to reduce to some set of facts about the actual agent that are quite independent of issues of consent. In short, I am generally skeptical about the ability of hypothetical consent to render an agent autonomous.

18. Moti Gorin, "Do Manipulators Always Threaten Rationality?," *American Philosophical Quarterly* 51, no. 1 (January 2014).

then go on to situate them in relation to the examples provided above in earlier sections.

According to BSV, manipulation is a process of interpersonal influence that necessarily either fails to engage the rational capacities of the influenced agent (that is, it bypasses them) or else engages these capacities in some way that undermines their function (that is, it subverts them). BSV captures science-fictional cases of manipulation of the sort frequently discussed in the free-will literature—for example, cases of direct neurophysiological interventions or high-tech brainwashing. It also captures more realistic cases in which a manipulator stimulates psychological states in the manipulee that interfere with the manipulee's ability to reflect on her situation or to act in light of her better judgment.

BSV can account for many cases of manipulation—probably most of them—and it can explain why manipulation is often associated with "pulling the strings" of the manipulee, with conceiving of others as "puppets" to be managed or handled. It can also explain the tendency to associate manipulation with deception and with the undermining of autonomy. Thus, BSV is quite plausible and has been advanced in one form or another by a number of philosophers writing on manipulation.[19] Writing in this volume, Allen Wood suggests that manipulation "influences people's choices in ways that circumvent or subvert their rational decision-making processes, and that undermine and disrupt the ways of choosing that they themselves would critically endorse if they considered the matter in a way that is lucid and free of error."[20] At one time, BSV was defended by two other contributors to this volume, Marcia Baron and Eric Cave. Baron concludes her (earlier) essay on manipulativeness with the claim that "manipulativeness...reflects a failure to view others as rational beings or an impatience over the nuisance of having to treat them as rational."[21] In his (earlier) paper,

---

19. See Marcia Baron, "Manipulativeness," *Proceedings and Addresses of the American Philosophical Association* 77, no. 2 (November 2003): 50; Tom Beauchamp and J. Childress, *Principle of Biomedical Ethics*, 6th ed. (Oxford: Oxford University Press, 2008): 133–34; Jennifer Blumenthal-Barby and Hadley Burroughs, "Seeking Better Health Care Outcomes: The Ethics of Using the Nudge," *American Journal of Bioethics* 12, no. 2 (2012): 5; Eric Cave, "What's Wrong with Motive Manipulation?" *Ethical Theory and Moral Practice* 10, no. 2 (2007): 138; Patricia Greenspan, "The Problem with Manipulation," *American Philosophical Quarterly* 40, no. 2 (Apr. 2003): 164; Claudia Mills, "Politics and Manipulation," *Social Theory and Practice* 21, no. 1 (Spring 1995):100; Lawrence Stern, "Freedom, Blame, and Moral Community," *Journal of Philosophy* 71, no. 3 (February 1974): 74.

20. Allen Wood, "Coercion, Manipulation, Exploitation," this volume,xx–xx.

21. Baron, "Manipulativeness," 50.

Eric Cave defends the claim that "successful motive manipulation…operates by bypassing an agent's capacities for control over her mental life."[22] Patricia Greenspan has also defended BSV, claiming that

> [A]s *an interference with rational self-governance*, the problem with manipulation is not just that it fails to respect some notion of personal separateness or boundaries between persons but rather that it undermines a basic assumption of interpersonal trust in groups that make claims on their members on grounds of fraternity among reasoning agents.[23]

In her essay on manipulation and politics, Claudia Mills suggests that manipulators influence manipulees by "offering…bad reasons, disguised as good, or faulty arguments, disguised as sound."[24] Scanlon, too, seems committed to something like BSV. As noted earlier, Scanlon's Principle M is meant to rule out one agent's leading another agent to form expectations based on intentionally misleading behavior on the part of the first agent. Again, on his view Principle M is a valid moral principle because "[c]onsidering the matter from the point of view of potential victims of manipulation, there is a strong generic reason to want to be able to direct one's efforts and resources toward aims one has chosen and not to have one's planning co-opted."[25] Insofar as the rational capacities play a central role in helping an agent direct her energies towards aims she has chosen, manipulation subverts these capacities.

Despite its plausibility I think BSV is false. Consider the following case:

> *Election*: Jones is running for president. He has never taken the time to educate himself about matters of public concern and in fact could not care less about politics. Jones is attracted to the presidency because he intensely craves attention and knows that those who occupy this office are constantly in the spotlight. In order to make himself politically salable Jones hires a stable of pollsters, speech writers, and acting coaches. He constructs a political platform with the maximal vote-getting potential, as determined by his polling experts. He also commits to following through on his campaign

---

22. Cave, "What's Wrong with Motive Manipulation?" 133.

23. Greenspan, "The Problem with Manipulation," 164 (emphasis mine).

24. Mills, "Politics and Manipulation," 100.

25. Scanlon, *What We Owe to Each Other*, 298.

promises once elected, since he calculates that this may help him win a second term and hence to extend his time as the center of attention. Though personally indifferent to the ideals reflected in the policies he publicly defends, Jones—with the help of his speechwriters and coaches—convincingly advocates for his platform in speeches and debates and garners enough support to win the election.

In *Election,* Jones behaves manipulatively. Nevertheless, Jones does not bypass or subvert the rational capacities of the citizens who vote for him. After all, Jones advocates in favor of policies that many citizens really do support and he commits himself to realizing the values of these citizens. Jones does not deceive anyone about what he intends to do when elected and those who vote for him do so on the basis of political preferences upon which (we may suppose) they have rationally settled.

BSV holds that manipulation always involves the bypassing or subversion of the manipulee's rational capacities, and yet *Election* is an example of manipulation in which the rational capacities of the manipulated agent are neither bypassed nor subverted. Therefore, despite its intuitive appeal and ability both to account for many cases of manipulation and to subsume other competing theories, BSV is false.

Manipulation and Reasons

I believe the plausibility of the accounts discussed so far—and of BSV in particular—is grounded in our sense that manipulation does not track reasons in the way some other less problematic forms of interpersonal influence do. That is, I think it is manipulation's failure to track reasons that renders it morally suspect. In this section I will provide a rough account of how I think manipulation fails to track reasons.

As a first step, consider Mills's insightful observation that

A manipulator judges reasons and arguments not by their quality but their efficacy. A manipulator is interested in reasons not as logical justifiers but as causal levers. For the manipulator, reasons are tools, and a bad reason can work as well as, or better than, a good one.[26]

---

26. Mills, "Politics and Manipulation," 100–101.

I think Mills gets something right here, but also that she overlooks a critical implication of her claim and thus misses something central about the nature of manipulation, namely that for those who care only about the causal efficacy of reasons or arguments—that is, for manipulators—the degree to which a particular reason or argument provides justificatory support will be irrelevant, and this will be as true with respect to *good* reasons and arguments as it is with respect to bad ones. Mills puts too much emphasis on the provision of bad reasons and arguments and consequently misses the crucial point, which is that for manipulators the justificatory quality of their means of influence just does not matter.

This point can be illuminated by contrasting the behavior of Jones in *Election* with the behavior of Smith, who is running for president in a nearby possible world. Smith and Jones are physically indistinguishable from one another and they run qualitatively identical campaigns from the point of view of voters. The difference between Smith and Jones is that Smith really does believe in the wisdom of the policies he proposes and he really does adhere to the values he believes will be realized by these policies. Smith wants to become president because he believes the policies he defends will be good for his country and its citizens. Most important, Smith believes the considerations that count in favor of his policies provide citizens with good (justifying) reasons to support his candidacy, and the reason-supportedness of these policies is what ultimately motivates Smith to seek public office. Put another way, the reasons Smith believes support his candidacy are the same reasons to which he appeals when he asks voters for their support. Unlike Jones, for whom the causal efficacy of his advocacy is the only aspect he considers, if Smith were to realize that one of the policies he favors is misguided he would make the relevant adjustments to his platform.

The salient difference between Smith and Jones—the feature that renders only the latter's behavior manipulative—is that the consideration that motivates Jones to run for office (i.e., that it will bring him a lot of attention) is completely independent of the consideration he invokes in trying to motivate voters to support him (i.e., that the policies he will implement are the best policies). For Jones the fact that there is good reason for a voter to see some policy implemented does not play a role in the explanation of why he publicly seeks to implement that policy—recall that he chooses policies strictly on the basis of their popularity. Similarly, in *Flattery* when Carlos compliments his boss Lucinda he is not motivated by his beliefs regarding the features of Lucinda's behavior that really do justify a compliment but, instead, by his desire to get into her good graces. That what he says happens to be supported from Lucinda's point of view by good reasons plays no role in the explanation of his behavior.

Both Jones and Smith intend to bring about behavior that is, from the perspective of voters, supported by good reasons. However, only Smith is motivated by the reasons he believes really do support the behavior he seeks to bring about, while Jones is completely indifferent to the justificatory dimension of the reasons to which he appeals, caring only about their causal efficacy. Thus, though Jones and Smith both intend to bring about reason-supported behavior, and though both Jones and Smith appeal to these reasons in asking for support, only Smith intends to bring about the reason-supported behavior *because* it is supported by reasons and only Smith would revise his plans if he were to come to believe that the behavior at which he is aiming is not, in fact, supported by reasons. The process of influence initiated by Smith tracks reasons; the process initiated by Jones does not.

In *Election*, the behavior at which Jones aims is in relation to those he seeks to influence supported by reasons, though this does not matter to Jones and plays no role in forming his intentions. I call manipulation of this type *non-paternalistic reasonable manipulation* (NPM). In other cases of manipulation, however, the reason-supportedness of the behavior does play a role in the intentions of the manipulator—that is, the manipulator aims at reasonable behavior *because* it is, from the perspective of the manipulee, reasonable. I call this sort of manipulation *paternalistic manipulation* (PM). *Dementia*, in which a concerned son manipulates his demented mother into admitting herself to the hospital for treatment, is a case of paternalistic manipulation. PM, like NPM, is reasonable—that is to say, the manipulator believes the behavior that is the upshot of the manipulation is, from the perspective of the manipulee, supported by good reasons. The difference between PM and NPRM lies in the motivational base of the manipulator. Paternalistic manipulators are motivated by the reason-supportedness of the behavior, while for non-paternalistic manipulators like Jones the reason-supportedness of the behavior is merely incidental and plays no direct role in explaining their intention to influence others.

However, despite aiming for behavior that is supported by reasons *because* it is supported by reasons, paternalistic manipulators still make use of *means of influence* that fail to track reasons. For example, Nathaniel encourages his mother, Mildred, to mistake him for his father. Nathaniel knows this belief does not justify his mother's going to the hospital for treatment. He makes use of his mother's belief solely because of the causal role he knows it can play and not because the content of her belief provides justificatory support for her action. Similarly, many of the "paternalistic libertarian" forms of influence defended by Thaler and Sunstein exploit cognitive biases such as the framing effect, anchoring, the default bias, and so on, which are psychological processes that do not track reasons.[27] Paternalistic manipulators typically choose manipulation only when reason-tracking forms of influence are unlikely to work and when they believe the reasons that support the behavior they seek to bring about are sufficiently weighty to justify non-reason-tracking means of influence.

Thus far I have discussed two types of manipulation, both of which involve manipulees being influenced in ways that lead to their behaving in reason-supported ways. But obviously there are many cases of manipulation that do not fit into either category because the manipulator is aiming at behavior he believes to be *unsupported* by reasons. *Unreasonable manipulation* (UM) is a form of influence in which an influencer aims to get the person being influenced to behave in ways the influencer believes to be unsupported by reasons, viewing the matter from the point of view of the manipulee.[28]

The sort of example that motivates the Harm-Based View of manipulation are also (typically) cases of UM. As I suggested when discussing the Harm-Based View, if an agent is sufficiently rational it will be difficult or impossible to get her to behave in ways she believes to be unsupported by good reasons. In such cases, a determined influencer who also believes the behavior she is seeking is unsupported by good reasons cannot appeal to what she thinks are good reasons. She might present bad reasons as good

---

27. Sunstein and Thaler, "Libertarian Paternalism," 1159–202. Cognitive biases do not track reasons because the explanation for why an agent chose as she did—suppose, for example, an agent is much more likely to choose option A than option B when option A is presented as the default option, even when option B is superior—makes no reference to reasons that could be invoked to justify that choice.

28. The account I am sketching here is similar to Robert Noggle's account of manipulative action. According to Noggle, "manipulative action is the attempt to get someone's beliefs, desires, or emotions to violate . . . norms, to fall short of . . . ideals" where the norms in question are the norms of belief, desire, and emotion, and the ideals are those of the influencing agent. I disagree with Noggle on several points, though I do not have the space here adequately to engage with his view. My main worry with Noggle's construal of manipulation is that it is not clear that it can easily account for paternalistic manipulation. Robert Noggle, "Manipulative Actions: A Conceptual and Moral Analysis," *American Philosophical Quarterly* 33, no. 1 (January 1996): 44.

ones or she may bypass the manipulee's rational capacities altogether, opting instead to stimulate a compulsion or to appeal to a misdirected or out-of-proportion emotion. UM fails to track reasons because it is not part of the manipulator's intention that the manipulee behave reasonably—on the contrary, here the manipulator consciously aims at behavior she believes is unsupported by reasons.

I have argued—in an admittedly sketchy way—that interpersonal manipulation, whether it is UM, PM, or NPM, fails to track reasons. Sometimes a manipulator will try to get others to behave in ways the manipulator believes are unsupported by reasons. Sometimes a manipulator will aim for behavior that happens to be supported by reasons, though the reason-supportedness of the behavior does not provide an independent motivational base for the manipulator. And finally, there are times when the reason-supportedness of the behavior does provide a source of motivation for the manipulator, though here the manipulator makes use of means of influence that do not track the supporting reasons.

On this view, the most salient elements of an interpersonal encounter in which one agent seeks to influence another are the motivations of the influencer, the particular means of influence chosen by the influencer, and the propositional attitudes and other mental states of the agent being influenced. In an ideal type of interpersonal influence, like rational persuasion with the right intentions, everything links up nicely: the motivations of the influencer are grounded in the reasons she believes really do support the behavior she seeks to bring about, the means of influence (e.g., sound argument) reliably "aim at" or "link up with" these reasons, and the mental states of the person being influenced also refer to the reasons that support the behavior. In cases of manipulation, there are breakdowns in these relations, breakdowns that can occur in more than one place. The location of the breakdown will determine whether the manipulation is reasonable or unreasonable, paternalistic or non-paternalistic.

Though I cannot argue for this claim here, I believe manipulation's failure to track reasons is what makes it morally impermissible (when it is). I believe this is true even when manipulation does not involve deception, harm, the bypassing or subversion of the rational capacities, or the violation of the manipulated agent's autonomy. Processes of influence that fail to track reasons can leave those who are influenced by them detached from an important aspect of reality, namely the considerations that ought to govern their behavior—their reasons. Influencing reasons-responsive agents via such processes displays a lack of respect for them as agents, and this is *pro tanto* wrong.[29]

Conclusion

I have argued that although it often does so, manipulation does not necessarily involve common wrongs like deception, harm, the bypassing or subversion of the rational capacities, or the violation of the manipulated agent's autonomy. Some of the accounts I have criticized—for example, the Harm-Based View—were not very plausible to begin with. Others are much more attractive. The Bypass or Subvert View in particular is quite plausible, at least initially, and a number of philosophers have defended it. However, despite its covering probably the majority of cases of manipulation, BSV cannot capture all of them. Consequently, we are need of an alternative account of interpersonal manipulation.

I then went on to sketch an alternative theory. According to this account manipulation is a process of interpersonal influence that deliberately fails to track reasons. Sometimes manipulators intend their manipulees to behave in ways they (the manipulators) do not believe to be supported by reasons. Sometimes manipulators aim at behavior they do believe to be supported by reasons, but here either they remain unmotivated by these reasons or they make use of means of influence that do not reliably track those reasons. Finally, I suggested that manipulation's failure to track reasons can help explain why manipulation is wrong (when it is wrong). Clearly much more needs to be said, both about what manipulation is and about what makes it wrong. For now, I hope to have accomplished two relatively modest things. First, I hope to have shown why some accounts of manipulation that initially might appear attractive—those that appeal to phenomena such as deception, harm, autonomy, and the rational capacities—do not work. Second, I have provided a sketch of what I believe to be a better theory, one that begins to provide a general explanation of the nature and ethical significance of interpersonal manipulation.

---

29. I discuss the ethics of manipulation in an unpublished manuscript.

4

The *Mens Rea* and Moral Status of Manipulation

Marcia Baron

MY AIMS IN this essay are twofold: to sort out what might be called the *"mens rea"* of manipulation, and to try to work out the moral status of manipulation.[1] Both are matters that I touched on only briefly in an earlier piece[2] where, in offering an account of manipulativeness, I had to take a stand, for purposes of clarity, on whether manipulation requires intent and whether 'manipulative' is best understood as allowing for the possibility that the quality or action described as manipulative is unobjectionable. I continue to think that manipulation requires intent (and continue to think that it need not be conscious intent). On the second matter, I took the position that it is not best understood as allowing for that possibility and that in that sense, 'manipulative' is best understood as a moralized term. (Note that this is a slightly different sense from that in which Allen Wood speaks of 'manipulative' or 'coercive' being moralized: by 'moralized' he means that "it is taken for granted, as part of the very meaning of the term, that what it refers to is immoral."[3] In holding that 'manipulative'

1. I would like to thank discussants at the Bowling Green State University 2012 workshop on manipulation for helpful remarks on an earlier version of this essay, and those who attended a mini-seminar I taught with Allen Wood at Stanford University in 2012 for incisive discussion of my earlier work on manipulativeness. Special thanks to Allen Wood for many helpful discussions and for comments on a draft of this paper; and to Christian Coons, Kate Manne, and Michael McKenna for insightful comments on the penultimate draft.

2. Marcia Baron, "Manipulativeness," *Proceedings and Addresses of the American Philosophical Association* 77, no. 2 (November 2003): 37–54.

3. Allen Wood, "Coercion, Manipulation, Exploitation," this volume, 18.

is a moralized term I was claiming not that it is part of the meaning of the term that what it refers to is *immoral,* but only that it is morally objectionable—but of course something can be morally objectionable yet be morally justified and in that sense not immoral.)

In this essay I revisit both issues. I explore in more detail than I did earlier what it means to say that manipulation requires intent; I argue that it does require intent; and I try to sort out the moral status of manipulation, exploring the possibility that (contrary to what I wrote in "Manipulativeness") 'manipulative' is not best understood as a moralized term and that manipulating another is sometimes morally unobjectionable. In discussing these issues, especially the moral status of manipulation, I am at the same time trying to bring out disagreements about the scope of manipulation. I do not, in this essay, offer an account of what manipulation is, but I am building on my "Manipulativeness" (which I stand by, apart from the position on whether it is better to understand 'manipulative' as a moralized notion).

A quick preliminary. With the aim of clarifying what I am up to and, in the case of (1) below, also of bringing to light a difference among philosophers that I think deserves to be flagged lest we talk past each other, I emphasize:

1. Unlike many philosophers who work on the topic of manipulation, I do not hold that if S is manipulated into doing *x*, S is not responsible for having done *x* (or for the consequences of having done *x*).
2. Relatedly, I am not interested in what the manipulated person should or should not have done; my focus is on the conduct (and sometimes the character) of the manipulator.[4]
3. Although it is understandable to take as paradigms of manipulation particularly egregious cases, I will not be doing so. I am more interested in the less egregious cases, where there is room for disagreement as to

---

4. This may be part of the explanation of some points of disagreements between Allen Wood and me, disagreements elaborated in his contribution and discussed briefly below; for although he shares my position on (1), and regarding (2), is not particularly interested in what the manipulated person should or should not have done, his account proceeds "from the standpoint of the person who is coerced, or feels coerced, and the account tries to say when, and why, such a feeling is correct" (21) and his discussion of manipulation is likewise more focused on what it is to be manipulated than what it is to be manipulative or act manipulatively.

whether the conduct is morally objectionable (and, for those resistant to allowing that manipulation is sometimes not morally objectionable, room for debate over whether the conduct counts as manipulation).

A comment on (1): The philosophical literature on manipulation has (at least) two very different entry points. One is a concern with freedom and moral responsibility, where the focus is on the effect of manipulation on the manipulee's freedom. In this literature it is widely assumed that being manipulated into doing *x* entails not being responsible for doing *x*. The other concern is what sort of manipulating (or would-be manipulating, for those who think it is not manipulation if it is permissible) it is permissible to do, with no particular interest in the degree of exculpatory force 'I was manipulated' has. There is room for a great deal of confusion if we do not bear in mind these two rather different philosophical reasons for taking an interest in manipulation, particularly if those with the first concern assume that those writing on manipulation share the assumption that the person who is manipulated into doing *x* is therefore not responsible for doing *x*.

Intent

'*Mens rea*' refers in criminal law to the "mental component" of a crime, or as it is sometimes put, the "mental state" (where, however, this can also encompass the absence, not merely the presence, of relevant "mental states").[5] In this context my interest is in the mental component necessary for something to count as an act of manipulation (and I do not mean to insinuate by my use of the term '*mens rea*' that manipulation should be thought of as a crime).

The position I took in "Manipulativeness" was that manipulation requires intent.[6] I also held that it does not require that one knows one is manipulating

---

5. Some legal scholars and philosophers of law understand '*mens rea*' more narrowly, so as not to encompass negligence. See, e.g., David Ormerod, *Smith and Hogan Criminal Law*,13th ed. (New York: Oxford University Press, 2011), 147.

6. So does being manipulative. Being manipulative contrasts in this respect with being intimidating. (Note that I am speaking here of being intimidating, not of the act of intimidating another; intimidating another does require intent. 'You intimidated me' should be retracted if it emerges there was no intent to do so.) One can be intimidating without meaning to be. This is true of many very smart, very articulate people (among others). It is also true of many smart, very articulate people that they are sometimes manipulative

or being manipulative.[7] I remain confident about the second claim. I believe the first claim is true, but I am not altogether confident. To figure out whether it is true, I'll need to address an unclarity. I'll explain the unclarity shortly, but first want to provide some motivation for the (rough) idea that manipulation requires intent.

Here is the thought: Suppose you agree to do something because you are nervous around the person who requested it, eager not to displease her, and fearful that you will displease her if you decline her request. You may feel you have no real choice. This seems to me not yet to be a case of manipulation. What is missing is her intent to get you to do what she wants and (but I shall revisit and modify this shortly) to do so by taking advantage of your eagerness not to disappoint her (perhaps also cultivating it, or speaking in a way that feeds your fear of her disapproval or rejection). She may not need to know that it is her intent to get you to do what she wants, but it has to be the case that it is.[8] Otherwise, she is not manipulating you.

There is a complication that needs to be borne in mind: the history of the relationship. Sometimes A feels manipulated even though in this particular instance B merely wants very much that A will do x and does not want to bring it about that A does x; in fact, B wants it to be the case that

---

without knowing it. They may think they are merely presenting strong arguments, and presenting them with conviction, but in fact they are determined to get their way. Without realizing it, they convey to their interlocutors that (a) they will not let matters rest until it is acknowledged that they are right, or [inclusive 'or'] (b) they will judge those who continue to hold an opposing view to be stupid or immoral. Department meetings in some philosophy departments are a good place to observe this phenomenon. Being manipulative involves one of the following: a recklessness or disregard for one's effect on others, a delight in controlling them, or a determination to have one's way, even if one has to resort to deception or to pressuring the others in a way that makes it hard for them to go against one's wishes. More on this below. Nothing analogous is true of being intimidating. Being intimidating sometimes does involve one or more of the qualities just mentioned, but it does not need to.

7. In holding that knowledge is not required, I differ from Robert Noggle who, in his "Manipulative Actions: A Conceptual and Moral Analysis," *American Philosophical Quarterly* 33, no. 1 (January 1996): 43–55, claims that it would be a flaw in an account of manipulation if the account entailed that one might "unknowingly perform manipulative actions" (the idea being not that one might not know what actions she is performing, but might not know that her actions are manipulative) (xx).

8. What might be an instance of manipulating without being aware of one's intent to get the other person to do (or feel) what one wants her to do (or feel)? Fortunately, another contribution to this volume provides a well-developed example (though the author doesn't commit to characterizing it as involving an unconscious intention, preferring to leave open the possibility that what is unconscious isn't an intention, but a motive). See the example of Joan in Kate Manne's contribution to this volume.

A does x "freely" (as B may think of it), not out of fear of displeasing or disappointing B. That A feels manipulated is not enough for this to count as manipulation. But suppose (here I am thinking of Olive and Verena in *The Bostonians*) that B has been working on A to, in effect, remake A in B's image of what A at her best can be. If A knows how invested B is in A as B's project (or simply in A's living up to B's expectations), it may well make sense to say that when A does x because she knows B badly wants her to do so, A not only feels but *is* manipulated by B. What this reflects is that manipulation is not always (if ever) best understood episodically, as an isolated event; it may need to be explained historically. You may be manipulated now thanks to months of prior actions that instilled (*inter alia*) fear of disappointing or fear of rejection. S's intent to get you to do what she wants might not be present right now; she wants you to do what she wants, but does not want it to be the case that she got you to do it. She may badly want to believe that she did not. Nonetheless, there was intent of a relevant sort earlier, intent to remake you into a different sort of person, and continuity between that intent and her ongoing investment in your acting as she hopes you will.

It is instructive to compare manipulating with insulting, and more specifically, to compare apologies for manipulating someone with apologies for insulting him or her. The following apology makes a great deal of sense, and it is not difficult to imagine a situation in which it is called for: "I am so sorry I insulted you. I didn't mean to; I didn't realize that what I was saying was insulting. I would never have put it that way if I had realized then what I now can see." One could of course instead say, "I am so sorry that what I said to you came across as insulting," but this is a different and more guarded apology (though not as stingy as "I am sorry that you feel that way," an apology whose condescending tone seriously undermines its claim to be an apology). In some circumstances it may be suitable, but in others "I am sorry I insulted you" is more appropriate, even if the agent did not intend to insult the person. Insulting another, in short, need not be intentional. It is, unfortunately, possible to insult someone without doing so intentionally.

By contrast, the following apology seems odd: "I am so sorry that I manipulated you [treated you manipulatively]. I didn't mean to; I didn't realize I was manipulating you, and I never would have acted as I did had I known."[9] What makes far more sense is: "I am so sorry that I spoke to

---

9. The infelicity does not lie in 'I didn't realize I was manipulating you'; I hold, as noted above, that one can manipulate another without realizing at the time that one is doing so.

you in a way that left you feeling as if you had no alternative but to accept my offer. I didn't mean it that way at all; I really wanted it to seem like an offer, not a demand, but I can see that I put you in an awkward position, and I apologize for that." Also possible (and I mention this in support of my claim that manipulation need not require awareness that one is manipulating the other): "I am so sorry about the way I treated you; I realize now that it was manipulative, and apologize for that. I guess I was so intent on getting you to give up your plan, which I thought really dangerous, that I went overboard." It appears, then, that an act of manipulation is necessarily intentional. If I didn't manipulate intentionally, I may have left you feeling manipulated, but I didn't manipulate you.

But there is some reason for uncertainty about what I have just written, namely an unclarity that renders it difficult to answer the question, "Does manipulating require intent?" What must one intend for the action to count as an instance of manipulating another? It makes sense to hesitate to affirm that manipulation requires intent when no account has been provided of just what the intent has to be.

So what exactly must one intend? What would make sense? Should we say that one must intend to manipulate the other? No, at least not under that description. That would unduly limit what can count as manipulation. So maybe this: to lead the other to do *x*, and to lead the other to do so by ___ [and here we would sketch methods the agent might employ, which would in fact be manipulative]? When, in the second paragraph of this section, I took a stab at spelling out the intent, that was the approach I took. I spoke of the agent's intent to get you to do what she wants, and to do so by taking advantage of your eagerness not to disappoint her (perhaps also cultivating it, or speaking in a way that feeds your fear of disapproval or rejection). But does manipulating have to involve intending specifically to take advantage of the person's eagerness not to disappoint or to employ some other strategy that, whether or not the agent thinks of it that way, is manipulative? I don't think so. The *mens rea* of manipulation can be a combination of intent and recklessness: the aim of getting the other to do what one wants, together with recklessness in the way one goes about reaching that goal.[10] In cases where one is culpably manipulative, one

---

I include 'I didn't realize...' in the infelicitous expression only to underscore the speaker's denial of intent—i.e., her claim that she would not have acted as she did had she realized that in so acting she was manipulating the other person.

10. For a different view of what one must intend, see Noggle, "Manipulative Actions."

is insufficiently concerned about the other *qua* agent. The recklessness amounts to a disregard for whether one is treating the other with respect.

This explication of the intent fits best, however, the cases where manipulating is clearly wrong. In other cases we may need to explain the *mens rea* component a little differently. That is as it should be: in cases where we are reluctant either to call it manipulation or, if we allow that manipulation need not always be wrong, reluctant to deem it wrong, one reason for our reluctance may be that the *mens rea* is (partially) missing.

This clarification should remove one reason for doubting that manipulation requires intent. The intent need not be intent to manipulate (though it can be). It can be intent to get the other to do *x*, along with insufficient concern about the other *qua* agent. The lack of concern is manifested in the way one chooses to get the other to do *x*, or one's willingness, when more appropriate ways prove ineffective, to resort to unsavory means. This captures the way we generally think about what is wrong with manipulation—manipulation of the non-sinister varieties, anyway. More sinister manipulation sometimes involves something worse—a delight in controlling another, for example. But when it does not (and sometimes when it does), manipulation generally involves a recklessness, a disregard for the other *qua* agent (though not necessarily a disregard for the other's welfare), a determination to bring about a particular result and a willingness to be very pushy or somewhat deceptive to reach that result.

I should add that my view is not merely that *if* the person manipulated is manipulated by one or more persons, it has to be the case that those doing the manipulating do so intentionally; I also hold that there is no manipulation without a manipulator. I may be the victim of circumstances, but the circumstances have not manipulated me. Only people can do that.

Likewise with coercion: there is no coercion without a coercer, and the coercer has to coerce intentionally. That coercion requires that the coercer coerce intentionally is, I think, evident—more evident, in fact, than that manipulation requires intent. Inadvertent coercion is more patently impossible than inadvertent manipulation. If I inadvertently park my car in such a way that my car blocks yours, preventing you from driving your car out of the lot, I have not coerced you into being late or into calling someone to come pick you up when you were unable to locate the jerk who parked so badly.

But does coercion really require a coercer? Or could it go like this: when there is a coercer, the coercion has to be intentional, but there need not be a coercer? After all, one can be forced by circumstances to do this or that. I agree: one can be forced by circumstances. But not coerced by circumstances. One can be forced either by (one or more) persons or by circumstances; one can be coerced only by people (or an individual person).

In his contribution to this volume, Allen Wood argues that one can be coerced by circumstances, and favors using 'coerced' and 'forced' as equivalent.[11] I think it preferable to treat them as nonequivalent, and not only because this follows standard usage in ordinary discourse. The experience of being forced by circumstances is quite different from that of being forced by a person (particularly if one thinks the person forcing her is wrong to do so). Being forced by circumstances to accept work that is dangerous, underpaid, and very distasteful is, to be sure, terrible; still, there is an added dimension to being forced (say) into prostitution by a particular person (or a group of persons, such as military officers) as compared with being forced into it by economic circumstances. (In comparing these, of course we need to imagine that the conditions into which one is forced are the same in each instance, recognizing that often they are not.) I believe Wood wants to de-emphasize the difference, perhaps in response to social and political views he and I both deplore, in particular, the view that people who are forced to accept terrible work conditions aren't *really* forced, and that it therefore should not be the concern of the state to try to bring it about that no one has no reasonable alternative to accepting such employment. But as long as we do not acquiesce to the claim that they are not really forced (and as long as we do not allow that forcing is not really a bad thing unless it is an instance of coercion), I see no reason to allow the fact that many people hold such deplorable social and political views to shape our thinking about the relation between coercing and forcing.[12]

---

11. Wood also suggests that one can be manipulated without there being a manipulator, and says that advertising "is a case in point, because it is not merely a practice engaged in by specific advertisers, but also a social institution that over time shapes people's habits and preferences" (39). It seems to me a stretch to claim that the institution manipulates; rather, advertisers, or groups composed of advertisers, manipulate.

12. There are other points of disagreement as well; e.g., Wood (26) says that "talk of coercion is most appropriate when the agent has exactly one acceptable alternative and takes it." Yet if the option the agent takes is fully acceptable, it seems odd to call it a case of coercion at all.

The Question of Moral Status

The question of whether to understand manipulation to require intent, and if so, what the intent should have to be, is one facet of the broader question of how broadly or narrowly to understand manipulation. The main divide, however, is between those who want to understand it narrowly enough that it comes out that manipulation is always wrong, and those (myself included) who do not wish to so constrain it. The divide here is not merely over how narrowly to define it, but more specifically over the aim to exclude from the category of acts of manipulation any action that is well-intentioned (or, in other possible versions, that is benevolent). Some wish to demarcate manipulative actions in such a way that it is clear that they are impermissible. To this end they want to exclude from the category actions which, while perhaps criticizable on other grounds, do not have the qualities that, it is claimed, are what make manipulative actions wrong.

Informing this disagreement on how broadly or narrowly to understand 'manipulation' are, as the above paragraph hints, normative disagreements. Some, often but not always Kantian, are troubled by the tactics used in manipulation, and take there to be a class of actions, appropriately classified as manipulation, that have in common that they employ methods that one should generally not employ; others see the problem in manipulation mainly to be the nefarious aims of the manipulator. The latter will understandably favor construing manipulation narrowly because they think the wrong of manipulation lies in the nefarious aims. I prefer a broader understanding of manipulation even though it does mean grouping the more sinister kinds of manipulation with the kinds that are problematic but not sinister. But I think this worth doing in part because the sinister aspects and the problematic but not sinister aspects are not disjoint. The aim affects how problematic the manipulation is, and if the aim is bad enough, makes the manipulation truly sinister.[13] I do not hold that manipulation is never justifiable. (I expect very few people would disagree, apart from those who understand manipulation so narrowly that there is little scope for justification.) But it is something that needs to be justified, and

---

13. Wood wonders in his contribution to this volume if I claim in my essay, "Manipulativeness," that "the worthiness of any end, taken by itself, is sufficient to justify manipulation as a means to it" (36). He correctly decides that I am not saying that. The position I took was that the worthiness of the end "can make what would otherwise clearly count as manipulative not so clearly manipulative" and that whether it does "depends on the techniques of manipulation that are employed"; see my "Manipulativeness," 46.

in those circumstances where it is justified, the manipulator's aim is part (but only part!) of the explanation of what justifies it.

Or *does* it always need to be justified? There is room for disagreement here. Once again, the question is complicated because it involves two issues: the question of what counts as manipulation—of how broad a swathe we want the word 'manipulation' to cover—and the question of the moral status of what is counted as manipulation. It will help to lay before us several examples and to consider, if we do view them as cases of manipulation and think that the manipulative conduct depicted is not wrong, why we think it is not wrong. What, more precisely, do we think when we think it isn't wrong? That it is justified? Usually. But always? Or do we take its moral status to be slightly higher: it never needed to be justified?

Before taking this up, I want to present an array of possible views as to how the moral status of manipulation should be understood. I do so in order to situate the narrower issue concerning moral status on which I'll focus in the context of other views concerning the moral status of manipulation, views I will not take up. Here is one way to divide up the possible views concerning the moral status of manipulation:

1. Manipulating people is invariably wrong. An account of manipulation that does not recognize this is *ipso facto* flawed.

There are two ways the position might be understood:

1a. Manipulation should be understood as wrong by definition, and any adequate account of manipulation will so understand it. 'A manipulated B' is similar to 'A murdered B' (despite murdering being a much graver wrong than manipulating) in that it is built into the concept of both manipulating and murdering that all such actions are wrong. If we ascertain that because of the circumstances A's action was not wrong, we retract the claim 'A murdered B' and say 'A caused B's death' (or perhaps 'A killed B, but the killing should count as manslaughter, not as murder'). 'A manipulated B,' on this view, works the same way. We retract the claim that A manipulated B if we find that A did not act wrongly, that under the circumstances, it was the best thing to do. Of course it is nonetheless consistent with this position to allow that A manipulated B but is not blameworthy; excusing conditions may apply. But it can never be justified.

1b. Manipulation is not wrong by definition, but it is always wrong. It can never be justified, but this is not a matter of definition. It simply is invariably wrong. (To borrow a helpful parallel from Allen Wood,[14] manipulation so understood has the moral status that abortion has in the eyes of those who believe that abortion is impermissible always, even to save the woman's life.)[15]

2. Manipulating people is not always wrong, but it is generally wrong. On this view, the word 'manipulated' functions in a way that is structurally more similar to that of the word 'killed' than to that of the word 'murdered.' Killing people is generally wrong, but not always; in some circumstances, it is permissible to kill in self-defense (or in defense of another). This option admits of some variation:

   2a. It is wrong in the way lying is wrong: it is always objectionable and to be avoided, but sometimes is the best option. It is an evil but sometimes the lesser of two evils (or the least of several evils). Unlike murder, which if justified is not murder at all, manipulating another can be justified without ceasing to count as an instance of manipulating another.

   2b. It is more often than not objectionable, but sometimes not at all objectionable; in this way, it has a somewhat higher moral status than does lying.

3. Manipulating people as such is not in the slightest wrong; it is an appropriate way of getting on in the world. As long as the manipulation is not coercive and as long as it does not involve deception, it is not wrong.

4. Manipulating people as such is not in the slightest wrong, as long as it is done for the benefit of the person manipulated. It is only wrong when it involves using people—that is, treating them as means to one's own ends (or to a third party's ends). Like (2), this option admits of some variation, but the variations need not concern us here if, as I think, (4) does not merit serious consideration.

I take (4) as well as (3) to be false and expect most readers do as well. Explaining why they are wrong would be a worthwhile project, but it is not my project. What about (1)? I do not see (1a) to be a serious option. Certainly as we now use 'manipulate,' it does not operate as 'murder' does. We cannot say "It was murder, but under the circumstances, it was justified"; by

---

14. See Wood's contribution to this volume.

15. With (1b), as with (1a), that it can never be justified does not entail that one could not possibly be excused for manipulating another.

contrast, "It was manipulative, but under the circumstances, it was justi-fied" does make sense. (1a) can make sense only if the idea is to stipulate that a justified act of manipulating another is, like justified murder and married bachelors, logically impossible. It is hard to see what reason there could be for favoring that. It would make more sense to favor either (1b) or (2a), and if (2a), perhaps adding that it would be rare for manipulation to be justified. I take (1b) to be implausible, though one could render it plausible by tailoring one's definition of 'manipulation' so as to exclude the cases that most tempt us to view manipulation as sometimes permis-sible. This would not be quite the same as defining manipulation in such a way that manipulation is wrong by definition, for the remaining instances of manipulation—all the cases not ruled out as not really manipulation—would not be wrong by definition. But the maneuver would be similar in that the wrongness of manipulation would be secured by defining the term so as to exclude the cases that challenged the thesis that manipulation is always wrong.

I take the serious choice to be between (2a) and (2b). But in case some are inclined toward (1), it is worth considering why the position that manipulation is invariably wrong might be attractive. I'll focus on (1b).

One reason why some may think of manipulation as invariably wrong is that the word 'manipulative,' at least when applied to persons, is always used pejoratively. Relatedly, we view manipulativeness as a vice, not as a virtue (or as neutral). If you have any doubt about this, a method Hume proposes and employs in the *Enquiry Concerning the Principles of Morals* for determining which qualities of character are virtues and which are vices might be a help: ask yourself whether or not you would desire to have the quality in question ascribed to you, and whether an imputation of the trait would proceed from a friend or from an enemy.[16] If anyone calls you manipulative, it is someone who (at least to that extent) does not like you.

It may be tempting to infer from manipulativeness being a vice, or from the fact that 'manipulative' as applied to persons is used pejoratively, that manipulation is always wrong. But that inference should be resisted. Think about why manipulativeness is a vice and why 'manipulative' as applied to persons has so strongly negative a connotation. To this end,

---

16. David Hume, *Enquiry Concerning the Principles of Morals,* in *Enquiries Concerning Human Understanding and Concerning the Principles of Morals,* 3rd ed., edited by L. A. Selby-Bigge (Oxford: Clarendon, 1975), 174. Of course, it is not a foolproof test; for one thing, it might reflect only what we generally regard to be a vice and what we generally regard as a virtue.

think about what we mean when we say someone is manipulative. We do not mean simply that he has certain skills. We mean that he is far too ready to manipulate people. His attitude toward others is all wrong. In judging manipulativeness to be a vice we generally have in mind such attitudes toward others as delight in controlling others or a readiness to see others as, in effect, pawns on a chessboard. Yet an act of manipulating another might not reflect these attitudes and dispositions. One might manipulate another reluctantly, judging it to be necessary under the circumstances yet regrettable. As observers, we might so judge the action, thus holding that manipulation is sometimes not wrong; there is no inconsistency in our judging this while at the same time believing manipulativeness to be a vice. Indeed, even in a case where we think the person's action reflects the character trait of manipulativeness, we might judge the action not to be wrong (while at the same time disapproving of the character it reflects), perhaps holding that under the circumstances it was the best (perhaps the only) option. Thus that manipulativeness is a vice—and that the word 'manipulative' when applied to persons is always pejorative—does not entail that manipulation is (or should be understood as) always wrong.

Now if the word 'manipulative' when applied to actions were always pejorative, this would lend somewhat greater support to (1). But it is not as consistently pejorative when applied to actions as it is when applied to persons. It is not hard to imagine someone saying, "Her action was manipulative, but it was necessary," and the speaker might add, "I'm glad she was willing to do what she did, but I am also glad that isn't the way she usually treats people." That said, it is rather unusual to call an action manipulative without intending thereby to criticize it, and that it is some-what unusual is a consideration in favor of (1). But it also lends support to (2a). Moreover, although it does not lend support to (2b), it tells against it less than one might suppose, for it might be unusual only or mainly for this reason: because calling an action manipulative may be taken to suggest something untoward about the agent's motive, we choose a term other than 'manipulative' if we do not intend any criticism of either the agent or the action.

What I have said about 'manipulative' as applied to actions applies for the most part to the verb 'manipulate' as well. Generally we do not say of someone that he manipulated another person unless we intend some criticism; still, one could say 'He did manipulate her, but it was the only option given her stubbornness, and given what was at stake.' Of course there is the complication that 'manipulate' can take objects other than people. I am concerned in this essay only with manipulating people, not with manipulating tools, genes, and other nonhumans. It is noteworthy, though, that even when the object is not a person, the word 'manipulate' often has a negative connotation. It does in "Shopkeepers and secular humanists may have successfully manipulated Christmas into an amalgam of potent sentiment and orchestrated debt," where the word 'manipulated' was presumably chosen over such alternatives as 'turned' or 'transformed' for its pejorative aspect, but not in "Hellerwork, Rolfing and Feldenkrais [techniques] focus on deep-rooted stress and tension, and by manipulating the body, they restore its flexibility and ease of movement" (to take two examples provided in the *Oxford English Dictionary*).[17]

All the considerations mentioned above that lend some support to (1) equally support (2a); and (2a) has the obvious advantage over (1) that it does not rule out, by fiat—as (1a) does—the possibility that manipulation can sometimes be justified, nor does it stack the deck—as (1b) probably will have to, in order to be plausible—by understanding 'manipulation' in such a way as to exclude the cases that tell against the thesis that manipulation is always wrong. I'll proceed, then, with the idea that the moral status of manipulation is best captured by either (2a) or (2b). I take it that manipulation is in fact sometimes justified. But for those who think that (1b) is plausible, I provide a list of examples that they would have to exclude as not really manipulation unless they are willing to maintain that these actions are wrong. To clarify: they would have to hold not merely that they are morally objectionable, leaving a moral residue, but that they are not justified.

Examples

Let's consider some examples that challenge the position that manipulation is always wrong. Although I offer them in part as a challenge for those who think that (1b) is plausible, I hope to draw from the examples further insight into manipulation and its moral status, including insight into why, when manipulation is not wrong, it isn't wrong. I am particularly interested in any light they shed on the question of whether we should accept (2a) or whether manipulation may have a somewhat higher status, as (2b) claims.

---

17. They are provided under 'manipulate.' The source provided by the *OED* for the first quotation is *Saturday Night* (Toronto, 1993) and for the second is *Elle* (1992). The brackets are the *OED*'s.

1. *A negotiator persuades the hostage taker to release the hostages.* Depending on how it is done, we might maintain that it is merely persuasive, not manipulative; but I don't think it is hard to imagine strategies that we would agree are manipulative, yet not morally wrong—unless of course we have a prior commitment to avoiding classifying as manipulative something that we do not think is morally wrong.

2. *Skillful, "by the book" interrogations.* The methods FBI agent George Piro employed that eventually led Saddam Hussein to disclose, *inter alia,* what happened to Iraq's weapons of mass destruction, included creating a sense that he (Piro) was all-powerful and seeing to it that Saddam felt, indeed was, completely dependent on him. Piro arranged with the guards that only he would wear a watch, so that Saddam would be able to find out what time it was only by asking Piro; Saddam could only acquire items he wanted, such as writing utensils and paper, by requesting them from Piro. Piro saw to it that he was the sole person with whom Saddam could converse, and he conversed with him extensively. He sometimes showed Saddam upsetting images (including that of the huge statue of Saddam being pulled down) in order to rouse his emotions, timing and calibrating it so as to increase the likelihood that Saddam would speak freely with him. Piro's actions toward Saddam seem clearly to be manipulative, yet not morally wrong.[18] The same is true of the actions of Ali Soufan, the FBI agent who succeeded in getting Abu Zubaydah to disclose to him a great deal of information about Al Qaeda and in particular, the 9/11 attackers, through "non-enhanced" interrogation.[19]

3. *Psychological strategies employed in self-defense to thwart an attacker.* Rather than hitting or kicking the attacker or using other physical force, you might purposely confuse him, psychologically disarming him, perhaps by leading him to think you are insane. You manipulate him, but it would be bizarre to claim that in so doing, you act wrongly.

---

18. For more details, see Scott Pelley's "60 Minutes" interview with George Piro, broadcast January 27, 2008, http://www.cbsnews.com/video/watch/?id=3756675n.

19. See Soufan's testimony to a Senate committee in *What Went Wrong: Torture and the Office of Legal Counsel in the Bush Administration: Hearing Before the Senate Committee on the Judiciary Subcommittee on Administrative Oversight and the Courts,* 111th Cong. 2009. http://www.judiciary.senate.gov/hearings/hearing.cfm?id=e655f9e2809e5476862f735da14945e6 See also Michael Isikoff, " 'We Could Have Done This the Right Way': How Ali Soufan, FBI Agent, Got Abu Zubaydah to Talk without Torture," *Newsweek,* April 25, 2009, and the 2010 film *The Oath,* by Laura Poitras.

4. *Tevye's dream in* Fiddler on the Roof *(slightly modified).* In the musical and the short story on which it is based,[20] the tale goes like this: A marriage has been arranged between Tsaytl, Tevye's daughter, and Lazar the Butcher, a wealthy widower. After sealing the deal with Lazar without consulting Tsaytl, Tevye learns from her that she absolutely does not want to marry Lazar and in fact has her own marriage plans. Tevye decides that Tsaytl should not be forced to marry against her will, despite the normal expectation that a girl will marry whoever is selected for her. He then wonders how to share all this with his wife, Goldie, and handles it by pretending to have a nightmare in which the deceased Grandma Tsaytl—their daughter's namesake—appears and offers her blessing for the marriage of young Tsaytl to Tsaytl's boyfriend. Also appearing in the dream Tevye pretends to have is Lazar's deceased wife. She threatens Tsaytl in the event that Tsaytl marries Lazar. This has the desired effect on Goldie: seeing Grandma Tsaytl's blessing not of the arranged marriage but of the marriage young Tsaytl wants, and believing that young Tsaytl might be endangered by the ghost of Lazar's dead wife if she marries him, Goldie agrees that Tsaytl should marry not Lazar, but the young man she loves.

The modification that is in order, for my purposes, is this. It was not indicated in the story that Goldie would otherwise have insisted on Tsaytl marrying Lazar the Butcher. But if we suppose that she would have, we can agree not only that what Tevye did was manipulative—that is obviously the case, with or without my modification—but also that it was morally permissible for him to be so manipulative, given the importance of allowing Tsaytl to marry the man she loves.[21] If the manipulation was unnecessary (and if he had good reason to think it was) then I would say it was not permissible. Manipulation of this sort should be a last resort.

5. *Getting a boss to do something that he would not consider doing unless he thought it was his idea.*[22] To this end, you introduce it in such a way as to induce in him the belief that it was his idea and that you are endorsing his idea, rather than that he is endorsing yours. (If desired. add that it is a very good idea, and good for the company, not only for the person whose idea it was.)

---

20. Sholem Aleichem, "Today's Children," in *Tevye the Dairyman and The Railroad Stories*, translated by Hillel Halkin (New York: Schocken, 1987).

21. We may nonetheless be troubled by his attitude: he evinces no regret at all in having to resort to these means, and indeed takes considerable pleasure in manipulating Goldie.

22. This is a modification of an example offered by Patricia Greenspan in "The Problem with Manipulation," *American Philosophical Quarterly* 40, no. 2 (April 2003): 156.

6. *An array of actions we might bring together under the heading of "sales techniques,"* excluding those that involve any of the following: deception, refraining from disclosing vital information, badgering, or (without disclosing this before the customers have parked) charging an enormous amount for parking unless one spends at least $20 in the store. I am thinking, rather, of "mood enhancers" such as boiling some water infused with cinnamon or vanilla to release a delicious, comforting aroma before showing the house to potential buyers, playing in one's shop music that is expected to incline customers to spend freely, and such strategies as placing chocolates near the cash register and arranging the traffic flow in the store so as to force people to walk by costly and tempting items.

These examples pose a challenge to the thesis that manipulation is always wrong, but how they challenge it may vary somewhat. The example of Tevye suggests only that manipulation is sometimes justified because it is the lesser of two evils. Although Tevye himself may have viewed it differently, what he did was morally objectionable. It was in need of justification. One might claim that this is true of all the examples: there is always something morally objectionable, in need of justification, but there is also a justification at hand. If so, that lends support to (2a).

But I think at least one of the cases is different. Boiling water with a drop of vanilla in it before potential buyers arrive, is, it seems to me, not morally objectionable at all. (It matters that the aim is not to cover something up, e.g., an odor of urine in the carpets.) No justification is needed for trying to induce, in that particular way, a sense of well-being in the house, a feeling that this could be a lovely home. I say 'in that particular way' because inducing it by hypnosis would be a different matter. If that is correct, it lends support to (2b): not only is manipulation sometimes justified by the particular circumstances but occasionally it does not even need justification.

One might argue that that is not the best way to think of the example. There are two alternative readings of it. We might say that there is a wrong, but one that it is simply very easy to justify: it is justified by the fact that one knows one is entering a situation where an effort is being made to sell one something. Or we might hold that what I have described is not manipulative in the slightest. Both are possibilities, but I want to explore the thought that manipulation, which (2a) compares to lying, may have a slightly higher moral status than lying. Lying always needs to be justified. Is the same true of manipulation?

There is reason to think that it is not. In this way, manipulation may not be morally on a par with lying and deceiving. The comparison here needs to be between benign manipulation and benign lying and deceiving. My thought, very roughly, is that benign manipulation is more nearly continuous with perfectly appropriate behavior, even valuable behavior, than is benign deception. The perfectly appropriate behavior I have in mind includes the following: We tell people certain things—things we hate to have to relay—at what we hope will be the right time so that they will not get mad at us, or not be terribly upset, or still be able to do well in an event of importance to them (a piano recital or an exam, for instance).[23] We ask irascible colleagues for their help in a departmental matter at a time when others are present, knowing this reduces the risk that they will refuse or blow up at us. I cannot think of anything that is both as continuous with deception as this is with manipulation and as fully innocuous. ('Innocuous' in fact may not capture it: such actions are arguably not merely innocuous but valuable.)

What might be some candidates? That is, what might stand in the same relation to deception that these stand in to manipulation, and have comparable value? Refraining from telling someone something that would be deeply upsetting to her; not sharing personal information about ourselves? But unless we have indicated that in fact we are holding nothing back, this would not count as deceiving, or even come close to it. A better candidate would be pretending to like a friend's new house. That does come closer. But I am reluctant to treat it as fully innocuous. It is more aptly regarded as something unfortunate, but justified—perhaps even required—by the circumstances. It is something best avoided but hard to avoid, and is justified by the fact that the alternatives are worse (assuming that they are worse, or at least that the agent reasonably believed they were). Framed differently: there is something regrettable about having to pretend to like one's friend's house.

In his "Casuistical questions" at the end of the section "On Lying" in *The Metaphysics of Morals*, Kant writes:

An author asks one of his readers "How do you like my work?" One could merely seem to give an answer, by joking about the

---

23. I have been helped in developing this thought by the opening paragraph of Claudia Mills, "Goodness as Weapon," *Journal of Philosophy* 92 (1995): 485: "Most of us spend much of our time trying to get other people to act as we would like them to act.... In this enterprise, we make use of a wide array of motivational levers; we take advantage of various sources of others' susceptibility to influence."

impropriety of such a question. But who has his wit always ready? The author will take the slightest hesitation in answering as an insult. May one, then, say what is expected of one?[24]

We regret having to lie, but if we cannot gracefully dodge the question, we judge it better to say what is expected than to be honest. But, apart from those contexts where it is unmistakably clear that the speaker really does not expect the truth at all, perhaps because the conversation is merely a quick exchange of salutations and pleasantries ("How are you?" said quickly in the corridor while heading to a meeting), having to be dishonest is regrettable. I take it that this differentiates it from the cases that stand to manipulation as this stands to lying—cases such as that of timing carefully when one tells another disturbing news or asks a somewhat brittle person to take on a departmental committee assignment.

In sum, I believe that the moral status of manipulation is slightly higher than that of deception. Both manipulating and deceiving are generally wrong, and both can sometimes be justified. But there are cases of manipulation (or if one prefers, quasi-manipulation) that are morally innocuous. They are not merely justifiable, and they leave no moral residue. I don't think there is anything that is equally morally innocuous and as closely related to deception as these cases are to manipulation.[25]

Strawsonian Reflections

The above examples lend support to the following: manipulation is not always wrong (though I would maintain that it usually is); and when it is not wrong, this usually is because under the circumstances it is justified. In those cases, there is still a moral residue, still something to regret. But in some cases there is nothing to justify; the manipulation (or if one

---

24. Immanuel Kant, *The Metaphysics of Morals*, in *Practical Philosophy*, edited by Allen Wood, translated by Mary J. Gregor (Cambridge: Cambridge University Press, 1996), 6: 431.

25. A possible candidate is surprise parties. I see these as not entirely innocuous, and regret having once been persuaded to host (more accurately, manipulated into hosting) one. The birthday celebrant is misled into thinking he is going to one sort of event (perhaps a very small gathering) and suddenly has to deal with a large number of guests, all focused on him. Worse, he may expect a quiet evening at home and then, without warning, finds he has to rise to the occasion when he may not at all be in the mood for hours of socializing.

prefers to consider it such, quasi-manipulation) not only is not wrong but is not even regrettable.

I mentioned earlier that I hoped that reflection on the examples might yield some insight concerning why, when manipulation is not wrong, it isn't wrong; and I had in mind more than simply that when it is wrong, this is sometimes because it is justified and sometimes because it was morally innocuous in the first place. In this section I draw from P. F. Strawson's "Freedom and Resentment" to suggest a further wrinkle to the story.

In several of the examples, the following is true: the person who is manipulated has done something that renders him or her a suitable subject for a dose—though only a small dose, barring the addition of further details—of what Strawson calls the "objective attitude."[26] If someone is so arrogant as to dismiss ideas unless he thinks he came up with them, then the only solution, if one has the unfortunate fate of having to work with such a person and cannot simply overrule or outvote him, is to give him the impression that the ideas that one thinks it important to implement in fact were his ideas. If someone is so bullheaded, so deaf to reason, as Goldie would have been had she insisted on forcing her daughter to marry against her will, she is appropriately viewed, in that limited context, anyway, as someone to be "managed."

One reason, then, why manipulation is in some instances not wrong is that the person with whom one is interacting is, in those circumstances, deaf to reason. Even so, manipulating the person generally leaves a moral residue. It is something to be avoided.

While warranted by certain sorts of conduct, it is dangerous to allow ourselves to view people as needing to be managed. There should be a very strong presumption against it, and against manipulating people on these grounds. This is of particular importance given how tempting it may be to resort to manipulation. It may be tempting simply in order to get one's way or to enjoy, for those who thrill to it, the sense of mastery. Added to that, any suggestion that if someone is deaf to reason, it is appropriate to view him as "to be managed" is dangerous given the common tendency to see someone who fails to be convinced by our excellent points as deaf to reason. Further adding to the risk that we will view others as to-be-managed is that, as Strawson observes, it can be fatiguing to engage with people in a

---

26. P. F. Strawson, "Freedom and Resentment," in *Freedom and Resentment* (London: Routledge, 2008): 9–10.

straightforward way.[27] Even when nothing about the behavior of the person calls for it, we may take up the objective attitude. Strawson writes, "We look with an objective eye on the compulsive behaviour of the neurotic or the tiresome behaviour of a very young child.... But we can sometimes look with something like the same eye on the behaviour of the normal and the mature. We have this resource and can sometimes use it: as a refuge, say, from the strains of involvement...."[28]

The examples of Tevye's dream and the arrogant boss suggest that a significant factor separating morally permissible from morally impermissible manipulation is whether our treatment of the person as someone to-be-managed is in fact called for. Is the goal so important and is the likelihood that the person can be convinced so slight as to warrant manipulating the person? (And is our lack of humility, our certainty that we are right, warranted?)

This same factor might be cited in explanation of the examples of the hostage-taker and the attacker. But although it is true that they merit taking up the objective attitude rather than the participant attitude, we would not need even to mention this to explain why manipulation is permissible in these circumstances. After all, it is obvious that manipulation is permitted in such cases because even physical force is permitted. It is a straightforward case of justification: something that in other circumstances would be wrong is permissible in these circumstances. Something similar might be said about the examples of interrogation.

Consider the very different case of manipulative but permissible sales techniques, bearing in mind that we may differ on which ones are permissible. The question is, when and insofar as they are permissible despite being manipulative, why is that? The reason is not that the *prima facie* wrong of manipulation is outweighed by the gravity of an evil to be prevented, nor that the person's behavior warrants treating her as someone to be managed. The explanation is more along the following lines: it is well understood that in shops (and during a showing of a house that is for sale)

---

27. It is worth bearing in mind that such fatigue (combined no doubt with other factors) may lead to other choices, such as opting for relationships that are, in effect, pseudo-relationships. Consider, for example, the stance of Benigno, a hospital nurse, toward his comatose patient, Alicia, in the 2002 film *Talk to Her* by Pedro Almódovar. Or Timothy Treadwell's intense love for the grizzly bears with whom he sought (with some success) to develop a rapport, as depicted in Werner Herzog's 2005 film *Grizzly Man*.

28. Strawson, "Freedom and Resentment," 80. The rest of the sentence is "or as an aid to policy; or simply out of intellectual curiosity."

people will be trying to get you to buy something, and that there are norms governing what methods can be employed. The manipulative methods are quite predictable: music, fragrance, skillful arrangement of the display items are all permitted, but offering a beverage spiked with something calculated to render you more pliable, game to spend a lot of money, is not. But it is not only the predictability. Also factoring in is avoidability and resistibility.[29] How easily can you avoid going into shops where these techniques are used? And how potent are the techniques? If we cannot buy our children shoes without encountering overpriced toys and candy strategically placed to maximize the chances that our children will wail—to our great embarrassment—unless we purchase one of these items for them, we may well object to this sale strategy. (Indeed, if the aroma of vanilla or cinnamon actually caused people to purchase houses against their better judgment, we would regard this strategy as morally impermissible.)

Where do these comments on the examples leave us? They confirm, first of all, that what differentiates impermissible from permissible manipulation is no one thing; no surprise there, since manipulation comes in many forms, as does wrongful conduct. Second, they provide an explanation of why there may be some temptation to opt for a definition of manipulation purposely made narrow enough to yield the result that manipulation is always wrong (possibly allowing that there might be drastic circumstances where it is the lesser of two evils). The explanation they suggest is that if we think of an account of manipulation as first and foremost telling us what is true, we will want one that recognizes that manipulation is not always impermissible. But suppose we instead think of an account of manipulation more pragmatically, attending to the effects of accepting one sort of an account rather than another. Given how quick people are (whether because they are ungenerous and mistrustful, or arrogant, or disrespectful) to see others as needing to be managed, and given how much some people enjoy the power they feel in manipulating others, it may seem unwise for an account of manipulation to announce that manipulation is sometimes permissible, especially if part of the explanation is that sometimes, some people need to be managed. So thoughts about the objective attitude support both the claim that an account of manipulation that says it is sometimes permissible is correct and—insofar as we are concerned

---

29. Avoidability and resistibility are likewise part of our assessment of advertising practices. See Eric Cave's discussion of subliminal advertising in his contribution to this volume.

about what it is good for people to hear—the claim that it is better for our account of manipulation not to say this.

Conclusion

I began by addressing the question of whether manipulation requires intent, and argued that it does, but that the object of the intent need not be to manipulate. The *mens rea* of manipulation can be a combination of intent and recklessness: one's aim is to get the other to do x, and one is reckless in the way one goes about reaching that goal. The manipulator may of course be worse than merely reckless, but this helps to pinpoint why we think the person culpable even when there is nothing worse in virtue of which we judge him culpable. To the extent that we think the person did not act recklessly, and did not exhibit insufficient respect for the manipulee *qua* agent, we may be hesitant to call it a case of manipulation, and if we do consider it manipulation, will regard it as justified manipulation. The remainder of my essay focused on the moral status of manipulation, distinguishing various views one could take on its moral status and putting forward examples aimed both to challenge the view that manipulation (unless carefully defined so as to rule out as not manipulation all cases that challenge the thesis) is never morally justified, and to help us choose between the position that it is sometimes never morally objectionable at all and the position that although always morally objectionable, it is sometimes morally justified. I explored and tentatively endorsed the position that sometimes it is not morally objectionable at all, differentiating its moral status from that of lying. Lying, even when justified, leaves a moral residue; by contrast, there are instances of manipulating another that do not. They are by no means typical; manipulation is usually wrong, and when not wrong, there usually is a moral residue—but not always—and in this way its moral status is higher than that of lying and deceiving.

5

A Framework for Assessing the Moral Status of "Manipulation"

J. S. Blumenthal-Barby

THIS ESSAY DEALS with the ethics of using knowledge about a person's particular psychological make-up, or about the psychology of judgment and decision making in general, to shape that person's decisions and behaviors. Various moral concerns emerge about this practice, but one of the more elusive and underdeveloped concerns is the charge of manipulation. It is this concern that is the focus of this essay.

The elusiveness and underdevelopment of the manipulation charge goes something like this: Person A describes a decision- or behavior-shaping practice (e.g., offering rewards, inducing affective states such as guilt or fear, presenting information in a certain order or tone) and Person B claims "That's manipulation, and therefore morally wrong!" This claim is usually followed by Person A's attempting to explain why instance *X* is *not* an instance of manipulation, and therefore morally permissible. This is the wrong response, I would argue. The more illuminating response would be to consider what if anything is morally problematic about manipulation. So, the discourse is underdeveloped in that it relies on intuitions that manipulation is morally wrong instead of providing arguments as to why and how it is, and it is elusive in that it is never quite clear on what exactly is meant by manipulation, descriptively speaking. For example, is any sort of intentional influence without the subject's knowledge manipulation? What about a case in which the subject is aware of the influence attempt but has trouble resisting it because it plays on desires or other parts of the subject's psychological make-up? Is that a case of manipulation as well?

The literature has been less than clear on this conceptual point. The following practices have all been described by philosophers as manipulation:

incentivizing, offering, increasing options, decreasing options, tricking, using (resistible) threats of punishment, managing information, presenting information in a way that leads to predictable inferences, deceiving, lying, making a false promise, withholding information or options, slanting information, providing irrelevant inputs or crowding out relevant inputs, exaggerating information in a misleading way, using misleading packaging or misleading images, creating impressions by imagery, using loaded language, trading on fear, subliminal suggestion, insinuations, flattery, guilt, appealing to emotional weaknesses or needs, initiating psychological processes that are difficult to reverse or that lead to predictable behaviors or decisions (e.g., the tendency to continue with an active decision even after becoming aware that it is more costly than originally thought, or the tendency to view an option as more desirable when shown its contrast), browbeating or otherwise wearing the person down, reverse psychology, and seduction.[1] Even if we were to achieve some clarity on the bounds of manipulation, doing so would fail to answer the central moral question, which concerns the moral status of any of these practices.

The moral status of any of these practices, I would argue, *depends*. That is, it is not the case that any of these practices traditionally labeled as "manipulation" are *ipso facto* morally wrong; nor is it even the case that any of these practices always has a single wrong-making feature (e.g., infringement on autonomy) that is always present but may be outweighed by other morally relevant factors such that the practice may be all things considered ethically permissible or morally right. What then does the moral status of these methods of influence that lie somewhere between reason and coercion *depend on?* I argue that the moral status depends on the extent to which the instance of influence (1) threatens or promotes autonomy; (2) has good aims and virtuous overtones or bad ones; and (3) fulfills or fails to fulfill duties, obligations, and expectations that arise out of the relationship between the influencer and influenced. I will explain in more

---

1. Ruth R. Faden and Tom L. Beauchamp, with Nancy M. P. King, *A History and Theory of Informed Consent* (New York: Oxford University Press, 1986), 261; Marcia Baron, "Manipulativeness," *Proceedings and Addresses of the American Philosophical Association* 77, no. 2 (November 2003): 29, 42; Robert Noggle, "Manipulative Actions: A Conceptual and Moral Analysis," *American Philosophical Quarterly* 33, no. 1 (January 1996): 43–55; Joel Rudinow, "Manipulation," *Ethics* 88, no. 4 (July 1978): 338–47; Claudia Mills, "Politics and Manipulation," *Social Theory and Practice* 21, no. 1 (Spring 1995): 100, 108–10; Judith Andre, "Power, Oppression and Gender," *Social Theory and Practice* 11, no. 1 (1985): 111.

detail the moral relevance of these factors, showing why each is necessary and demonstrating how they work in specific cases.

Before doing so, a minor terminological note. Henceforth I will refer to the aforementioned practices not as "manipulation" but as *non-argumentative influence*.[2] Non-argumentative influence is influence that operates either by bypassing a person's awareness or by relying on facts about the subject's psychology, such as knowledge about his emotions, how he perceives things, how he makes judgments and decisions, and what he desires. It is in contrast to influence that operates by engaging with a person's rational capacities and offering him reasons and arguments (i.e., rational persuasion), and to influence that operates by force or severe threats of harm (i.e., coercion). In using the term "non-argumentative influence" instead of "manipulation," I hope to avoid any automatic negative associations and assumptions about moral status and thereby address the central question of what if anything is ethically problematic about these forms of influence and when.

Autonomy

The majority of writing on the morality of non-argumentative influence is infused with condemnation of it. The foundation of much of this is the claim that non-argumentative influence somehow interferes with an agent's autonomy. Melissa Seymour Fahmy condemns non-argumentative influence by arguing, "to interfere in the lives of others without their consent is to usurp their authority to direct their lives as they see fit."[3] Eric Cave makes a similar argument in previous work and in this volume, claiming that when A induces B to behave differently than she otherwise would have via non-argumentative influence, A undermines B's capacity to manage her concerns since B cannot manage her concerns effectively while A is doing so. Cave argues that non-argumentative influence violates "modest autonomy," where modest autonomy means that "To act autonomously, an agent need only act from concerns not thrust on her by others in ways that

---

2. J. S. Blumenthal-Barby, "Between Reason and Coercion: Ethically Permissible Influence in Health Care and Health Policy Contexts," *Kennedy Institute of Ethics Journal* 22, no. 4 (2012): 345–66.

3. Melissa Seymour Fahmy, "Love, Respect, and Interfering with Others," *Pacific Philosophical Quarterly* 92, no. 2 (June 2011): 183.

overwhelm her capacity for control over her own mental life."[4] James Stacey Taylor builds absence from non-argumentative influence into his definition of autonomy, arguing that a person is autonomous with respect to a choice that she makes if and only if (i) the information on which she based the choice has not been affected by another agent with the end of leading her to make a particular choice, or a choice from a particular class of choices; or (ii) if it has, then she is aware of this.[5] He writes, "It is clear that the successful manipulation of a person into performing an action that she would not have otherwise performed would serve to compromise the manipulee's autonomy with respect to her manipulated actions."[6] He recounts the story of Shakespeare's *Othello* where Iago insinuates to Othello that his wife Desdemona is having an affair by arranging for Othello to overhear certain conversations and planting suggestive objects such as a handkerchief until Othello becomes convinced and jealous enough and kills Desdemona. Taylor writes, "Since Othello was manipulated by Iago into smothering Desdemona, he lacked autonomy with respect to his decision to do this, for it was not he, but Iago, who was the font of this decision. It was not Othello, but Iago, who originally decided to cause Desdemona's death; Othello was merely the instrument through which he brought it about."[7]

In response to the claim that non-argumentative influence poses a threat to autonomy, Sarah Buss has produced a compelling counter-argument. Buss's argument consists of two main claims. First, she argues that, at least on a compatibilist account, we consider people to be self-governing or autonomous despite the fact that there is a past and an external world that influences their current mental states and actions, and that non-argumentative influences are no different; if the past and the external world do not pose threats to self-governance or autonomy then neither does non-argumentative influence from others.[8] Second, she argues that

---

4. Eric M. Cave, "What's Wrong with Motive Manipulation?" *Ethical Theory and Moral Practice* 10, no. 2 (December 2006): 138. Cave reiterates this position in this volume, but here he allows for a "broad" notion of modest autonomy such that someone could consent to have his or her motives or concerns managed by another via non-argumentative influence. In this rare instance, non-argumentative influence (what Cave calls "manipulation") would be compatible with autonomy; "Unsavory Seduction and Manipulation," this volume, xxx–xxx).

5. James Stacey Taylor, *Practical Autonomy and Bioethics* (New York: Routledge, 2009), 7–8.

6. Taylor, *Practical Autonomy and Bioethics*, 41.

7. Taylor, *Practical Autonomy and Bioethics*, 4.

8. Sarah Buss, "Valuing Autonomy and Respecting Persons: Manipulation, Seduction, and the Basis of Moral Constraints," *Ethics* 115, no. 2 (January 2005): 212.

many well-informed, self-governing agents would endorse a policy that involved being influenced by non-argumentative forms of influence (e.g., seduction), and though she does not spell this out, this sort of endorsement would result in the influence's being compatible with autonomy under accounts such as John Christman's,[9] where a person's development of some desire is autonomous only if the person "would not have resisted that development had [he] attended to the process [by which it was developed]."[10] Incidentally, Harry Frankfurt has made a point similar to Buss's first claim when he writes "We are inevitably fashioned and sustained, after all, by circumstances over which we have no control.... It is irrelevant whether those causes are operating by virtue of the natural forces that shape our environment or whether they operate through the deliberatively manipulative design of other human agents."[11] For Frankfurt, of course, what matters for autonomy is whether a person is wholeheartedly behind the desires that move him to act, regardless of the origin of those desires.

I think that Buss succeeds in countering the prevailing view that non-argumentative influence, or what has traditionally been called manipulation, is always incompatible with autonomy. When then is it incompatible with autonomy? Let me make a couple of modifications to the Buss–Frankfurt claims and then offer some criteria that allow us to assess the extent to which an instance of non-argumentative influence is compatible with autonomy. The main modification that I would make is to reject the equivalence of a non-argumentative influence that occurs undirected from the environment (e.g., a song that comes on the radio and influences someone

---

9. Moti Gorin makes a similar point in this volume ("Towards a Theory of Interpersonal Manipulation," xx–xx), arguing that manipulation and autonomy are compatible on internalist accounts (since an agent could be manipulated to have her first- and second-order desires achieve coherence and hence to be autonomous) and on mixed externalist (i.e., attitudinal historical) accounts such as Christman's (since it is an open question as to whether or not the agent authorizes the process by which her desires or behaviors were formed). Thus, Gorin, myself, Buss, Christman, and Frankfurt all hold a similar position on the compatibility of manipulation and autonomy—namely, that it *may* be the case that an agent is manipulated (or influenced via non-argumentative means by another agent) and still autonomous. John Christman, "The Historical Conception of Autonomy," in *The Politics of Persons: Individual Autonomy and Socio-Historical Selves* (New York: Cambridge University Press, 2009).

10. Christman, "Historical Conception of Autonomy," 11.

11. Harry Frankfurt, "Frankfurt-Style Compatibilism: Reply to John Martin Fischer," in *Countours of Agency: Essays on Themes from Harry Frankfurt*, edited by Sarah Buss and Lee Overton (Cambridge, MA: MIT Press, 2002), 28.

to behave romantically, or the natural absence of an important piece of information that influences the direction of someone's decision) and one that occurs directed at someone from someone else (e.g., A knows about B's weakness for jazz and so puts on a jazz CD to influence B to behave romantically, or A withholds an important piece of information from B to get B to make a particular decision).[12] Why is this distinction important for autonomy? To see the importance we need only consider why it is that we think that something like slavery is so morally egregious: it is not just because the slave is not able to govern himself, it is because he is governed by someone else. The master has imposed his will on the slave in a way that the slave would not endorse. And the second modification I would make to the Buss account is to emphasize the significant difference between contexts of seduction and romance, which Buss focuses her analysis and claim of endorsement on, and other contexts. It may be that most of us would endorse, or at least not repudiate, being moved to love someone via non-argumentative influences such as romantic gestures, but this sort of endorsement is not likely to be the case in many other instances of non-argumentative influence, such as if I am moved to consent to a surgery for my elderly grandmother via the non-argumentative influence of guilt used by my physician to induce me to consent.

Thus, the criteria that I would offer to allow us to assess the extent to which an instance of non-argumentative influence is or is not compatible with autonomy are as follows:

1. The extent to which the non-argumentative influence attempt blocks or burdens options; and
2. The extent to which the person influenced is aware of and endorses, or were he were aware would endorse, the non-argumentative influence attempt as a process by which his desires, decisions, or actions were formed.

These are of course not new or novel criteria, as they stem largely from neo-Frankfurtian theories of autonomy such as Christman's, but it is

---

12. Cave also resists this equivalence in his essay in this volume ("Unsavory Seduction," xxx), writing, "from a moral standpoint, we can distinguish between nonrational motivational change or stasis resulting from either environment or non-negligent accident and such change or stasis that is planned, anticipated, or caused accidentally but negligently by another. If the above observations about modest motive autonomy are correct, then cases of the latter evince a morally reproachable form of disrespect."

Moral particularism - no general rules

worth explicitly outlining them as the key normative questions that should be asked when considering the compatibility of non-argumentative influence and autonomy, instead of assuming or tautologically holding that non-argumentative influence interferes with autonomy.

Before continuing on to the other morally relevant factors and developing the rest of the framework, however, it is worth pausing to address an important question and to make an important observation. The important question is whether an agent whose autonomy is impaired by one instance of non-argumentative influence can have his autonomy further impaired by another one. Consider Johnny who decides to start smoking after much non-argumentative influence from tobacco companies, a process of desire formation that he does not endorse upon reflection. Thus, Johnny is not autonomous with respect to his desire to smoke. Johnny's physician decides to use counter non-argumentative influence—let us say extremely frightening videos—to try to get Johnny to stop smoking. How is it even possible that the physician's actions could impair Johnny's autonomy with respect to his smoking, given that he is already non-autonomous with respect to that decision? In other words, if Johnny's autonomy is at a zero, so to speak, how could it go any lower? Investigating this in great depth would take us too far afield, but my intuition is that one way in which it could is that this further manipulation (which, let us say, Johnny would not endorse, either) makes it harder for Johnny to recover and govern himself, and in that sense does pose a *further* threat to autonomy.

There is, as I mentioned, an important observation with respect to the impact of non-argumentative influence on autonomy as well. Earlier I defined "non-argumentative influence" as influence that operates *either* by bypassing a person's awareness *or* by relying on facts about the subject's psychology such as knowledge about his emotions, how he perceives things, how he makes judgments and decisions, and what he desires. It strikes me that the former type is the most threatening to autonomy. Before I elaborate, let me make a brief conceptual point, and that is that the "or" is not meant to be an exclusive *or*. Often instances of non-argumentative influence that bypass a person's awareness do so by relying on knowledge of facts about their psychology (e.g., that he does not notice information that is placed in the middle instead of first or last, or that he simply follows what is presented as the norm or the default without even realizing it). But many instances of non-argumentative influence that rely on knowledge of facts about a person's psychology (e.g., what he desires, how he perceives things) do so in a way that the subject is very well aware of (e.g., inducement of desire or guilt).

It strikes me that autonomy is more threatened by the types of non-argumentative influence that bypass an agent's awareness. After all, if autonomy involves governing oneself, this requires some degree of awareness and control over one's actions and reasons for acting. The importance of this is acknowledged in most accounts of autonomy, including Christman's, which is illustrated by his inclusion of the hypothetical, "*were* she aware of the process of desire/belief/decision/action formation...*would* endorse." One way to put this is that most accounts of autonomy require some sort of "responsiveness to reasons," whether those reasons are found in the demands of some external normative framework or inside a person's own desires and preferences. Thus, a non-argumentative influence that bypasses a person's awareness is one that gives him little chance to endorse it or not endorse it as the process by which his decisions and behaviors are formed. Of course, it is possible that the agent would meet the criteria to satisfy the hypothetical—that is, he *would* endorse it—but epistemologically we have very little insight as to whether the person would endorse this process that he is not aware of. Thus, the epistemic and justificatory burden is placed on the influencer who is bypassing the agent's awareness to make the case that the agent would in fact endorse it as a process by which his desires, decisions, and behaviors were formed and as such it is autonomy preserving.

Now, onto what I take to be the second morally relevant consideration for the moral status of non-argumentative influence: whether it has good aims and virtuous overtones or bad ones.

Aims and Overtones (Virtuous or Vicious)

One objection that has been raised against non-argumentative influence is that the practice is often aimed at bad ends or involves non-virtuous elements such as dishonesty or violation of trust, disrespect, arrogance, predatoriness, and laziness. Laziness, because it takes more effort to sit down and try to convince someone of a point or a course of action by laying out arguments and responding to objections and questions than it does to appeal to his emotions or set up the environment a certain way. Predatoriness, because, as Colin McGinn notes, the influencer studies human weakness and plays on anxieties and insecurities;[13] and as Marcia Baron notes, exploits emotional

---

13. Colin McGinn, *Mindfucking: A Critique of Mental Manipulation* (Durham, UK: Acumen, 2008), 46–47.

needs or a sense of indebtedness.[14] Arrogance, because of the hubris involved in thinking that I know better than you what is good for you *and* that you are not capable of understanding what is best and why.[15] This harkens back to Aristotle's argument that tools of rhetoric are to be used when dealing with "people whom one cannot instruct," such that non-argumentative influence becomes necessary when the quality of the audience degrades.[16] And, disrespect, because, as Fahmy claims, to use non-argumentative influence is to treat the subject as a child,[17] and as Robert Noggle claims, is to degrade her and treat her as less than a person and more like a machine whose levers can be pushed and pulled.[18] Marcia Baron, Allen Wood, and Kate Manne all make similar claims in this volume about viewing others as mere play things, not taking them seriously, and being "too ready" to manage them.[19] And finally, dishonesty or violation of trust, since non-argumentative influence involves dealing with others in a less than straightforward way, which may damage interpersonal trust.[20]

But as Baron points out in earlier work, non-argumentative influence can also involve virtue, and of course, good aims. Baron writes, "the person who has the virtue corresponding to manipulativeness—a virtue for which we do not, I believe, have a name—knows when it is appropriate to try to bring about a change in another's conduct and does this for the right reasons, for the right ends, and only in instances where it is warranted (and worth the risks), and only using acceptable means."[21] She cites the examples of persuading a reluctant friend or spouse to seek medical help or prodding an untenured friend with a slim publication record to produce. To *not* use non-argumentative influence at certain times or to adhere to a form of fanatical straightforwardness is actually a vice, Baron argues, a vice of isolationism. I think that she is right. Baron gives the example of not stopping a

---

14. Baron, "Manipulativeness," 50.

15. Baron, "Manipulativeness"; Fahmy, "Love, Respect, and Interfering with Others," 184.

16. Aristotle, *The Rhetoric and Poetics of Aristotle* (New York; McGraw-Hill, 1984), 22.

17. Fahmy, "Love, Respect, and Interfering with Others," 179.

18. Noggle, "Manipulative Actions," 52–53.

19. Baron, Wood, and Manne essays in this volume.

20. Patricia Greenspan, "The Problem with Manipulation," *American Philosophical Quarterly* 40, no. 2 (April 2003): 160; McGinn, *Mindfucking*, 27–28; Stanley I. Benn, *A Theory of Freedom* (Cambridge: Cambridge University Press, 1988), 134.

21. Baron, "Manipulativeness," 48.

friend from driving home drunk. To not use a form of non-argumentative influence, such as hiding the keys or distracting the friend by tempting him with a cup of his favorite coffee, is to exhibit the vice of isolationism. To quell potential dismissals of this example owing to the subject's intoxication, let me offer another example. Imagine a person whose friend and roommate is overweight and developing diabetes. The person creates an environment that non-argumentatively influences the roommate to eat healthier by stocking the cupboards with healthy snacks and priming the roommate to take walks by leaving running magazines and shoes out around the apartment.[22] In these cases, the use of non-argumentative influence, I would argue, involves the virtues of respect for the worth of others, kindness, and courage. It is hard to say there is any dishonesty involved—after all, it is not the case that the friend is putting distorting mirrors up around the apartment to get the roommate to see himself as more overweight than he actually is. It is also hard to say that there is laziness involved. In fact, it would be easier to present the friend with a simple argument full of statistics about why he should lose weight. And it is also hard to say that there is any disrespectful, predatory, or arrogant behavior.

Thus, whether practices of non-argumentative influence are ethically problematic via ends or virtue-based concerns depends. Although usually associated with vicious traits such as disrespectful, predatory, and arrogant, the use of "manipulation" or non-argumentative influence can aim at good ends and be motivated from and exhibit virtuous traits such as kindness, courage, and respect for the worth of others. Our intuitions about the extent to which an instance of non-argumentative influence exhibits virtue or vice depends in part on the context in which the non-argumentative influence takes place or, to be more specific, on the relationship between the influencer and the influenced, and the duties and boundaries that arise out of that relationship. So, on to the next factor relevant to assessing the moral status of interpersonal influence: the relationship between the influencer and the influenced, and the duties, obligations, and expectations that arise out of that relationship.

Relationship Between Influencer and Influenced

Consider the difference between two cases: (1) the government begins priming people to eat healthier by an advertising campaign that vividly

---

22. John Wryobeck and Yiwei Chen, "Using Priming Techniques to Facilitate Health Behaviours," *Clinical Psychologist* 7, no. 2 (October 2003): 105–108.

illustrates the negative health and aesthetic consequences of obesity, playing on both fear and ego; and (2) a wife begins priming her husband to eat healthier by reminding him of his father who died young of a heart attack, playing on a fear she knows he has, and also occasionally pointing out how attractive he looks after he has just exercised, playing on his ego. The latter case is one that is familiar and usually considered unobjectionable. As a member of the audience where I presented this paper remarked about the latter case, "What's the big deal with that example of manipulation? My wife knows a thousand psychological tricks to use on me, and it would be odd to say that my autonomy is impaired or that something is morally problematic about what happens in such routine interactions." His remark serves as a reminder about the importance of separating the various moral concerns about manipulation (e.g., perhaps the spouse example *does* pose a threat to autonomy, but is not morally concerning all-things-considered for other reasons), and also about the importance of the context in which the manipulation occurs, particularly the context of the relationship between the two parties.

Thus, the reason why we find the spouse case generally morally unproblematic and the government case potentially concerning is the difference in duties, obligations, and expectations that arise out of those two relationships. It is entirely reasonable to think that the wife has an obligation to care for the well-being of her spouse, and that to some extent he has an obligation to care for his health for her benefit. Moreover, we expect this sort of non-argumentative influence from our spouses, and view it as occurring fairly routinely in our interactions.[23] It is less clear that the state has an obligation to care for the well-being of its citizens in anything more than a negative sense of protecting them from harm, nor that the citizens have an obligation to care for their health for the sake of the state.

Before moving on, I want to note a way in which the relationship or legitimacy factor ties the other factors together. The extent to which it is morally problematic if autonomy is not protected or promoted, or good ends are not promoted, depends in part on the relationship between the influenced and the influencer. For example, a doctor may have an obligation to work to enhance a patient's autonomous decision making, whereas an agent

---

23. Marcia Baron makes a similar point about manipulation in this volume ("The *Mens Rea* and Moral Status of Manipulation," xxx), arguing that one circumstance in which it might be justified is when there is a normative expectation of it.

of the state, or an advertiser, does not have that obligation. Thus, a case of non-argumentative influence used by a doctor that threatens autonomy to some extent and fails to promote the patient's best interests is morally worse than a case of non-argumentative influence used by a state institution or advertiser that threatens autonomy to some extent or fails to promote the subject's best interests. Moreover, the doctor who knows his or her patient well is more likely to be able to use non-argumentative influence to produce good consequences for the subject of the influence since she knows the patient's goals and values, which is perhaps not the case with the state or an influencer far removed from knowledge of the subject's goals and interests.

The Challenge of a Pluralistic Framework

One challenge to any pluralistic account of the ethical permissibility or impermissibility of non-argumentative influence, such as the one I am suggesting,[24] is how to deal with cases where an instance of non-argumentative influence is problematic with respect to one normative feature (e.g., autonomy) but not another (e.g., promotion of good ends and virtue over vice) and to come to an all-things-considered judgment about ethical permissibility. This is a challenge that needs to be taken up, given that, as I have argued, the moral status of the wide variety of practices encapsulated by the term "manipulation" depends, and depends on a wide variety of factors. It is not always the case that influencing another non-argumentatively by bypassing or countering his reasoning capacities is morally wrong, nor is it even always the case that it infringes on autonomy or involves vices such as disrespect or arrogance. Moreover, even if an instance of non-argumentative influence did, say, infringe on autonomy, we may still find it morally permissible for other reasons, given that autonomy is not the only appeal that generates normative reasons. So, we are left with a much more complex picture that requires us to evaluate particular instances based on the moral framework and then come to an all-things-considered judgment about the ethical permissibility, which will involve weighing some moral reasons against others.

---

24. Incidentally, most other authors in this volume end up relying on a pluralistic account as well (e.g., holding that even if manipulation violates autonomy or respect [for reasons or for agents], it may still be morally justified on other grounds). Cave is explicit about this pluralism, noting that autonomy is not the only or overriding good ("Unsavory Seduction," xxx), as is Baron, noting that manipulation may be justified if it is the lesser of two different moral evils ("The *Mens Rea*," xxx).

I am not going to resolve this issue in this essay, but let me make some suggestions. There are several avenues one can pursue in response to this challenge: (1) commit to one of the moral reasons (e.g., autonomy) in an absolutist sort of way or grant it "lexical priority" in a Rawlsian sense;[25] (2) take a *prima facie* approach inspired by W. D. Ross;[26] or (3) take a moral particularist approach inspired by Jonathan Dancy.[27] I am going to set aside the absolutist approach, for it is the easy (yet most unattractive) response, and instead focus on making an initial sketch of the Ross and Dancy approaches to the problem. In *The Right and the Good*, Ross developed a theory of *prima facie* duties such that there is no master moral principle or duty, but instead that there are a plurality of duties and moral reasons that we ought to consider in determining what we ought to do, all things considered. Ross did hold, however, that some of these duties are more important than others (e.g., the duties related to personal relations, such as non-maleficence, fidelity, reparation, and gratitude are more weighty than the duty to promote a maximum aggregate of good).[28] That might offer us some guidance, but unfortunately Ross does not provide us with an algorithm for coming to an all-things-considered determination of what we ought to do, but instead refers to the notion of a "considered opinion" that "rests with perception."[29]

Dancy's moral particularism is not going to offer us an algorithm either, but it does offer an additional tool that may be useful. Particularism allows for a feature to have one moral valence in one case and another in a different case. So, for example, impairment of autonomy might have more of a negative moral valence in one case of non-argumentative influence than in another. For instance, in a case where we think that the obligations and expectations regarding autonomy that arise out of the relationship between the influencer and the influenced are strong (e.g., physician–patient), non-argumentative influence that impairs autonomy may have more of a negative moral valence than in one where they are weak (e.g., advertiser–consumer, or even wife–husband). If this is correct, then one of the places to start with the assessment of the moral status of an

---

25. John Rawls, *A Theory of Justice* (Cambridge, MA: Harvard University Press, 1971).

26. W. D. Ross, *The Right and The Good* (New York: Oxford University Press, 1930).

27. Jonathan Dancy, *Ethics Without Principles* (New York: Oxford University Press, 2006).

28. Ross, *The Right and The Good*, 19–30.

29. Ross, *The Right and The Good*, 19, 30–33, 42.

instance of manipulation or non-argumentative influence is by assessing the obligations and expectations arising out of the relationship between the influencer and the influenced, considering them as one moves through the moral framework and assessing the extent to which the influence threatens or promotes autonomy, virtue and vice, and good aims and consequences over bad ones.

Conclusion

The central moral question with respect to any practice described as "manipulation" is *whether* it is ethically permissible. Practices described as "manipulation" are better described as practices of "non-argumentative influence," since this description avoids any automatic and undefended assignments of negative moral status. Non-argumentative influence is influence that either bypasses or counters a person's reasoning capabilities. The moral status of non-argumentative influence *depends* and *depends on* the extent to which the instance of influence (1) threatens or promotes autonomy; (2) has good aims and virtuous overtones or bad ones; and (3) fulfills or fails to fulfill duties, obligations, and expectations that arise out of the relationship between the influencer and influenced. This framework is a pluralistic one, and presents the usual challenge of pluralistic frameworks, which is "weighing" some moral reasons against others. Moral particularism, with a focus on spelling out the duties and obligations that arise from the relationship between the influencer and the influenced in a particular case, is a useful theoretical framework for helping us to come to an all-things-considered judgment about the ethical permissibility of non-argumentative influence in a particular context.

6

Manipulation as an Aesthetic Flaw

Claudia Mills

MOST OF THE rich and growing philosophical literature on manipulation examines manipulation as an ethically problematic way for one individual to influence another so that she will subsequently act as the manipulator intends.[1] However, "manipulation" can be a term of aesthetic as well as of ethical condemnation. Works of art such as films, novels, and even songs or musical scores are frequently criticized for being "manipulative." Manipulation in this latter context has received insufficient philosophical attention, and certain proffered analyses of manipulation in the philosophical literature define it in such a way as to exclude manipulation in art. In this essay I seek to provide an analysis of manipulation as an aesthetic flaw, both because this is an independently interesting domain to explore and with the hope of supporting a broader and more inclusive account of manipulation that will work in both ethical and aesthetic contexts.

The Special Features of Aesthetic Manipulation

Current accounts of manipulation tend to focus narrowly on manipulation that seeks to get someone else to act in a certain way. Even where manipulation is not defined within the parameters of one person's influencing another to take a given action, the language invoked in many accounts directs our attention toward manipulating another's actions, invoking the

---

1. I am grateful to Keith Nightenhelser for helpful comments on an earlier draft of this essay and to Christian L. Coons for helpful comments on a later draft.

common comparison of manipulator to puppeteer. Consider accounts of seduction, sometimes included within the general category of manipulation: most seducers are interested not so much in seducing the person to fall in love with them as in seducing the person to have sex with them. While it is beyond the scope of this essay to canvass the existing philosophical literature to ascertain the degree to which it focuses on the domain of action, Sarah Buss opens her frequently cited essay on manipulation and seduction by calling attention to manipulation as a threat to "the self-governed (and self-governing) *activity* we call 'making up one's own mind about how to *act*.'"[2] In this volume, J. S. Blumenthal-Barby contributes an essay that "deals with the ethics of using knowledge about a person's particular psychological make-up, or about the psychology of judgment and decision making in general, to shape that person's *decisions and behaviors*."[3] While many accounts certainly allow for manipulation of others' less voluntary subjective states such as beliefs, desires, and feelings, philosophical examples of alleged manipulation, such as Anne Barnhill's carefully crafted cases in this volume, tend to be cases where A's manipulation results in some *action* by B in accordance with A's intentions: canceling a trip, making an offer on a house, engaging in sexual activity.[4] This is as it should be: ethics is concerned centrally with how we act toward others, including how we influence others to act.[5]

Many works of art, however, are not produced with any intention of causing their audience to alter subsequent behavior, and so when works of art are criticized as "manipulative," it is not because of problematic influence leading the audience toward any desired action. Of course, in creating their art works, some artists are politically and ethically motivated to try to get others to act. Upton Sinclair, in writing *The Jungle*, was obviously trying to get his readers to protest working conditions in the meat-packing industry; John Steinbeck, in *The Grapes of Wrath*, was obviously trying to get his readers to care about the conditions of California migrant workers

---

2. Sarah Buss, "Valuing Autonomy and Respecting Persons: Manipulation, Seduction, and the Basis of Moral Constraints," *Ethics* 115 (January 2005): 165 (italics mine).

3. J. S. Blumenthal-Barby, "A Framework for Assessing the Moral Status of 'Manipulation,'" this volume, 121 (italics mine).

4. Anne Barnhill, "What Is Manipulation?" this volume.

5. Of course, manipulators get us to act by altering our mental states, such as beliefs, desires, and intentions, so aesthetic manipulation and action-focused manipulation both ultimately involve a focus on altering our mental states.

and to take political action on their behalf. But such cases are arguably the exception rather than the rule in art. Indeed, one key difference between art and propaganda seems to be the degree to which the latter is focused on getting someone else to act, to the exclusion of any other objective. Although many works of art seek to awaken the conscience and engage us ethically and politically, with a view toward our translating this engagement into action that makes a difference in the world, most do not.

In addition to being primarily action-focused, some accounts of manipulation (including my own earlier work in this area) are narrowly (and I would now say, excessively) cognitive and rationalistic. I once wrote: "A manipulator tries to change another's beliefs and desires by offering her bad reasons, disguised as good, or faulty arguments, disguised as sound."[6] In this volume, both Barnhill and Moti Gorin have rightly called me to task for that claim. Barnhill is correct that this definition is too narrow; her example of a home-seller trying to influence a home-buyer to make an offer on a house by baking cookies so that the house will exude an enticing, cozy aroma "is not an instance of purporting to offer reasons or arguments."[7] This is because it isn't an instance of offering someone *reasons* at all. Likewise, Gorin points out correctly that a manipulator is perfectly willing to offer a good reason if the good reason, rather than the bad reason, will be more casually efficacious (which is often the case); however, manipulators offer the good reason only because it is more effective at getting another to act, only because it proves to be a superior causal lever, not because it points another in the direction of truth. His alternative account of manipulation is that "manipulation is a process of interpersonal influence that deliberately fails to track reasons."[8] This is a clear improvement over my earlier proposal. However, his account retains some of the rationalistic flavor of my earlier account. Even this kind of greatly improved reasons-based analysis of manipulation fails to capture in a comfortable way what is going on with manipulative art, given that we generally do not expect art, manipulative or non-manipulative, to track *reasons* at all.

Before proceeding further, let me say that I'm going to be assuming in what follows that "manipulation" is generally a term of condemnation.

---

6. Claudia Mills, "Politics and Manipulation," *Social Theory and Practice* 21, no. 1 (Spring 1995): 100.

7. Barnhill, "What Is Manipulation," this volume, 60.

8. Moti Gorin, "Towards a Theory of Interpersonal Manipulation," this volume, 97.

(Marcia Baron addresses the moral status of manipulation at length and in depth in her insightful essay for this volume.) While sometimes we hear "manipulation" used admiringly as synonymous with a certain kind of skilled mastery in eliciting audience response to an artwork ("Hitchcock was a consummate manipulator"), I will treat the charge of aesthetic manipulation—manipulativeness as a quality of a work of art—as generally involving aesthetic criticism, even while noting that there is no precision or rigor in how the term "manipulation" is used in this context. But there are three reasons one might think that aesthetic manipulation, however much it tells against the *aesthetic* quality of an artwork, will not be *morally* problematic, or will certainly be far less morally problematic than standard instances of interpersonal manipulation. In closing, I will suggest a reason why we might think that aesthetic manipulation is, or certainly can be, morally problematic nonetheless.

First, the effects of aesthetic manipulation tend to be more limited and circumscribed. Often an encounter with a work of art provides a contained and bounded experience with little lingering effects on how we live out the rest of our lives, so that encounters with aesthetic objects may seem to be too insignificant to be subject to serious moral evaluation. However, this seems to be the case only for lesser works of art or for less sensitive individuals. And even inferior films and novels may affect us in powerful ways for the rest of our lives: fostering phobias, setting up unrealistic expectations for romantic love, and so forth. So I mention this first possible distinctive feature of aesthetic manipulation only to set it aside. The other two features of aesthetic manipulation, by contrast, do indeed mark a significant difference from most cases of manipulation more generally.

Next, manipulation standardly is covert rather than overt. In contrast, when we engage with a work of art, we usually do so knowing that it is an object that has been consciously and deliberately constructed by the artist to elicit a desired response in the audience. Both Gorin and Barnhill point out that manipulation does not need to involve deception or covertness; these are not defining features of manipulation necessarily present in all cases of what we could agree to be manipulation. But most manipulators seek to hide the degree to which they are angling to achieve their desired result and would find the success of their project seriously compromised if their manipulative intentions were revealed. This is not true of aesthetic manipulation, at least for the most part. When we read a novel or a poem, see a film or play, look at a painting or listen to a symphony, we know that it was fashioned by someone bringing artistry to bear on the goal of eliciting a desired response.

Finally, in cases of aesthetic manipulation, the person being manipulated generally accepts the manipulative experience voluntarily—indeed, often pays money for the privilege of being affected in this way. To the degree that violations of autonomy are taken to be at the heart of what is wrong with interpersonal manipulation, manipulation of a specific kind will not be wrong in cases where we autonomously sign up to be manipulated in that specific way. And this is typically what happens with manipulation in art.[9]

What Makes a Work of Art Manipulative?

It will turn out to be more difficult than one might think to unpack exactly what is involved in the criticism of a work of art as manipulative. I will review a number of common ways in which critics charge that a work of art (often a film) is manipulative and conclude that most of these fail to capture what makes manipulation aesthetically problematic. There is no rich body of scholarly literature on this topic for me to survey. Instead, I enter this arena of discourse by canvassing pre-theoretical intuitions expressed in Internet discussions of manipulation in film, where accusations of manipulation are especially prevalent, in order to survey ordinary-language uses of the term in this context.[10] We also need to distinguish judgments that a work as a whole is manipulative from judgments that some particular element of the work (for example, one individual scene within the work) is manipulative.

The charge that a film is "manipulative" has been unpacked in several leading ways. First, a film can be criticized as manipulative when the filmmaker is overly directive in controlling the viewer's response to the film ("*I* prefer to decide how I'll react to a film"). Second, a film can be criticized as manipulative when the filmmaker's attempt to control the viewer's

---

9. Here our knowledge of genre plays an important role in the voluntariness of our exposure to a work of art. While we generally do not sign up to read a book or see a film with full information about particular details of its plot and presentation (thus making our consent to the experience less than fully informed), we do know its general genre: mystery, "chick flick," comedy, "slasher film." So we are aware of, and agree to undertake, the *kinds* of experiences we are going to be having when we open the cover or enter the theater.

10. E.g., in the extensive comments posted on Roger Ebert's website, rogerebert.com, and the website mubi.com ("an online cinema and community for people who love film"), which hosted a forum on the topic "What qualifies a film as being manipulative?" with a follow-up discussion, "What's so wrong with well-done manipulation?"

response to the film is too transparent to the viewer ("I could clearly see how the filmmaker was trying to affect me"). Third, a film can be criticized as manipulative when the response that the film elicits is somehow inappropriate (e.g., eliciting more emotion than is warranted—for example, when the film is a "tearjerker" or "weepie" that involves the mere pushing of the viewer's "emotional buttons"). I address these in turn, pointing out problems with understanding aesthetic manipulation in each of these ways. I then propose an alternative account of aesthetic manipulation that will align it with the most successful accounts of manipulation more generally.

Consider first the charge that a filmmaker is overly directive in controlling the viewer's response to a film. Here the thought is that the filmmaker is bent on having the viewer respond to the film in a certain fashion, rather than "leaving it up to the viewer" how to respond. The opposite of a manipulative film, understood in this way, would be a film that has a more open-ended resolution, more scope for the viewer to debate how to respond, more complex characters that aren't so easily classified as heroes or villains, good guys or bad guys, less "black and white," if you will, and more shades of gray. *Crash* and *Slumdog Millionaire* are two films that are frequently criticized for being manipulative in this way, in contrast to films such as *The Bicycle Thief*, which are held to exhibit more respect for the viewer as an autonomous agent. To return to one common image of manipulation, the manipulative filmmaker is acting as a puppeteer, moving as puppets both his characters (so that what they do seems predictable and overly scripted, rather than growing organically out of the story as it unfolds) and his audience, so that they will cry, laugh, or gasp on cue. The non-manipulative filmmaker treats both his characters and his audience with greater respect: one might say that the non-manipulative filmmaker regards his audience as intelligent and discerning rather than addressing his work to some assumed lowest-common-denominator, easily influenced mass public; the non-manipulative filmmaker respects his viewers as able to respond to a challenging, complex story in a range of possible ways.

In response, I argue that, other things equal, it is not aesthetically problematic that a filmmaker utilizes all his artistry to elicit a particular desired response, or series of responses, to his film. This can be a sign of commendable attention to the aesthetic qualities of the film and concern to give the audience a maximally satisfying film-going experience. Why shouldn't the director want us to laugh at comic pratfalls, or weep at poignant losses, or cower in terror as the villain closes in for the kill? Alfred

Hitchcock is widely quoted as saying, "I enjoy playing the audience like a piano." That consummate artistry has gone toward getting me to respond in the way a director or author intends does not ground the charge that a work of art is manipulative, if this is intended to mark an aesthetic flaw.

Consider next the charge that a work of art is manipulative, not because the director tries too hard to "push our buttons," but because we can *see* exactly how those buttons are being pushed (here, too, *Crash, Precious*, and *Slumdog Millionaire* come in for criticism as manipulative). The film-maker, or author, or songwriter is too transparent in his attempts to "get to us," and so we "see through" the attempts: we can't help but pay too much attention to "the man behind the curtain." Many country-western songs create the impression that the songwriter is just trying to find stock ways of making us weepy as we sit in a bar. And so, if we don't happen to be sitting captive in a bar, we turn off the car radio in disgust.

I am willing to grant that overly obvious manipulation can indeed be an aesthetic weakness in a work of art, but here the problem is simply that the intended manipulation is ineffective. These are examples of ways in which attempted manipulation can fail: instead of crying, we roll our eyes; instead of laughing, we feel embarrassed by the joker and his lame joke. But we want to understand not why failed manipulation is aesthetically problematic—that's too easy—but why successful manipulation can be.

Now, sometimes it will be the case that attempted manipulation is successful on some audience members but not on others; it works on me, but it fails on you. Here *you* can see how clumsily obvious the attempted manipulation was, but *I* cannot. But in some cases, the most psychologically and philosophically interesting ones, aesthetic manipulation can work on me even as I realize I am being manipulated.

Thus, I take most seriously the third way of fleshing out the accusation that a film is manipulative: that the response elicited by a film is somehow inappropriate, that it gets us to elicit more emotion than is somehow "warranted." We react in this way to a film when despite its "trying too hard" and too obviously to move us, it actually succeeds in doing so. We don't want to cry, because we see how hard the filmmaker is trying to get us to cry, and yet we cry anyway—despising ourselves, and resenting the filmmaker for getting us to do so.

Tears in particular seem to elicit this response of self-loathing and resentment when we feel that they are "unearned." We might sometimes find ourselves being frightened by movie violence despite seeing through the filmmaker's attempt to frighten us, or laughing at lame jokes despite seeing clearly the pitifulness of this transparent attempt at humor. But with both of these responses, we aren't drawn in emotionally to the same degree as when we are "forced" to cry. I'm straining to think of a case when I've been really frightened by what seem to be cheesy film effects; at best, I might be startled by a sudden loud noise on the soundtrack. Here I might have the grudging response, "Okay, you got me!" Then I might hasten to tell myself that I wasn't really frightened, just caught off guard by a merely physical reaction to a merely physical stimulus. With laughter at lame jokes, sometimes it isn't so much that I'm laughing at the joke, but laughing at the joker for failing so badly in his joke-telling; human beings do seem to be constructed to be able to find humor in others' misfortunes, where these are not too serious or painful. Just as I might laugh when someone slips on a banana peel (so long as the person isn't actually injured by the fall), so I might laugh at a misfired joke about someone slipping on a banana peel. So it isn't the joke itself that tickles my funny bone, but the comic effect of the entire situation. For this to kick in, I'd probably have to see the comedian actually making the joke; with merely awful attempts at humor in a film (where the filmmaker remains an invisible presence behind the camera), I'd probably just groan without emitting any chuckle, however forced.

But with certain overly obvious sad films, songs, and stories, sometimes I actually do weep. Even as I see through the clumsy, cheesy attempt to move me, I'm moved. My eyes fill up with actual tears, and then actual tears trickle down my cheeks—this, even though I can see so plainly that the filmmaker is trying to wring those tears out of me. It's unearned weeping that most galls us as manipulative. We protest against being manipulated in this particular way, perhaps because it's difficult for us to deny the reality of our response, however unmerited we may take it to be.

This way of understanding aesthetic manipulation—that we are "forced" to have "unwarranted" emotions in response to a work of art—is on the face of it a puzzling charge. If a film depicts a very sad event, such as a prolonged death from cancer, why would tears in response to such an event be inappropriate? "Tearjerkers" are often criticized as manipulative: books or films or songs that pile on sad events, like death, lost love, family estrangements. But these *are* sad events. Why would tears in response to such an event be inappropriate, or unwarranted, or too much? Yes, country-western songs tell lugubrious tales about death by car accident, cancer, suicide. But how can we say that sad emotions in response to such events are inappropriate?

I pause to note that sometimes works of art get us to have sad emotions in response to events that in the scheme of things are fairly trivial. I have been deeply moved, even as an adult reader, by children's books that focus on small sadnesses in a child's life. I've gotten a lump in my throat when Ramona Quimby in Beverly Cleary's *Ramona the Pest* thinks that her kindergarten teacher doesn't love her anymore. Here, as an adult reader, I can see that Ramona is mistaken about this, and that even if she isn't, even if her teacher is indeed temporarily irritated with her, this will pass, and causing others to be temporarily irritated with us is a part of life. But Cleary's artistry here is such that I identify with Ramona completely, I inhabit her viewpoint completely, and so I can see how something that may be "objectively" small can feel subjectively huge to Ramona. Sometimes, however, when we are caused to feel deep emotions over something trivial, we resist. The best example here is the 1960s hit song "MacArthur Park," which has soaring, heart-wrenching vocals expressing anguished despair, and invoking a corresponding emotional response in the hearer, over...a cake left out in the rain! I loved the song when I first heard it, and I find it hard even now to resist sharing the vocalist's heartfelt torment, but then I remember that he is singing about a ruined cake, for which he'll "never have the recipe again," and I feel embarrassed that I'm manipulated into getting a lump in my throat as I listen.

So manipulative art causes the viewer to have non-ideal emotional reactions, reactions that are unwarranted in some way. But to repeat my earlier question: How can it be that viewers consider a film to be manipulative in getting us to cry over sad events, when the events depicted (unlike the melting of a cake in the rain) *are* indisputably sad? How is our sadness in such a case "excessive," or "not the right amount"?

The answer, I submit, goes something as follows. The events portrayed by a fictional work of art are not real events. So we cannot simply argue that the same response that is appropriate to a real event of the sort depicted is automatically appropriate to a similar fictional event. Hamlet was right to wonder how we are able to identify with fictional characters enough to be emotionally engaged with their plight: "What's Hecuba to him, or he to Hecuba / That he should weep for her?" Blakey Vermuele, in her recent book *Why Do We Care about Fictional Characters?*, argues that fictional characters are more similar to real people than is often thought; she maintains that we encounter even many "real" people as fictional characters, as when we "encounter" celebrities or other figures in the news only through media reports of their doings, rather than first-hand as family, friends, colleagues, neighbors whom we care about within the actual experience of our daily lives. She argues that "the reasons that we care about literary characters are finally not much different from the question of why we care about other people, especially people we have never met nor are ever likely to meet";[11] this is because we have a human hunger and "need to know what other people are like, not in the aggregate, but in the particular."[12] But it seems to me that misfortunes and triumphs suffered by fictitious creations should matter to us less, for there was no *actual* human suffering and joy involved, except that experienced vicariously by readers and viewers (where here the "suffering" generally does not count as a negative in any utilitarian calculus, because it forms part of the larger pleasure of interacting with a work of art, as art). So we can't just read off what emotional reactions are appropriate to real-life tragedies and assume that the same reactions are appropriate to tragedies in fiction.

I argue that we judge emotional responses to a piece of fiction to be appropriate not only by considering the events depicted in that piece of fiction but, even more so, by considering the artistic quality of the piece of fiction and of particular elements in it. If we are to be justified in weeping over imagined or fabricated events, which never really happened, we feel that this needs to be in response to the artistry with which those events are depicted. Filmmakers who are denounced as manipulative tend to be perceived as trying to obtain their results simply by means of depicting stock sad events (e.g., heaping up tragedy upon tragedy) rather than by selecting and depicting these with admirable artistic skill. When we succumb to the manipulation and cry the intended tears, we tend to resent the filmmaker for dragging this undeserved response from us, as well as to blame ourselves for being so susceptible to certain emotive levers.

Here is where the language of "button pushing" is invoked. This kind of button-pushing can occur with a range of emotional responses: laughter, fear, sadness. Young children (and also some immature adults) laugh when certain words are said: "poop," "pee-pee," "bottom," "underpants." These words push their laughter buttons. Likewise, we squirm or startle at the sight of blood, even stage blood. And we have our crying button pushed by the thought of certain tragic life events. It's too easy to push

11. Blakey Vermeule, *Why Do We Care about Literary Characters?* (Baltimore: Johns Hopkins University Press, 2009), xiii.

12. Vermeule, *Why Do We Care*, xii.

these buttons. Anybody can do it. We want to cry only over real sad events; or fictional sad events that earn this response through the artistry with which they are depicted; or perhaps, the artistry earns our engagement with the work, which then elicits these appropriate emotional responses.

Now, of course, there is considerable and unresolvable controversy over what counts as artistry. Here is where I locate the ultimate source of difference in our assessment of films as manipulative or not. Many of the films frequently criticized as manipulative, mentioned above, are also major award-winners, taking home even the ultimate accolade of the Academy Award for best picture of the year, so extremely sophisticated viewers, including professional film critics, are on record as thinking that these films did indeed exhibit skilled filmmaking of the highest order. There is no universal agreement about excellence in art, no indisputably objective standards by which it can be judged. So if judgments of aesthetic manipulation are parasitic on judgments of an artwork's quality, disagreements regarding the latter will result in disagreements regarding the former; we may also disagree about whether some particular element of the work is aesthetically problematic.

But while judgments of aesthetic manipulation are *parasitic* on judgments of an artwork's quality, they are not *identical* to such judgments. The charge that an artwork is manipulative is more than the charge that it is simply a bad piece of art. Instead, it is the charge that the work of art tries to elicit—and in the case of many if not all audience members, succeeds in eliciting—an emotional response that is unwarranted by the quality of the work. Generally, it succeeds by presenting situations that are genuinely sad, or would be sad if they took place in real life, but as merely fictional sad situations we feel they need to elicit an emotional response from us in terms based not only on their content but also on the artistry of their style of presentation.

Now, the account that I have just given addresses only manipulative works of *fiction,* as I have made use of the distinction between fiction and reality in giving my analysis of how we should reply to this third charge of aesthetic manipulation. How can this account address charges of manipulation in documentary films, which are showing real events that are truly sad? If, in depicting genuinely sad real-life events, a documentary film is judged to be manipulative, this cannot be because the emotions it elicits are inappropriate to the events depicted. Here I can no longer appeal to the gap between the real and the fictional to ground a response. The *New York Times* recently reviewed a satirical film about documentary filmmaking,

The Woman in the Septic Tank; in the film, cynically ambitious filmmakers are making a documentary about poverty, called *With Nothing*, designed to "pile on the pathos" in hopes of winning prizes at international film festivals. "Wow, perfection," the fictional director of this fictional documentary says, when the filmmaking team "find a slum with children picking through mountains of garbage."[13] Here the audiences targeted by these fictional filmmakers aren't being led to weep about fictional poverty, but about actual, terrible, life-crushing, soul-destroying poverty. And let us assume for the sake of the argument that the fictional filmmakers do end up producing a brilliant film of high aesthetic quality that merits the coveted prizes it ends up reaping. Yet the filmmakers do seem as manipulative as can be. I will return to this case below.[14]

In this section I have argued that aesthetic manipulation involves eliciting an emotional response to a work of art that is inappropriate because it is unearned by the artistic merits of the piece. Where the work of art is a representational work, depicting genuinely sad events, sad emotions in response to those events are in some sense appropriate, but because the events depicted are fictitious events, we want to be moved by them only if they are depicted with appropriate artistry. I will offer a refinement of this account below to deal with manipulative works of art that elicit emotion from actual (rather than fictitious) sad events, such as a manipulative documentary.

Manipulation as an Attempt to Elicit an Emotional Response that Violates Norms and Ideals

What light, if any, does my proposed account of aesthetic manipulation shed on the issue of manipulation more generally? I argue that it works to support the account of manipulation given by Robert Noggle, who defines interpersonal manipulation in this way: "There are certain norms or ideals that govern beliefs, desires, and emotions. I am suggesting that

---

13. Rachel Saltz, "Let's Film These Poor People; Maybe We'll Get Rich," *New York Times*, May 22, 2012, C3.

14. Also, some works of art might be called manipulative even though they don't depict any events at all, such as an over-the-top schmaltzy piece of purely instrumental music. Such music seems to be trying to elicit certain emotions in us and might succeed in doing so with some audiences. Here, too, the music just seems to be pushing certain "buttons" of an automatic aural/emotional response. We can say that the response is unearned because the methods of producing it lack appropriate musical artistry.

manipulative action is the attempt to get someone's beliefs, desires, or emotions to violate these norms, to fall short of these ideals."[15] Note that Noggle's
account discusses "norms" and "ideals" that should govern the formation of
our beliefs, desires, and emotions, not "reasons" that should govern them.
Thus, his account does not suffer from the bias toward the rationalistic and
cognitive that I criticized above in my own previous account of manipulation,
as well as in recent attempts to improve upon it.[16] Noggle's account, I argue,
is broad enough to include aesthetic manipulation, as I've analyzed it, within
its scope. Where manipulation is an aesthetic flaw, it is because we desire to
have our emotional responses to a work of art be governed by aesthetic ideals: by the quality of the work of art, as art, rather than by the mere content
of what that work of art depicts. A manipulative work of art is one that tries
to get us to respond in a way that falls short of these ideals. Noggle's account
is thus capacious and flexible enough to accommodate both interpersonal
manipulation of the standard sort and aesthetic manipulation of the sort
I am focusing on here.

Noggle relativizes his account of the relevant ideals to what the "actor
[manipulator] takes to be the victim's ideal conditions."[17] Given that we
seem to lack an "'objective standard' for appropriate emotion," we need
to relativize the standard either to "what the person being influenced
believes are the ideal settings for her," or to "what the *influencer* thinks are
ideal settings *for the person being influenced*."[18] Noggle opts for the latter
choice, both because it preserves "a conceptual parallel with lying" (where
"I lie if I tell you something I do not believe, whether or not that thing
is true"[19]), and because "if we do not define manipulative action relative
to the beliefs of the actor, then it would be possible—even common—to
unknowingly perform manipulative actions."[20] Manipulation, for Noggle,
is "an intentionally characterized action."[21]

---

15. Noggle, "Manipulative Actions," 44.

16. In the final analysis, I read Gorin's appeal to the failure of manipulation to "track reasons" as in the spirit of Noggle's account; it's only a small change to expand "track reasons"
to "track norms and ideals," which may or may not be understood as "reasons."

17. Noggle, "Manipulative Actions," 47.

18. Noggle, "Manipulative Actions," 47 (italics in original).

19. Noggle, "Manipulative Actions," 47.

20. Noggle, "Manipulative Actions," 48.

21. Noggle, "Manipulative Actions," 48.

Is this what we want to say about aesthetic manipulation? In opposition to Noggle on this point, works of art are often criticized as manipulative even though we have no evidence that the *artist* was trying to get us to fall short of her *own* judgment of what the audience's ideal emotional response would be to the work. Many people produce works of art that are obvious, heavy-handed, emotionally inept, and otherwise flawed in a seemingly manipulative way without at all *trying* to do so. They just aren't very good at making art. Yet many of these flawed works of art do succeed in connecting with their audience in the desired way. Now, sometimes creators of an artwork do seem to aim merely at pleasing or pandering to the public. We judge such artists to be complacent and lazy: "hacks." While they weren't trying to make a bad film on purpose, they seem to be indifferent to quality, targeting their efforts only on easy and predictable ways to elicit emotional response. This kind of case fits comfortably within my account. What's more difficult is when the artist does indeed seem to have tried her hardest to make a film or write a book that was good. Perhaps those who criticize the film as manipulative do so with the thought that it's hard to believe that anyone could produce a film so heavy-handed in its emotional register without doing so on purpose, or at the least proceeding with insufficient artistic care. But we could easily be wrong about this. If so, then my account of aesthetic manipulation begins to part company with Noggle's general account of manipulation.

A special feature of aesthetic manipulation is that we talk not only about the *artist* as manipulative but also the *work of art* itself as manipulative. In either case, aesthetic manipulation seems less fully intentional than on Noggle's account. The earnest but incompetent artist does not intend to have her work elicit an unwarranted emotional response (*she* believes the response *is* warranted), but we still might find ourselves saying that, as an artist, she is at least obliquely manipulative in that she produces *work* that is manipulative. In saying that the artwork she produces is manipulative, of course, we recognize that artworks are not the kinds of things that are capable of intentions, so no intentionality can be imputed to them. So at this point we seem driven to characterize manipulative action in a way that Noggle would reject: rather than identifying manipulation in terms of the artist's own (intentionally violated) ideals, we "appeal to objective ideals, hope that the problem of formulating them does not turn out to be intractable, and then either attempt to construct the appropriate ideal or wait for someone else to do so."[22] But this does indeed capture how

---

22. Noggle, "Manipulative Actions," 47.

we make judgments of aesthetic manipulation in many cases. When we level a charge of aesthetic manipulation, an appeal to objective ideals of aesthetic quality does seem to be playing a role in our critical judgment. If we were to appeal only to evidence about the artist's own manipulative intentions, we would arguably have less disagreement over whether or not an artwork is manipulative, and we would require biographical evidence to settle the dispute, rather than debate the artwork's merits.

Whereas some artists elicit an objectively *inappropriate* response to their work without intending to (the not-very-good filmmaker just discussed), others might elicit an *appropriate* response to their work that nonetheless feels inappropriate because they themselves—the creators of the art work—don't share the objectively appropriate emotional response to the events they are depicting. The *viewer's* emotional response is appropriate; the *artist's* own emotional response is not. We are now in a position to see how the fictional documentary *With Nothing*, as portrayed in the satiric film *The Woman in the Septic Tank*, can be manipulative, even though it is indeed objectively ideal to respond to portrayals of terrible poverty by being outraged, saddened, and deeply moved in exactly the same way that the filmmakers hope we will be. The filmmakers in this example aren't trying to get their audience to have a non-ideal response to the events they are portraying in the film. But *they themselves* have a non-ideal response to these events. No one should see starving children picking through garbage in a slum and think, "Wow, perfection."

To return to Gorin's analysis of manipulation, these filmmakers are like the manipulators who actually offer *good* reasons to get someone to act as they desire, but offer them with fundamental indifference to their goodness, offering them only because the good reason happens to be an effective causal lever in the circumstances. Cynical documentary filmmakers are offering genuinely sad, real events that trigger genuinely sad, appropriate responses—but they would have offered us anything to get us to respond in this way. We end up having the response they want us to have, in alignment with their single-minded, ambitious focus on their own fame and fortune, but the fact that they themselves do not share this response suggests that they are acting manipulatively. It isn't quite right to say that they intend for us to have an inappropriate emotional response to the film, and we do end up having an appropriate emotional response, but that response is different from their response: they intend for us to feel what they themselves do not feel, just as the liar intends his victim to believe what he himself does not think—although what the victim ends up believing may in fact turn out to be true.

I want to close with one final claim about aesthetic manipulation. Above, I argued that there are several reasons to think that aesthetic manipulation will not be morally problematic in the way of much other manipulation: it often makes less of an impact on our lives, it's overt rather than covert and so lacking the deception present in many standard cases of manipulation, and most important, the individuals undergoing aesthetic manipulation sign up for the experience voluntarily. They are puppets, if you will, who actively seek out their puppeteer. Nonetheless, the analysis of aesthetic manipulation offered here reveals a way in which it is often evidence of a moral flaw in an artist. The cynical filmmaker, the pandering filmmaker, and the lazy filmmaker all exhibit a failure to view their audience with respect. Noggle holds that "Acting manipulatively toward someone... is an affront to her as a rational and moral being."[23] I want to say that aesthetic manipulation is often an affront to someone as an emotional being. The artist who offers the public work that is crassly calculated to push emotional buttons and affective levers in a mechanical way without committed attention to artistic excellence exhibits a kind of contempt for others that is a moral flaw. Not all aesthetic manipulators do this—we can't say this of the earnestly inferior artist discussed above—but many aesthetic manipulators clearly fail to respect their audience as individuals who deserve to experience appropriate emotional responses to a work of art. Instead, they view them only with the shrewd gaze of the puppeteer. Where this is so, aesthetic manipulation is not only an artistic flaw, but a moral flaw as well.

---

23. Noggle, "Manipulative Actions," 52.

7

Information Manipulation and Moral Responsibility

Todd R. Long

I. Introduction

In previous work, I have argued that we can be morally responsible for our actions in cases in which we act on the basis of manipulated information, even if the manipulation is so radical that we would not have performed the relevant actions had the manipulation not occurred.[1] In so arguing, I have focused primarily on metaphysical conditions for moral responsibility. Here I focus on broadly epistemic matters. My goal is to advance our knowledge about information manipulation and moral responsibility in a way that yields philosophically satisfying responses to some criticisms of my previous work.[2,3]

In section II, I provide two cases to support and anchor subsequent discussion of my thesis. In section III, I entertain and reject an initially appealing objection, according to which relying on *false information*

1. Todd R. Long, "Moderate Reasons—Responsiveness, Moral Responsibility, and Manipulation," in *Freedom and Determinism*, edited by Joseph Campbell, Michael O'Rourke, and David Shier (Cambridge, MA: MIT Press, 2004): 151–72.

2. For criticism of Long, "Moderate Reasons-Responsiveness," see John Martin Fischer, "Manipulation and Guidance Control: A Reply to Long," in *Action, Ethics, and Responsibility*, edited by Joseph Campbell, Michael O'Rourke, and Harry Silverstein (Cambridge, MA: MIT Press, 2010): 175–86; Christopher Evan Franklin, "Plausibility, Manipulation, and Fischer and Ravizza," *Southern Journal of Philosophy* 44, no. 2 (2006): 173–92; Eddy Nahmias, "Review of Freedom and Determinism," *Notre Dame Philosophical Reviews*, June 11, 2005, http://ndpr.nd.edu/review.cfm?id=2841; James Steadman, "Moral Responsibility and Motivational Mechanisms," *Ethical Theory and Moral Practice* 15 (2012): 473–92.

3. For this essay, my thanks go to John Martin Fischer, Michael McKenna, Michael Weber, audiences at my presentations at the 2012 Bowling Green Workshop in Applied Ethics and Public Policy, the philosophy department at University of Nevada Las Vegas (2011), the Northwest Philosophy Conference (2007), and the Inland Northwest Philosophy Conference (2006).

prevents moral responsibility. In section IV, I defend my use of the term 'moral responsibility,' and I offer an account utilizing Aristotelian epistemic conditions for voluntariness. In section V, I respond to additional broadly epistemic objections—from John Martin Fischer and Christopher Franklin—which contend that information manipulation can preclude moral responsibility by restricting the *control* one has over one's actions.

II. The Family Policy Cases

Consider the following case:

> *Family Policy:* You live in a suburban subdivided neighborhood, and you are the father or mother of a four-year-old daughter. Your neighbors, who also have a young daughter, have been good friends during the past two years. The two girls have been accustomed to playing together, and they have, with their parents' permission, freely moved between the two houses during afternoon playtime. But, your neighbors have had to move away. One morning a police officer comes to your door and explains that a convicted sex offender will begin renting the neighboring house in one week. The police officer gives you all the details that she is legally allowed to divulge, including the claim that a police officer will drive by the street daily and a parole officer will check in weekly with the sex offender. Dismayed by the news, your spouse and you deliberate about what to do. You realize that your financial and work situation will not allow you to move right away. After careful, prolonged deliberation, you enact a family policy according to which your daughter will henceforth not be allowed to go outside of the house for any reason without overt parental supervision.

I take it that your action of enacting this family policy is an uncontroversial example of an action for which a person is morally responsible. After all, you do not engage in the action as a result of a psychological compulsion, a drug addiction, or any other kind of obvious responsibility precluding condition. It is a rational decision based on careful, reflective deliberation and it is consonant with the kinds of preferences, desires, and values that make up your character. I intend for this example to strike all non-skeptics about moral responsibility as a paradigm example of morally responsible action.[4]

---

4. Add any additional details that you think are needed.

Now consider a variation which is exactly like the first, except for the following facts:

Manipulated Family Policy: The person who comes to your house and explains that a sex offender will be moving next door is not a police officer. She is a fake who has been paid by an enemy of yours to impersonate a police officer for the purpose of causing you emotional distress. However, you have no reason at all to think that she is a fake. Indeed, she is actually wearing a police uniform issued by your city, and her conversation with you is completely convincing. Suppose that the fake police officer says exactly the same words, with the same inflection and body language, as does the actual police officer in *Family Policy*. She is such an excellent actor that only technology such as a lie detector test would reveal her deception. In this *Manipulated Family Policy* example, you deliberate just as you deliberated in *Family Policy*, and the outcome of your deliberation includes your enacting a family policy of not allowing your daughter to leave the house without overt parental supervision.

Are you morally responsible for enacting the family policy in this second example? I think that you are. Just as it is with the first case, your action is not a result of a psychological compulsion, drug addiction, neurological disorder, or any other obvious responsibility precluding condition. In both cases, you deliberate on the basis of information that you have non-culpably acquired and which you have excellent reason to believe is true. In both cases, your action is consonant with the desires, preferences, and values that make up your character. In both cases, the *way* you deliberate to your decision is the same. Thus, your way of deliberating and acting on the basis of that deliberation is not manipulated at all. All that is manipulated is the information that you have to go on in your deliberation. In my view, *information manipulation does not, by itself, preclude morally responsible action*. A consequence of this view is that *we can be morally responsible for actions that we would not have performed if the information manipulation had not occurred*.

III. No-Falsehood and Similar 'Intuitive' Objections

I think it is pretty obvious that you are morally responsible for enacting the family policy in *Manipulated Family Policy*. However, a number of critics have resisted my view.[5] One line of resistance is motivated by an epistemic matter understood along the lines of what I call the 'No Falsehood' principle:

No Falsehood: if one acts on the basis of *false* information, then one is not morally responsible for that act.

Variations on *No Falsehood* have appeared in the literature. For instance, James Steadman has us consider a case in which "Linda votes for McCain instead of Obama, because she possesses a number of false beliefs about where he stands on the issues (perhaps there was a misprint in her local newspaper, so that remarks by Obama were inadvertently attributed to McCain)."[6] Steadman's idea is that, because Linda engages in practical reasoning on the basis of many false beliefs, we should think that the psychological process constituting her practical reasoning is defective enough that Linda is not morally responsible for her voting for McCain. But, why think that practical reasoning on the basis of false beliefs renders the reasoning process defective in a way that pertains to moral responsibility? An answer offered is that "we would...not hesitate to absolve Linda of any responsibility for her (deluded) choice."[7] Because your action in *Manipulated Family Policy* is also based on many false beliefs, perhaps we would not hesitate to absolve you of responsibility.

However, from the fact (if it is a fact) that we would not hesitate to absolve Linda of responsibility for the relevant action, it does not follow that Linda lacked moral responsibility for her voting. Indeed, it would be possible to *absolve* someone of responsibility for an action only if the person were *responsible* for the action. This just follows from the fact that absolution is the act of freeing one from an obligation or of remitting a sin: just as I must have an obligation in order to be freed from it, so must I have committed a sin for it to be remitted.

But, perhaps by 'absolved' Steadman intended something like, 'we wouldn't *blame* Linda under the circumstances if we knew about them' (any more than we would blame you in *Manipulated Family Policy*). The

5. See Fischer, "Manipulation and Guidance Control"; Franklin, "Plausibility, Manipulation, and Fischer and Ravizza"; and Steadman, "Moral Responsibility and Motivational Mechanisms."

6. Steadman, "Moral Responsibility and Motivational Mechanisms," 484.

7. Steadman, "Moral Responsibility and Motivational Mechanisms," 484.

relevant circumstances involve Linda's acting on the basis of false beliefs that (we may suppose) she has non-culpably acquired. Similar circumstances are part of a fanciful case from Franklin wherein Judith punches Judy on the basis of misleading evidence about Judy induced in Judith (without her knowledge) by a manipulator. Franklin concludes, "Such a situation would seem to render Judith more pitiable than morally culpable."[8] Such sensible ideas might motivate endorsement of a *No Falsehood* principle by means of the following argument: if one acts on the basis of false beliefs that one has non-culpably acquired, then one is not morally culpable for the action; and, if one is not morally culpable for an action, then one is not morally responsible for that action; so, if one acts on the basis of false beliefs that one has non-culpably acquired, then one is not morally responsible for that action.

It is true that in many (but not all) cases of information manipulation, we would not, if we knew about the manipulation, think that the agent was morally *culpable* for the action, for 'culpable' means "deserving blame"; and, it is true that in many such cases we would pity the relevant agent; but, it does not follow that the agents lack moral responsibility for what they do in light of the information they have. After all, in some cases of information manipulation in which we would pity the agent because of the manipulation (e.g., *Manipulated Family Policy*), the agent deserves *praise* for what she does in light of her information; but, she can deserve praise only if she is morally responsible for what she does.

It may well be true that neither Linda (in Steadman's case), nor Judith (in Franklin's case), nor you (in *Manipulated Family Policy*) is blameworthy. It doesn't follow that they are not morally responsible for their actions. After all, it is extremely plausible that, if you are morally praiseworthy for your action in *Family Policy*, then you are morally praiseworthy in *Manipulated Family Policy*; for we may suppose that in each case you did what the most morally upstanding, perfectly rational person in your circumstances would do in light of the information you had to go on. But, of course, you are morally praiseworthy for an action only if you are morally responsible for that action.

Consider now an epistemically motivated legal motivation for *No Falsehood*. In discussing the voluntariness required for legal consent for a contract, Joel Feinberg says that the voluntariness of one's agreement is

---

8. Franklin, "Plausibility, Manipulation, and Fischer and Ravizza," 187.

always lessened by an induced false belief that is germane to the agreement.[9] Of a case in which a seller induces a false belief about a product in a buyer, Feinberg writes: "Depending on how vital a role the belief in question plays in the buyer's motivation, its falsity will diminish to a proportional degree the voluntariness of his consent."[10]

Imagine a case in which the seller of a house lies to a buyer about features of such great importance to the buyer that he would not have bought the house had the seller not lied about those features. Feinberg would judge the buyer's consent to the deal as being so low on the spectrum of voluntariness that it falls below what ought to be the legal standard for lawful consent. Such a judgment coheres with our sense that the fraud involved in the case is severe enough that the buyer deserves significant compensation. One might easily infer that the buyer did not voluntarily sign the home ownership papers; and, because involuntary action is a sign of an action for which one is not morally responsible, one might infer that such a case reveals a reason to think that acting on the basis of false information can preclude moral responsibility for the action. Such a thought might well motivate a view along the lines of the *No Falsehood* principle.

However, reflection reveals that Feinberg is not using 'voluntariness' (and its cognates) in a way that pertains to *moral responsibility*. The relevant question for us is whether the buyer is morally responsible for buying the house. Suppose that the buyer has excellent reasons to think that, if he buys the house, he will thereby achieve his selfish desire to force his wife to get a well-paying job against her will and despite her deeply held, epistemically rational belief that her staying home with her young children is best for the family. I take it that, regardless of whether the buyer is deceived by the seller's lies about the condition of the house, the buyer is *morally blameworthy* for buying the house (add whatever details you think are needed). But, he is morally blameworthy for buying the house only if he is *morally responsible* for buying the house; and, he is morally responsible for buying the house only if he *voluntarily* bought the house (in whatever sense of 'voluntariness' pertains to moral responsibility).[11]

---

9. Joel Feinberg, *The Moral Limits of the Criminal Law: Volume 3: Harm to Self* (New York: Oxford University Press, 1986).

10. Feinberg, *Moral Limits of the Criminal Law*, 274.

11. In section IV, I discuss what I take to be the relevant sense of 'voluntariness.'

Clearly, then, the notion of voluntariness we assume when we think about the buyer's moral blameworthiness is different from the one Feinberg says pertains to legal consent. It remains very plausible that the fraud perpetrated by the seller is severe enough to justify legal compensation to the buyer. If we want to explain this justification by means of a concept expressed by phrases such as 'the voluntariness required for legal consent,' then so be it. But, the example reveals the mistake in thinking that legally useful senses of 'voluntariness' and 'responsibility' are directly relevant for assessing claims of moral responsibility.

Whatever are the motivations of various self-proclaimed intuitive judgments about 'moral responsibility,' I think that non-skeptics about moral responsibility should resist any principle along the lines of *No Falsehood* for the general reason that it cuts against their non-skepticism. Consider criminal jury trials. It is no secret that criminal trial lawyers, both for the defense and for the prosecution, are trained to provide misleading information, designed to manipulate jurors, as it serves their clients. The goal of each side is to spin the trial evidence in order to get a desired judgment. In closing statements, the prosecution routinely tells the jury that the defendant is guilty, and the defense routinely claims that the defendant is innocent. It follows that one of them tells the jury a falsehood of great importance. Thus, criminal trial jurors routinely deliberate on the basis of false (and often manipulated) information. Does it follow that jurors routinely lack moral responsibility for their judgments? I don't think that any non-skeptic about moral responsibility thinks so. In typical cases, jurors deliberate on the basis of the information they receive at the trial and the judge's orders, doing their best to make a fair, just judgment. Their judgments are typically not the result of psychological compulsions, physical addictions, irresistible impulses, or the like. They are typically the result of more or less rational deliberation, and thus bear the hallmark of voluntary, responsible action.

There is another reason for non-skeptics about moral responsibility to deny a principle along the line of *No Falsehood*. It is epistemically possible that a radical skeptical scenario obtains. Perhaps we are in the Matrix, or we are brains-in-vats, or a Cartesian evil genius is radically deceiving us. If any such skeptical scenario were to obtain, then we would almost always decide to act on the basis of false information. However, even if we are in such a scenario, that fact itself is no more a reason to deny that we are morally responsible for our decisions than it is to think that we would lack epistemic justification for our typical beliefs (the latter is a lesson from what epistemologists call the *New Evil Demon Problem* for reliabilism).[12]

This argument from the possibility of a radical skeptical scenario is germane to one of Steadman's proposals for distinguishing between normal psychological mechanisms, which he thinks yield morally responsible action, and defective psychological mechanisms, which he thinks yield actions for which the agent is not morally responsible. Referring to the mechanism-based understanding of moral responsibility developed by Fischer and Ravizza, Steadman claims that a "mechanism [that] has too many false beliefs about the choice at hand" is "a deluded mechanism," which is to say that it has a particular kind of defect or abnormality that renders it inapt to yield decisions and actions for which the agent is morally responsible.[13] Steadman says that we can distinguish normal practical reasoning mechanisms from abnormal/defective ones in the following way:

> [W]e can say that a practical-reasoning mechanism is normal (at least with respect to its rational reasons for action) if the number of occurrent belief-inputs relevant to the choice at hand (both true and false) is at least half the number that occurs in the life of an agent on normal occasions of action. Given this, we can say that the mechanism is abnormal when the number of such inputs falls either above or below the normal range.... We can say that a mechanism ... containing a number of *false* beliefs *above* this range is abnormally *delusive*.[14]

---

12. See Stewart Cohen, "Justification and Truth," *Philosophical Studies* 46 (1984): 279–96. Suppose you have an introspectively identical twin whose information about the external world is manipulated by a Cartesian evil demon. By hypothesis of the example, your demon-world twin has the same evidence as you, and this suggests that your twin is epistemically rational in believing the same propositions that you are, despite the fact that almost all of your twin's beliefs are false (and believed on the basis of unreliable sources). The intuitive judgment is that misleading information does not preclude epistemically rational beliefs. Although beliefs are not actions, I can think of no principled reason for holding that one can have an epistemically rational belief on the basis of false information but one cannot make a morally responsible decision on the basis of false information.

13. John Martin Fischer and Mark Ravizza, *Responsibility and Control* (Cambridge: Cambridge University Press, 1998); Steadman, "Moral Responsibility and Motivational Mechanisms," 484.

14. Steadman, "Moral Responsibility and Motivational Mechanisms," 484.

This idea assumes the following *No Falsehood*–like principle: *if the number of false beliefs involved in one's practical reasoning is abnormally high, then one is not morally responsible for actions that are outputs of that practical reasoning.*

Although it is worthwhile to look for ways to distinguish between responsibility-producing and responsibility-precluding psychological mechanisms, reflection on the argument from the possibility of a radical skeptical scenario gives us a good reason to deny this *No Falsehood*–like principle. For if we happen to be in a radical skeptical scenario, then we routinely engage in practical reasoning on the basis of a massive number of false beliefs. But, that fact would not prevent our being morally responsible for what we decide to do in light of the misleading information we have. Consider the skeptical scenario depicted in the movie *The Matrix*.[15] Before Neo is removed from the Matrix, virtually all of his decisions are made on the basis of a massive amount of false information. On Steadman's way of individuating mechanisms, Neo's mechanism of practical reasoning almost always contains a super-high level of false beliefs relative to what we take our typical practical reasoning mechanisms to contain. Thus, Neo's mechanism is, according to Steadman's idea, severely abnormal and defective. But, I find no reason to suppose that Neo is not morally responsible for the voluntary decisions he makes in light of the misleading information he has to go on. Now if the Matrix is directly causing Neo's desires, preferences, and values, then there is some plausibility in thinking that he is not morally responsible for the actions that flow from his practical reasoning; but, the mere fact that he engages in practical reasoning on the basis of false beliefs, even if the number is highly abnormal, does not, by itself, prevent his being morally responsible for the decisions he voluntarily makes in light of the information he has to go on.

IV. Voluntariness as a Theoretical Constraint for 'Moral Responsibility'

I have made claims that are in tension. In response to some resisters to some of my views about moral responsibility, I have criticized the reliance

---

15. *The Matrix* depicts a world in which most humans are unwitting, energy-yielding slaves of super-intelligent machines, which electro-chemically stimulate their bodies so that it appears to them that the world is just like it appears to us. If I were in the Matrix, then I would think that I am in an office typing out a sentence, but I would actually be naked in a pod hooked up to the machines' supercomputer.

on self-proclaimed intuitive judgments about 'moral responsibility,' but in defense of some of my own views I have implicitly, at least, appealed to intuitive judgments about moral responsibility. Although I think that my commentary has been instructive inasmuch as I have appealed to reasons that I expect to have widespread appeal among theorists about moral responsibility, I now want to acknowledge that I do not think that my appeals to intuition are decisive. Here is why: the term 'moral responsibility' is a term of art, which has been used in a variety of ways (a fact that explains *many* misunderstandings among philosophers working in this area).

Ordinary people do not go around talking about who is *morally responsible* for this or who has *moral responsibility* for that. They do sometimes talk about *responsibility*, they sometimes say things like, "what he did was *wrong*" (and occasionally, "*morally wrong*"), they are sometimes concerned with whether someone should be *praised* or *blamed* ("You shouldn't *blame* her: she didn't know any better"), and they are sometimes interested in basic *desert* ("He might have received the maximum sentence, but he *deserved* far worse"). These observations show that ordinary people care about matters that may sensibly be referred to under the label 'moral responsibility,' but the term itself is surely not in ordinary use as are other terms of philosophical interest, such as 'knows,' 'beautiful,' and 'good.' For this reason, it is a mistake to think that one has settled some philosophical dispute by appealing to what are supposed to be common intuitions about 'moral responsibility.' However, we can hope to make some philosophical progress by stipulating the conditions for the term's application, in light of theoretical needs and concerns.

The term 'morally responsible' has been employed by philosophers as a means of expressing the claim that one's actions are caused by, or explained by, or otherwise suitably related to, central features of one's *personhood* such that one is "an apt candidate for the reactive attitudes" and associated reactive responses such as praise/blame and reward/punishment [16] or such that "there is an 'entry' in one's 'moral ledger.'"[17] Understood in these ways, 'morally

---

16. Fischer and Ravizza, *Responsibility and Control*, 7. Similar views include those by David Copp, "Defending the Principle of Alternate Possibilities: Blameworthiness and Moral Responsibility," *Nous* 31, no. 4 (1997): 441–56; and Jay Wallace, *Responsibility and the Moral Sentiments* (Cambridge, MA: Harvard University Press, 1994).

17. Michael Zimmerman, "Taking Luck Seriously," *Journal of Philosophy* 99, no.11 (2002): 555. For similar views, see Joel Feinberg, *Doing and Deserving* (Princeton: Princeton University Press, 1970); Jonathan Glover, *Responsibility* (New York: Humanities, 1970); Herbert

responsible' is used to evaluate persons in some way. Which way? The philosophical literature features a variety of answers from a variety of perspectives. I am motivated by a guiding concern among quite a few philosophers,
and it is this: Quite apart from considerations about legality, the needs of
society, our actual epistemic limitations when we consider real-world cases,
and what makes us justified in praising/blaming or rewarding/punishing
others, *what are the conditions for correct evaluations of persons in light of what
they actually deserve?* On my view, this issue of basic desert explains what is
plausible about both the apt-candidate-for-reactive-attitudes approach and
the entry-in-one's-moral-ledger approach to fixing a sense of the term 'morally responsible.'

What could make something a candidate for deserving moral praise or
moral blame? As Aristotle pointed out, one deserves praise or blame only
for actions that one performs *voluntarily*.[18] Contemporary theorists of metaphysical freedom or moral responsibility can be taken to be attempting to
provide conditions for the relevant kind of voluntariness. No doubt we
need *metaphysical conditions* to do this work, but Aristotle rightly pointed
out that there are also *epistemic conditions* for voluntariness: "Everything
that is done by reason of ignorance is non-voluntary" (III. 1. 1110b.20). To
act voluntarily, Aristotle said, one must not be ignorant "of who he is, what
he is doing, what or whom he is acting on, and sometimes also what (e.g.,
what instrument) he is doing it with, and to what end (e.g., for safety), and
how he is doing it (e.g., whether gently or violently)" (III.1.1111a.3–6).

As these claims strike me as correct, I conclude that necessary conditions for being a candidate for deserving moral praise or moral blame
include some freedom-relevant metaphysical conditions as well as some
Aristotelian epistemic conditions. But, such conditions are not sufficient.
Here is why: It is possible for one to satisfy the metaphysical (non-epistemic
freedom-relevant) conditions of many popular theories of free will/action,
and also to satisfy the Aristotelian epistemic conditions, but not to have a
'moral sense' of the sort that courts try to establish the presence of in cases
in which the sanity of a defendant is in question. Typical four-year-old
children are plausible examples of persons who routinely perform voluntary actions, but, lacking sufficient understanding of the concepts of moral

---

Morris, *On Guilt and Innocence* (Berkeley: University of California Press, 1976); Michael
Zimmerman, *An Essay on Moral Responsibility* (Totowa, NJ: Rowman and Littlefield, 1988).

18. Aristotle, *Nicomachean Ethics*, in *A New Aristotle Reader*, edited by L. L. Ackrill
(Princeton: Princeton University Press, 1987), Book III, chap. 1.

right and moral wrong, they do not satisfy even the weakest standard for competence to stand trial in a criminal case against them. Consequently, it seems entirely appropriate to say that such persons lack *moral responsibility* for what they do. The same goes, it has been argued, for psychopaths.[19] Thus, it seems to me that in order for one to be morally responsible for *X*, one must satisfy both metaphysical and epistemic conditions for voluntariness and one must satisfy an additional epistemic condition having to do with one's understanding that *X* is either morally good or bad.

With these considerations in mind, I offer the following account of moral responsibility:

S is *morally responsible* for event *E*, which is a consequence of a basic action *A* performed by S if, and only if,

(i)   S satisfies the metaphysical conditions for free action with respect to *A*;[20]
(ii)   at the time of S's performance of *A*, S knows that *E* will occur as a result of S's performing *A*, and S is epistemically rational in believing that *E* is causally sensitive to S's performing *A*;
(iii) at the time of S's performance of *A*, S believes, or S is epistemically rational in believing, that *E* is either morally good or morally bad.[21]

What is the relation between 'moral responsibility' and praiseworthiness/blameworthiness? If you are morally responsible for *X*, does it follow that you are either praiseworthy or blameworthy for *X*? Some theorists think so, but others think (as I do) that to be morally responsible for *X* is to have satisfied a very important necessary, but not sufficient, condition for being praiseworthy/blameworthy for *X*. Here is a theoretical motivation for this view: Suppose that we know that your action satisfies the conditions of well-known theories of free will/action or moral responsibility. Do we thereby know whether you deserve moral praise or moral blame for your action? Not on theories such as Timothy O'Connor's libertarian agent-causal theory or Fischer and Ravizza's moderate reasons-responsiveness theory,

---

19. For example, see Neil Levy, *Hard Luck: How Luck Undermines Free Will and Moral Responsibility* (New York: Oxford University Press, 2011), 119–20.

20. I am, of course, waving my hand here in an attempt to remain as theoretically neutral as I can for the purposes of this essay.

21. These conditions are consistent with the issues I discussed above: metaphysical (non-epistemic conditions) are expressed in (i), Aristotelian epistemic conditions are expressed in (ii), and a 'moral sense' condition is expressed in (iii).

for instance.[22] For one can satisfy those conditions whether or not one believes, or has epistemic justification for believing, that the action is good/ bad. But, surely a person's being *deserving* of moral blame, for instance, depends on whether at the time of action the person believed, or had good reason to believe, that the action was bad; for, if the person justifiably believed that the action was good, then the person wouldn't *deserve* blame for the action even if that action were objectively bad.[23]

This seems to be a lesson from the observation that one can do the objectively wrong thing for the right reason (and thereby not deserve blame for the action), and one can do the objectively right thing for the wrong reason (and thereby not deserve praise for the action). I infer from these considerations that moral praiseworthiness or blameworthiness depends on epistemic facts about one with respect to whether a given action (or consequence thereof) is good or bad—epistemic facts which go beyond the epistemic facts that are relevant for assessing whether one satisfies the conditions of many leading theories of free will/action that seek to explain an action's being under the freedom-relevant, voluntary control of an agent. Such considerations provide a (and my) theoretical reason to distinguish between being morally responsible for X and being morally praiseworthy or blameworthy for X.[24]

V. The Lack of Epistemic Control over Manipulated Information

Family Policy is a paradigm example of praiseworthy, morally responsible action. Not only does it satisfy the three conditions of my account of moral responsibility, but also it is a case in which you had excellent reason—all your evidence considered—to believe that enacting the family policy was the best thing to do in your circumstances. Indeed, we can suppose that your enacting the family policy in your circumstances was the best decision that would be made by the most rational, morally upstanding human being in your situation.

---

22. Timothy O'Connor, *Persons and Causes* (New York: Oxford University Press, 2000); Fischer and Ravizza, *Responsibility and Control*.

23. I am not claiming that the epistemic conditions suggested here are sufficient for moral praiseworthiness/blameworthiness.

24. A different reason is offered by Fischer and Ravizza, *Responsibility and Control*, page 8, who say that the distinction is reasonable on the basis of the existence of what they call 'morally neutral' behavior.

Now, suppose, as I have intended for you to do all along, that you hold fixed all these facts when you turn your attention to *Manipulated Family Policy*. Clearly, if my conditions for moral responsibility are satisfied in *Family Policy*, then they are satisfied in *Manipulated Family Policy*. The only difference in the cases is that in the latter, you deliberate on the basis of false, manipulated information. I have been arguing that false information, by itself, is not a relevant difference between the cases.

That seems to leave just the bare difference of information manipulation. Why would the mere fact that the information we rely on is manipulated prevent us from being morally responsible for what we do in light of it? Is it because *we are not in control of the information* when it is manipulated? Surely not. Note that in our everyday lives we are very rarely in control of the information we rely on in our practical reasoning. I swerve my car to the left because I get visual information that you have entered the right side of my lane. I don't control this visual information I rely on. It comes to me by virtue of my happening to be where I am in the road at the same time that you happen to be where you are in the road, and my having my eyes open and focused on the road. I go to the faculty meeting partly because my boss told me that I had a faculty meeting. I was not in control of this information. My boss told me, and I heard it, but I didn't control that. I press the "p" key on my keyboard partly because of my visual and memory information about where the "p" key is located and I want to type "press," but I do not control the information I have about where the "p" key is located on my keyboard. Indeed, every day, virtually all day long while we are awake, we are engaging in practical reasoning on the basis of information that we do not control, and yet we non-skeptics about moral responsibility do not think that these facts, by themselves, prevent moral responsibility for what we do in those situations. But, if we can be morally responsible for what we do in ordinary cases when we do not control the information we rely on, then why think that our lack of control in cases of information manipulation prevents moral responsibility?

Franklin and Fischer have individually attempted to answer this question. Each of their responses may be understood as providing a broadly epistemic reason to challenge my claim that information manipulation does not preclude moral responsibility.

Franklin's Epistemic Control Challenge

Franklin responds to my line of reasoning where he writes about 'PAs' (abbreviating 'pro-attitudes': attitudes that can motivate us to action):

Long is correct that we are not often in direct control of our acquisition of PAs. Nevertheless, it is plausible to think that agents exercise a sort of indirect control over the acquisition of these PAs. It is implausible to think that agents can form PAs simply in virtue of an act of will, but this is not to say that agents cannot exercise control insofar as choosing what sort of environments or contexts to place themselves in. Again, consider John who may not be able to prevent his forming desires and beliefs about stealing by a sheer act of will, but he can perform an act of will to avoid circumstances that allow or make probable the forming of such a desire or belief.[25]

Franklin's idea is that a necessary condition for moral responsibility is that we have at least indirect control over the pro-attitudes that have some role in what we do.

I do not deny that we can exercise indirect control over some of our pro-attitudes, such as some of our beliefs and desires. Nevertheless, there is a significant problem with Franklin's proposal. To appreciate it, let us consider the context of Franklin's commentary. He is attempting to explain why agents whose pro-attitudes are induced (in a certain way) by an external manipulator are not morally responsible for their actions. Toward that end, he claims that, in order for us to be morally responsible for our actions that result from practical reasoning, we must be morally responsible for having the pro-attitudes that play a role in our practical reasoning; although we may rarely have *direct control* over our having the pro-attitudes that we rely on, we can exercise *indirect control* over them in a way that renders us morally responsible for them. This indirect control involves an epistemic requirement. Let us consider Franklin's account of moral responsibility for acquiring a pro-attitude:

> EC: Agent A, who is in context C, is morally responsible for acquiring pro-attitude PA, iff A could reasonably come to have known that the forming of PA is probable given C.[26]

My first criticism is that it is entirely mysterious how the truth of a counterfactual about what I would be reasonable in believing could, by itself, be *sufficient* for being *morally responsible* for anything. Recall that

---

25. Franklin, "Plausibility, Manipulation, and Fischer and Ravizza,"181–82.

26. Fischer and Ravizza, *Responsibility and Control,* 181.

Franklin's idea is that we exercise *indirect control* over our having the pro-attitudes that play a role in our practical reasoning just when EC is satisfied with respect to all the relevant pro-attitudes. But, satisfying EC is woefully insufficient for exercising actual *control* over what we acquire.

In light of this criticism, one might want to hold that satisfying the condition of EC is only a *necessary*, but not sufficient, condition for being morally responsible for acquiring a pro-attitude. Perhaps there is some additional condition that would be sufficient for that purpose. But, even if that is so, there is a serious problem with the general strategy, and it is this: a person can be morally responsible for an action even when the person does not indirectly control the pro-attitudes that have some role in that person's practical reasoning. Consider a variation on John Locke's locked-room example.[27] Suppose that you are taken while sleeping and without your knowledge into a room in which there is a person you have been longing to talk to. Upon awaking, you open your eyes and see the other person. You do not even indirectly control your seeing the other person when you open your eyes. Nevertheless, the information you acquired by seeing the other person was a crucial input to your process of practical reasoning that resulted in your starting a friendly conversation with the other person. Surely you can be morally responsible for starting such a conversation even though you did not exercise control, direct or indirect, over your acquiring that pro-attitude.

Another general problem concerns distinguishing the pro-attitudes that constitute, or partly constitute, what Fischer calls one's 'normative orientation' (which he identifies as one's standing dispositions, values, and preferences), and the kind of pro-attitudes that I have been drawing attention to: rational pro-attitudes that one acquires via one's new experiential information about the world.[28] Critics of my claims about my *Schmidt* Frankfurt-type example (discussed below, in the section "Fischer's Epistemic Control Challenge") tend not to appreciate the relevance of the distinction.[29] When I say that

27. John Locke, *An Essay Concerning Human Understanding*, edited by Peter H. Nidditch (Oxford: Clarendon, 1979), Book 2, chap. 21, sec. 10.

28. John Martin Fischer, "Manipulation and Guidance Control."

29. Steadman, "Moral Responsibility and Motivational Mechanisms," 486–91, seems to appreciate the relevance of the distinction but assumes that the pro-attitudes that I say are induced in Schmidt by the manipulator refer "to the *strength* of Schmidt's nonrational reasons" (such as "positive feelings that Schmidt has for Hitler"). But, that is not the way my case goes at all. The manipulation is of Schmidt's *information*, which yields *reasons* he has that indicate to him Hitler's suitability for office. In the original essay (Long, "Moderate Reasons-Responsiveness," 164–65), I identify the relevant reasons as being furnished by Schmidt's *evidence*. The reasons are thus *not* nonrational.

input (information) manipulation does not preclude moral responsibility for action, I am not talking about the manipulation of pro-attitudes that are part of one's normative orientation. To put the point in terms of Fischer and Ravizza's moderate reasons-responsiveness theory (discussed below), the inputs that are manipulated in my *Schmidt* test cases are not pro-attitudes that (partly) constitute Schmidt's psychological mechanism of practical reasoning. Although Fischer and Ravizza have been criticized for not providing details about how to individuate these psychological mechanisms, they have been explicit about the fact that these psychological mechanisms do not themselves include the inputs. They are thinking of the entire process of practical reasoning that produces an action as a causal chain that runs from one's new experiences in the world, through one's own way of deciding what to do, to a decision and sometimes to an associated bodily action.

One's new experiences in the world yield the 'reasons' that are the 'inputs' to the psychological mechanism. The psychological mechanism itself works on the new inputs. That mechanism is some complex involving one's 'normative orientation' (one's standing desires, preferences, and values) and one's own way of deciding. Whatever imprecision there is in Fischer and Ravizza's notion of the relevant kind of mechanism, the crucial point to see is that, when they talk about an agent's reasons as inputs, they do not intend to include as inputs the agent's longstanding desires, preferences, and values;[30] so, if such things count as pro-attitudes, then they are the kinds of pro-attitudes that help to constitute the person's psychological mechanism.

Now we are in a position to understand the problem with Franklin's proposal. Although there is some plausibility to the claim that, in order to be morally responsible for an action, a person must exercise some control over whichever pro-attitudes partly constitute the person's relevant psychological mechanism, it is entirely implausible to suppose that a person must also control the inputs to that psychological mechanism. After all, the inputs are typically new beliefs one has as a result of one's new experiences in the world. I am currently not moving toward you with a bandage. But, were I to have the experience as of seeing blood running profusely from your head (and thus to gain a reason for action), I might (given the kind of person I am) then decide to move toward you with a bandage and try to stop the bleeding. It is true that I can control many of my decisions

---

30. If they *do* intend to include as inputs the agent's longstanding desires, preferences, and values, then the response (which I discuss below) by Fischer ("Manipulation and Guidance Control") to Long ("Moderate Reasons-Responsiveness") is inexplicable.

about where I will go and what I will do, but if I am living even a marginally normal human life, I cannot control all the new information (the inputs) I rely on for action no matter where I go or what I do. Nevertheless, I can be morally responsible for whatever I do in light of that new information.

Fischer's Epistemic Control Challenge

Fischer has also challenged my view about information manipulation on the basis of a worry about a lack of control, which has a broadly epistemic component.[31] Because Fischer's objection directly treats my *Schmidt* example in light of his and Ravizza's theory of moral responsibility, a brief description of both will be helpful.

Fischer and Ravizza (hereafter F&R) say that their 'moderate reasons-responsiveness' theory (hereafter, MRR) specifies the freedom-relevant necessary and sufficient conditions for moral responsibility. MRR is distinctive in that it focuses on the psychological *mechanism* involved in actions that flow from a responsibility-yielding process.

The general idea of MRR is that, for any morally responsible act by an agent, the agent has some relevant psychological mechanism—for which the agent has taken responsibility—that receives as inputs the agent's reasons and produces the act as an output. The mechanism must be such that its outputs (actions) can vary due to the combination of its inputs (reasons) and the nature of the mechanism itself; and, the agent must be capable of recognizing the agent's reasons such that they make some orderly sense in light of the agent's values and beliefs.[32] These are, I think, plausible conditions on moral responsibility.

However, I have shown[33] that there is trouble for the way in which F&R say that their theory applies to Frankfurt-type examples.[34] F&R say that in any actual-sequence of a Frankfurt-type example the conditions of MRR are satisfied but that in any alternative-sequence the conditions of MRR are not satisfied, because the mechanism operant in any alternative-sequence is *different* from the mechanism operant in the actual-sequence. Nevertheless, I provided a new Frankfurt-type example in which the mechanism at issue

---

31. Fischer, "Manipulation and Guidance Control."

32. For the details, see Fischer and Ravizza, *Responsibility and Control,* 69–91, 241–44.

33. Long, "Moderate Reasons-Responsiveness."

34. A huge body of literature on Frankfurt-type examples derives from Harry Frankfurt, "Alternate Possibilities and Moral Responsibility," *Journal of Philosophy* 66, no. 23 (1969) 829–39.

is the *same* in both the actual-sequence and some alternative-sequences. The only pertinent difference in the sequences is the *inputs*, not the mechanism. So, if anything like my example is possible, it cannot be that all possible alternative-sequences utilize different mechanisms than do actual-sequences.

The interesting upshot, I argued, is this: F&R's theory allows agents to be morally responsible for their actions even when their information about the world has been so severely manipulated that they would not have performed the relevant actions had the input-manipulation not occurred. Not only do these results follow from F&R's theory, but also, as I argued, these are the *correct* results: even if external manipulation that controls the *entire deliberative process* (including the inputs *and* the mechanism) precludes moral responsibility on the part of the agent for acts that are outputs of that process, external manipulation that controls only some *inputs* to the agent's mechanism—but not the mechanism itself—does not preclude responsible action by that agent.

Because Fischer's objection concerns details of my *Schmidt* Frankfurt-type example, it will be helpful to summarize it:

Schmidt is a high-ranking official in the German government just before Hitler's rise to power. Having had excellent moral training as a child, Schmidt has developed into a person with outstanding moral judgment. Now Schmidt must cast the deciding vote to determine whether Hitler will be given supreme power. Schmidt and Hitler are long-time acquaintances. During the early years of their friendship, Schmidt gained extremely good reasons to believe that Hitler would be a fine, morally upstanding leader of Germany. But, in recent years, Schmidt has gained disturbing evidence that Hitler has intentions of building up a master race of Aryans and ridding the country of non-Aryans. Schmidt deliberates. Waiting in the wings is Block, a malevolent person with extraordinary causal and predictive powers. If it becomes clear to him that Schmidt is going to vote against Hitler, Block will take effective steps to ensure that Schmidt votes *for* Hitler. Otherwise, Block will do nothing.

In the *actual-sequence* case, Schmidt deliberates and votes for Hitler on his own. This is a standard case of weakness of will. F&R's theory correctly implies that Schmidt is morally responsible for his voting, and it is consistent with the plausible view that Schmidt is blameworthy. In each *alternative-sequence* case, the situation is such that, were Block not to intervene, Schmidt would vote against Hitler.

I developed two alternative-sequence test cases.[35] In the first case, one minute before Schmidt votes, Block adds new inputs (reasons-yielding information) to the very same mechanism that is operant in the actual-sequence case. Such reasons could come in various forms (such as Schmidt's confident beliefs based on experiences as of his having had credible testimony explaining away the disturbing evidence he had recently gained about Hitler). These reasons are, when combined with his deliberative voting mechanism, powerful enough such that Schmidt votes for Hitler. In the second alternative-sequence test case, a minute before Schmidt votes, Block removes inputs (reasons) from the very same mechanism that is operant in the actual-sequence. These inputs are in the form of Schmidt's recent memories indicating Hitler's diabolical intentions; so, when Schmidt deliberates, the inputs (reasons) he has to go on are, concerning Hitler, positive and powerful enough such that Schmidt votes for Hitler.

In these two test cases, Block manipulates the inputs to Schmidt's own deliberative voting mechanism, but Block does nothing to Schmidt's deliberative mechanism itself. Because that mechanism satisfies MRR in the actual-sequence, it satisfies MRR in my alternative-sequence test cases; accordingly, Schmidt is morally responsible for voting for Hitler in those cases. Of course, it is very plausible that he is not blameworthy for voting for Hitler in the test cases; after all, in those cases Schmidt, deliberating on his own, does what a perfectly reasonable, morally upstanding person would do, given the reasons he actually had (just as we may suppose you do in *Manipulated Family Policy*). That Schmidt is morally responsible but not blameworthy in these two test cases is entirely consistent with MRR. I concluded that F&R's theory gets the right results in all these cases.

Fischer's Response to *Schmidt*

Fischer objects on the grounds that Block's manipulation is sufficient to make the relevant mechanism in the alternative-sequence test cases a *different* mechanism from the one in the actual-sequence case.[36] Although Fischer agrees with me that there is no significant difference between my two test cases, his response focuses on the first test case:

> Note that Long begins by saying that Block swings into action "a minute before Schmidt casts his vote." This suggests something

---

35. In the original paper (Long, "Moderate Reasons-Responsiveness") they are called 'Block/Schmidt case 2' and 'Block/Schmidt case 3,' respectively.

36. Fischer, "Manipulation and Guidance Control."

important—or perhaps subtly frames the description in such a way that it would naturally suggest that "something" to the reader. The suggestion in question is that the implantation or manipulative induction of "reasons" is done immediately prior to the choice and subsequent behavior, and that there is thus no reasonable or fair opportunity for Schmidt to reflect on or critically evaluate the new input in light of his standing dispositions, values, preferences, and so forth.

I contend that when "inputs" are implanted in a way that does not allow for a reasonable or fair opportunity for the agent to subject those inputs to critical scrutiny in light of his or her normative orientation, then such manipulation does indeed remove moral responsibility. Such manipulation typically "changes the mechanism." On the other hand, if an "input" is artificially implanted in such a way as to leave it open to the agent (in a reasonable and fair way) to critically scrutinize and reflect on the new input, then this sort of manipulative induction of inputs *may well be* compatible with moral responsibility for the choice and subsequent behavior. Such manipulation could leave the ordinary mechanism of practical reasoning intact.

Long's examples are underdescribed in precisely this way—he does not make it explicit whether Schmidt has a reasonable and fair opportunity to evaluate the mysteriously appearing inputs in light of his overall normative orientation—his other values, preferences, and so forth. As I pointed out above, his description *suggests* that Schmidt would not have such an opportunity, and thus it is plausible (in my view) that such manipulation would rule out moral responsibility.[37]

Fischer's point, I take it, is as follows: because Schmidt's 'normative orientation' (i.e., his standing dispositions, values, preferences, etc.) is part of his ordinary practical reasoning mechanism, Schmidt's not having filtered his new inputs through his normative orientation entails that his ordinary practical reasoning mechanism has been bypassed in the test cases; thus, Fischer claims, Block's manipulation 'changes the mechanism.'

I detect two arguments for the crucial premise. According to the weaker argument, my test cases do not *make clear* that Schmidt has a fair

---

opportunity to reflect on his inputs in light of his normative orientation. The stronger argument relies on the premise that, if Schmidt has *only one minute* to deliberate on the *mysteriously appearing inputs* to Schmidt's psychological voting mechanism, then it is reasonable to think that Schmidt fails to have a fair opportunity to critically reflect on the new inputs in light of his normative orientation. Each argument says, in effect, that there is some broadly epistemic requirement for moral responsibility that Schmidt fails to satisfy in light of the way his information is manipulated by Block.

Reply to Fischer

With respect to the weaker argument, I did not explicitly say that Schmidt had a fair opportunity to reflect on his inputs in light of his normative orientation, but a charitable reading of the example easily includes the relevant feature.[38] Moreover, all that matters is whether such a thing is possible. I hereby make it explicit: During that minute before he votes, Schmidt very carefully considers his evidence in light of his standing dispositions, values, and preferences. He finds it obvious that his voting for Hitler is precisely what a morally upstanding, reasonable, strong-willed person—such as he takes himself to be—would do in light of the total evidence he has; and, he is right about this: anyone who had Schmidt's reasons and normative orientation but voted against Hitler would be weak-willed or witless or wicked. Schmidt votes in perfect consonance with his normative orientation. Block's manipulation does nothing to Schmidt's standing dispositions, values, and preferences. Because this is a way things could go, we should conclude that Fischer's weaker argument provides no reason at all to think that Block's input manipulation amounts to a change in the mechanism.

Fischer's stronger argument relies on these assumptions: (i) Schmidt is not given enough *time* to deliberate before his voting; and (ii) the inputs *mysteriously appear* to Schmidt. There are excellent reasons to think that the timing of Block's manipulation is irrelevant. For rhetorical structure, I said that Block takes action *one minute* before Schmidt votes. But, I might have chosen five seconds, or five hours, or longer. Let us consider cases in which Schmidt has more or less time to deliberate.

---

38. I did strongly suggest the feature in saying of Schmidt: "he was no helpless victim. No one caused him to act by bypassing his deliberative voting mechanism. Schmidt actually weighed reasons in a regularly reasons-responsive way, and his deliberative voting mechanism was weakly reactive to reasons"; Long, "Moderate Reasons-Responsiveness," 166.

Suppose that Block intervenes *24 hours* before Schmidt votes, by giving Schmidt inputs (reasons) that Schmidt finds compelling, in light of his normative orientation, to vote for Hitler. So long as, during that 24-hour period, Schmidt does not gain evidence indicating Hitler's wicked intentions (and there are *many* possible ways this could occur), Schmidt could spend 24 hours considering his evidence in light of his normative orientation, and then vote for Hitler.

Now suppose that Schmidt has only *10 seconds* to deliberate. Given his total evidence at the time, it could seem perfectly obvious to him that voting for Hitler would be consonant with his normative orientation. Indeed, someone like Schmidt might be able to realize this in little more than an instant. The same sort of thing goes in more ordinary situations when we have little time to reflect on new information in light of our normative orientation. For instance, someone sees an automobile accident on a stretch of otherwise deserted road, sizes up the situation almost instantly, and phones authorities to report the accident. Such a person can quickly filter her new inputs through her normative orientation such that she is morally responsible for making the call. Such cases reveal that it is a mistake to think that there is a restrictive necessary condition involving timing for having a fair and reasonable opportunity to filter one's reasons through one's normative orientation.

In footnote 3, Fischer says that he does not intend his objection to depend essentially on the timing involved; that is, the fact that Schmidt has only one minute to deliberate does not, by itself, show that he fails to have fair opportunity to filter his inputs through his normative orientation.[39] It only 'suggests,' Fischer says, that Schmidt fails to meet the condition. But, because things could go as I've described them, the fact that Schmidt has one minute to deliberate is irrelevant to the substantive issue of whether F&R's theory allows morally responsible actions to flow from deliberative processes that involve manipulated inputs.

The only other claim Fischer provides in support of the key premise is that the inputs Schmidt receives from Block are 'mysteriously appearing.' But, this is not the case. As I mentioned in the original paper, Block has the power to give Schmidt reasons in such a way that Schmidt has no awareness of psychic incongruence. From Schmidt's perspective, it does not seem to him that random ideas have popped into his head from

---

39. Fischer, "Manipulation and Guidance Control," 184–85, fn. 3.

nowhere. From his perspective, it seems just as it does when you are deliberating on the basis of what seems obviously to be veridical memory.

I conclude that Fischer has provided no good reason to claim that the psychological mechanism in my test cases is different from the psychological mechanism in the actual-sequence. Thus, Fischer's epistemic requirement that the relevant kind of control involves one's having a fair opportunity to filter one's new information through one's normative orientation provides no good reason to deny that MRR allows for morally responsible behavior to flow from psychological mechanisms whose inputs have been so severely manipulated that the agent would not have engaged in that behavior had the inputs not been manipulated.

VI. Conclusion

I understand the temptation to think that information manipulation precludes moral responsibility, for one can imagine the manipulator smirking in the shadows as his nefarious plot yields the desire of his wicked motivations: a voluntary act by a benighted agent. Such manipulation reduces the agent's autonomy! It reduces the agent's control! True enough, but sober reflection reveals limitations of autonomy and control as ordinary facts about our everyday lives. Other people frequently intrude upon our cognitive economy by exerting volitional pressure on us to do (or not do) something; and, non-agential causes are always constraining our opportunities for action. In ordinary situations when we are not the object of a manipulator, we are nevertheless always at the mercy of our epistemic circumstances, and there is nothing that we can do to control them while living anything like a normal, human life. Indeed, untold causal conditions, which affect our epistemic circumstances, are outside our control. As Fischer points out, "there are infinitely many factors over which I currently have no control, which are such that, if they were to occur, I would cease being as I am (and behaving as I do).... And yet this does not in itself seem to expunge or etiolate my agency and my moral responsibility."[40]

I agree. I have been pointing out that such factors include the new information that we rely on in practical reasoning. Indeed, I think that we are never off the moral hook just because the new information we

---

40. John Martin Fischer, "The Cards That Are Dealt You," *Journal of Ethics* 10 (2006): 116.

are relying on is manipulated, even if we know nothing at all about that manipulation. Those of us who are persons who have not lost control of ourselves or become insane (or the like) do not escape moral responsibility for what we do in light of our epistemic situations, manipulated or not. Information manipulation may be so vicious that we are not blameworthy, or it might be so virtuous that we are not praiseworthy. It may be so fraudulent that it prevents our satisfying a reasonable standard for legal consent. It may be so cunning that we fail to have even indirect control over the information we rely on. But, I remain confident that most of us are morally responsible for what we do in light of the evidence we have to go on. Information manipulation does not preclude moral responsibility.

8

Unsavory Seduction and Manipulation

Eric M. Cave

Unsavory Seduction

In a scene from early on in Neil Strauss's *The Game*, billed as an insider's view of pickup artist subculture, the protagonist meets Ross Jeffries, an established figure within this subculture, at a local restaurant. Jeffries demonstrates the effectiveness of his "Speed Seduction" techniques to the protagonist and another aspiring pickup artist by turning them on a convenient waitress. As the other two look on, Jeffries asks the initially disinterested waitress questions that evoke in her remembered feelings of sexual attraction, then hypnotically "anchors" these feelings to various gestures, touches, and objects. By strategically employing these gestures, touches, and objects to evoke psychological and physical responses in his target over the course of his dinner, Jeffries succeeds in linking the waitress's feelings of sexual attraction to himself. He thereby converts her initial sexual disinterest to sexual willingness, seducing her—at least if we understand seduction broadly as the conversion of initial sexual unwillingness to willingness to have sex based on sexual desire.[1]

Some ways of seducing another, on this broad understanding of seduction, are innocuous. Suppose I hope to have sex with you, but you are

1. For a defense of this broad understanding of seduction, see Eric M. Cave, "Unsavory Sexual Seduction," *Ethical Theory and Moral Practice* 12 (2009): 235–45.

unwilling. I believe that you would become sexually willing if we had a significant emotional connection. I therefore arrange to spend time with you doing something we both enjoy, then more time talking about our shared activity, seeking to forge such a connection. If things work out as I hope, I will have seduced you, but not in a way that is morally problematic, at least not absent some further story.

But Jeffries's seduction of the waitress is different. Jeffries does not seek to convert the waitress to sexual willingness by altering himself or his relationship with her so as to more fully satisfy her preferences, desires, or needs. Rather, he seeks to bring about such a conversion by altering her motives. And he seeks to alter her motives not by rational argument, or even by clever suasion, but by using fairly crude conditioning techniques to hamper the exercise of her rational capacities as fully as he can. Such motive altering, rationality hampering seduction strikes many of us as morally problematic, as involving a wrongful element significant enough to render it, on balance, wrongful in at least some circumstances. Or so I shall suppose.

I should clarify who *we* are. For my purposes, *we* are college- and university-educated denizens of large contemporary Western democracies like the United States, the United Kingdom, the Netherlands, or Australia. Individuals fitting this description have been exposed to an overlapping set of core works of art, literature, history, natural science, philosophy, and social science. As a consequence, such individuals (*we*) are apt to exhibit some convergence in their (*our*) moral judgments across various domains.

Consider advertising. We regard much advertising as innocuous, but not all of it. In 1957, market researcher James Vicary claimed to have substantially increased sales of food and drink in a theatre by flashing "Drink Coca Cola" and "Hungry? Eat popcorn" for one-thirtieth of a second at five-second intervals during the showing of the film *Picnic* over a six-week period. Although the study turned out to be a hoax, there was considerable public outcry about the practice, dubbed by Vicary *subliminal advertising*.[2] Subliminal advertising attempts to create demand for a product by altering the motives of consumers through means that severely hamper exercise of their capacities to evaluate these alterations.[3] Within a few years of Vicary's

---

2. See A. R. Pratkanis, "The Cargo-Cult Science of Subliminal Persuasion," *Skeptical Inquirer* 16 (1992): 260–72.

3. In his contribution to this volume, Allen Wood argues that this description properly applies to most, if not all, advertising. I am somewhat sympathetic to this claim, though I regard it as too controversial to take as a starting point here.

hoax, countries such as Australia, the United Kingdom, and the United States banned it (either legislatively or through the relevant regulatory bodies). Over the years, studies of subliminal stimuli have yielded mixed results, with only some providing evidence for the motivational efficacy of such stimuli.[4] Subliminal advertising is nonetheless still widely regarded as morally problematic among my intended audience.

There are other domains in which being both motive altering and rationality hampering renders a practice morally problematic. Recruitment to religious cults comes to mind, as does the making and dissemination of propaganda and the rearing and education of children sufficiently developed to reason for themselves. Appeal to even this partial list of practices suggests that across various domains, the combination of being rationality hampering and motive altering inclines us to wonder whether a given practice is ultimately immoral or innocuous, and to regard this issue as requiring further analysis to settle. For this reason, it is no great stretch to suppose, as I have, that we would converge in regarding Jeffries-style seduction as morally problematic.

I suppose that I could continue to use *Jeffries-style seduction* to refer to what I take to be a recognizable category of morally problematic seductions. But this term is cumbersome and not particularly apt. From here on, I shall instead use *unsavory seduction* to refer to this category, which consists of all conversions to sexual willingness accomplished by altering a target's motives in ways that hamper the exercise of her rational capacities.[5]

The boundaries of this category are rendered indistinct by cases in which it is not clear whether a target's motives have been altered or the exercise of her rational capacities hampered. Likely, the phenomenon I am calling *unsavory seduction* shades into other forms of sexual pursuit, just as subtle forms of product placement in films shade into subliminal advertising. Specifying unsavory seduction's boundaries precisely is ancillary to my main interest here, so I shall set this issue aside.

---

4. For a review of some of the relevant studies, see Kathryn T. Theus, "Subliminal Advertising and the Psychology of Processing Unconscious Stimuli: A Review of Research," *Psychology and Marketing* 11 (1994): 271–90. For a more recent review that argues against the real-life efficacy of subliminal advertising, see Sheri J. Broyles, "Subliminal Advertising and the Perpetual Popularity of Playing to People's Paranoia," *Journal of Consumer Affairs* 40 (2006): 392–406.

5. From here onwards, I shall frequently use "her," "hers," and "she" inclusively, to refer to female or male agents. Context will make apparent when I am instead using these terms in their usual, noninclusive way.

Although we got an initial fix on unsavory seduction by thinking about Ross Jeffries's "Speed Seduction" techniques, it can be accomplished by any means of intentionally altering another's motives that hampers the exercise of her rational capacities: emotional appeals, habituation, wearing down the other's resistance, temptation, and the list goes on.[6] Of course, unsavory seduction can also be accomplished using uncontroversially immoral techniques such as deception or extortion. If what I have said so far is correct, such seduction is doubly morally troubling. It belongs to a category of seduction that is morally problematic even when it is not accomplished by means of such techniques. And it is accomplished by means of techniques that render any seduction morally troubling. I shall set aside such morally mixed cases of unsavory seduction to focus on a puzzle arising for pure cases of this phenomenon.

A Puzzle

So we seem to recognize a moral difference between seducing someone and unsavorily seducing someone. But there is nothing morally problematic about just trying to alter someone's motives to try to get her or him to do what you want. This is a fairly common, and morally unobjectionable, application of rational argument. And there is nothing morally problematic about motivating someone in a way that hampers the exercise of her rational capacities. Coaches and athletic trainers of various sorts do this all the time, and few believe that they transgress morally in so doing.[7] So if there is nothing generally wrongful in altering another's motives, and there is nothing generally wrongful in hampering the exercise of another's rational capacities, then how can there be anything generally wrongful involved in unsavory seduction?

Here I want to make some progress toward articulating and defending a plausible solution to this puzzle. To do so is to articulate an account of the unsavoriness of unsavory seduction. A plausible such account must mesh with relevant commitments, beliefs, and judgments exhibited widely among those whose practices it is supposed to illuminate. By attending to

---

6. Arranging for another to become "ego depleted" surely belongs on this list as well. For a discussion of this phenomenon, see Michael Cholbi's contribution to this volume.

7. For more examples of perfectly acceptable interpersonal nonrational engagement, see Kate Manne's contribution to this volume.

some of the most important of these, we can identify a set of desiderata that a plausible solution to the above puzzle must satisfy.

One such judgment has to do with unsavory seduction's moral status. We do not regard unsavory seduction as morally innocuous. And as the comparison to subliminal advertising suggests, we do not judge it to be categorically immoral, either. Rather, we regard it as morally problematic, as involving a wrongful element or elements significant enough to render it, on balance, wrongful in at least some circumstances. Thus, as a first desideratum, a plausible account of unsavory seduction's unsavoriness should render it morally problematic, not morally innocuous or categorically immoral. "Morally problematic" here is just a less daunting synonym for "*pro tanto* immoral"; it is not an indicator of the degree of seriousness of the wrong involved in unsavory seduction.[8] And a plausible account should establish that unsavory seduction is morally problematic by appealing to rationally defensible commitments, ones supported by reasons most of us would not regard as eccentric or crazy.

Another such judgment is that much of what we humans do, in contrast with unsavory seduction, is morally innocuous. We exhibit considerable convergence in our judgments about what sorts of activities are morally innocuous rather than being morally problematic or categorically immoral. This suggests a second desideratum: a plausible account of unsavory seduction's unsavoriness should not be so broad in its implications as to condemn as morally problematic human activities widely judged morally innocuous.

Finally, if what I have said so far is correct, we judge all non-penumbral cases of conversion to sexual willingness accomplished by altering a target's motives in ways that bypass her rationality morally problematic. Thus, as a third desideratum, a plausible account of unsavory seduction's unsavoriness ought to be inclusive enough to condemn all unambiguous instances of this phenomenon as morally problematic. That is, it ought to so condemn all conversions to sexual willingness accomplished by what counts uncontroversially among us as rationality hampering alteration of a target's motives.

---

8. As I suggest in this essay's final section, the wrong-making element in unsavory seduction may vary from one sort of case to another, leaving room for the wrong involved in unsavory seduction to range from not so serious to quite serious. Further exploration of this aspect of a pluralistic account of unsavory seduction may bring me to rethink my choice of *unsavory seduction* as a term of art (as *unsavory* may turn out to be too pale a descriptor). I thank an anonymous referee for Oxford University Press for prompting me to think about the differing degrees of wrongness that might be involved in unsavory seduction on a pluralistic account of this phenomenon.

Other things being equal, a given solution to the above puzzle is more plausible than another to the extent that it satisfies more of these desiderata more fully than does the other. In what follows, I shall consider a manipulation account of unsavory seduction's unsavoriness. Even if this account does not satisfy all three of the above desiderata fully, its shortcomings might point the way toward a proposal that does.

Modest Motive Autonomy

Central to this manipulation account is a conception of autonomy articulated most precisely by philosophers thinking about agency. On this conception, autonomy is acting from a motivational set with the right sort of history.[9] Think of persons as having motives. And think of them as having the capacity to reflect rationally on their motives, and to revise them or not based on such reflection. Generically speaking, an agent acts autonomously if her action is caused by a motive acquired via the appropriate engagement of her capacity to rationally manage her own motives. Otherwise, she acts less than autonomously.

Historical principles of autonomy are most frequently mobilized as understandings of the nature of autonomous action. But they have moral implications as well. Let us say that a historical principle of autonomy is immodest if it appeals to specific, substantive, and controversial requirements of rationality and self-awareness. Such a principle is modest if it appeals to general, formal, and relatively uncontroversial such requirements. Engaged in theorizing about morality, modest historical principles of autonomy are more plausibly mobilized than immodest ones. Here I shall appeal to a modest such principle, one that I shall call *modest motive autonomy*. According to this principle, agents ought (morally) to take care not to undermine others' capacity to rationally supplement, winnow, reorder, revise, or retain any of the dispositions capable of moving them to action.

The notion of rationality, as applied to the having and adjusting of motives, requires some discussion. Expanding on a suggestion by Derek Parfit, let an agent's having a given motive be rational if she or he has it

---

9. See John Christman, "Autonomy and Personal History," *Canadian Journal of Philosophy* 21, no. 1 (1991): 1–24; John Martin Fischer and Mark Ravizza, *Responsibility and Control* (Cambridge: Cambridge University Press, 1998): 170–206; Alfred Mele, *Autonomous Agents: From Self-Control to Autonomy* (New York: Oxford, 2001), 144–73.

in response to beliefs the truth of which would give her reasons to have that motive.[10] Let a reason to have a motive be a consideration grounded in facts favoring having this motive. On the view defined by these two claims, what makes an agent's having a given motive rational is not the truth or falsity of the beliefs upon which this motive depends. It is, rather, that having this motive is a response, on the part of the agent involved, to beliefs implying that she has fact-based considerations that favor having this motive.

Thus, as I shall understand it, *rational to have a given motive* means roughly *has a motive in response to true or false beliefs about the favorableness of having this motive*. From my failure to have a given motive rationally in this sense, it does not follow that my having this motive is irrational. I fail to have my preference for the color green over the color blue rationally, but it is not an irrational preference. It is nonrational in the sense that I do not have it in response to beliefs about the favorableness of my having it.

We can readily extend this account of the rationality of an agent's having a given motive to an agent's making a change in her motives. On this extension, an agent's making a change in her own motives (adding a motive, deleting one, expanding or contracting a motive's object, etc.) is rational if the agent involved makes this change in response to beliefs about the favorableness of making this change. According to this extended account, the rationality of motive change turns on its being a response to certain beliefs of the agent, not on the quality of the evidence for these beliefs, or on their truth or falsity.

By appealing to this account of what it is for an agent to rationally have a motive and to rationally make changes in her motives, we can unpack one of the key components of modest motive autonomy: the notion of undermining another agent's capacity to rationally manage her motives. To say that one agent undermines this capacity of another is to say that the first induces changes or stasis in the second's motives by means that make it more difficult, or even impossible, for the second to change her motives or to retain them based on beliefs about the favorableness of making this change or not doing so.

---

10. See Derek Parfit, "Rationality and Reasons," in *Exploring Practical Philosophy: From Action to Values*, edited by Dan Egonsson, Jonas Josefsson, Bjorn Petersson, and Toni Ronnow-Rasmussen (Aldershot: Ashgate, 2001), 17–39. Thanks to Justin d'Arms for pointing me toward Parfit's account.

Unpacking the rest of modest motive autonomy is straightforward enough. To say that agents ought to *take care* not to undermine others' capacity for rational motive management is just to say that agents ought to be mindful of this capacity in others, and to avoid doing things purposefully, knowingly but not purposefully, or accidentally that tend to undermine this capacity in the manner described above.

Modest motive autonomy aims to protect a certain capacity of persons that many deem worth protecting. But no one thinks that this capacity of persons is the only aspect of persons worth protecting, or even that of the aspects of persons worth protecting, this one is overridingly important. Thus, modest motive autonomy is best understood as one among a number of plausible moral constraints. Monolithic attempts to reduce the multiplicity of plausible moral constraints to a single unifying principle have not proven very plausible. Let us instead opt for the alternative, a moral pluralism on which multiple plausible and mutually irreducible moral constraints, including modest motive autonomy, must be traded off against one another differently in different contexts.

Before bringing modest motive autonomy to bear on unsavory seduction, let us consider some preliminary worries about even applying it within the arena of human sexual pursuit. One might worry, for instance, that its implications in this realm are too immodest to be plausible, even absurd. Consider that this principle might seem to prohibit particularly attractive people from engaging in such routine activities as bathing and brushing their hair, lest they inadvertently inflame others to the point of undermining their capacity to rationally manage their own motives.[11] This would be absurd, of course, and reason enough to reject modest motive autonomy, at least within the realm of human sexual pursuit.

Bathing and grooming cases do not seem like a plausible threat to modest motive autonomy because it is hard to imagine their having more than negligible effects on other people's motivations. To fall afoul of this principle, an action must tend to make it more difficult or impossible for others to change their motives in response to beliefs about the favorableness of doing so. But outside of atypical cases, the causal effects of being clean and well coiffed seem too weak to justify ascribing this tendency to bathing and grooming.

---

11. Thanks to Marcia Baron for raising this worry about an earlier iteration of modest motive autonomy.

We can imagine such atypical cases, I suppose—cases involving either remarkably attractive or remarkably susceptible individuals, or perhaps both. In such cases, exposure to a freshly bathed and groomed attractive person might move an onlooker to feel or want or do something in a way that does not involve her beliefs at all. But even in such cases, I doubt that modest motive autonomy would commit us to denying the relevant attractive people the prerogative to bathe and groom, for any plausible moral pluralism will include principles protecting these prerogatives that will tend to trump modest motive autonomy when it comes to matters of personal hygiene.

One might regard as more worrisome a case in which a person splashes on cologne in the hope that it will subliminally dispose those in whom she is most interested to desire her. With the advent of modern plumbing, cologne splashing is not as plausibly included as bathing or brushing one's hair under principles protecting individuals' prerogatives to maintain their own hygiene. But glossy magazine advertisements notwithstanding, cologne splashing does not seem remotely likely to have effects on those exposed to it that undermine their capacity for rational motive management.

Again, we can imagine atypical cases where particular individuals are rationally compromised by cologne splashing. In such cases, however, modest motive autonomy's implication that others ought to take care not to undermine the capacity of such individuals for rational motive management is not absurd. This is, after all, how we think that others ought to conduct themselves around individuals adversely affected by cologne in other ways—for instance, those who are allergic to it.

Substances that can be splashed on to undermine others' rational capacities are presently something of a seducer's pipe dream. But they have real-life analogs. For instance, people vary in how charismatic they are, and very charismatic people may be able to deploy their magnetism and charm to generate or amplify sexual desire for themselves in others or to dissolve others' inhibitions. Doing so will violate modest motive autonomy, at least in cases where magnetism and charm do not operate by inducing in others beliefs about the favorableness of desiring the charismatic person sexually or of abandoning their inhibitions.

But the implication that very charismatic people ought to take care not to undermine others' capacities for rational motive management is not absurd. We insist that very gifted students take care not to undermine others' capacities for learning in the classroom, and that very strong people take care not to injure others in their physical interactions. With greater gifts sometimes come greater responsibilities. By the same reasoning, it is not absurd to suggest that people with extraordinary charisma ought to take similar care around others who might be especially susceptible to their magnetism and charm.

So modest motive autonomy is not readily reduced to absurdity by a consideration of its implications within the realm of human sexual pursuit. But one might worry instead about how it handles cases in which targets consent to having their capacity for rational motive management undermined. Consider a variation on the case of Jeffries and the waitress in which the waitress gives robustly informed and voluntary consent to having Jeffries turn his seductive techniques on her during dinner.[12] A success on Jeffries's part would undermine the waitress's capacity to rationally manage her motives, at least if we focus on the span of time during which she is serving Jeffries dinner. Reasoning thus, one might conclude that modest motive autonomy condemns Jeffries's actions in this case as morally problematic. And one might think this implausible, as there can be nothing wrong with treating someone precisely as she consents to be treated, at least outside of cases involving significant risk of grievous injury to the consenter.

This type of case raises an important point about the exercise of the capacity to rationally manage one's own motives. An agent might exercise this capacity by reserving the prerogative to evaluate and adjust her motives at every choice point. Or she might do so by adopting plans that forfeit the prerogative to evaluate and adjust her motives at some choice points. A narrow reading of modest motive autonomy protects only the first of these means of rationally managing motives. A broad reading of this principle protects both the first and the second. To handle cases like the one involving Jeffries and the consenting waitress, I shall opt for a broad rather than a narrow reading of modest motive autonomy. On such a reading, an agent's capacity to rationally manage her own motives is not undermined when others make it difficult or impossible to evaluate and adjust her motives in accordance with the plan, short term or long term, of the agent involved.

But how explicit and specific must an agent's plan be to exculpate others' interfering with or blocking her efforts to evaluate and adjust her motives within a given context? One might think that merely by entering

---

12. I thank David Shoemaker for calling this sort of case to my attention.

certain arenas, a typical nightclub perhaps, or speed-dating night at the local public library, agents evince plans encompassing the possibility of others trying to thrust motives on them in ways undermining their capacity for rational motive management. Were this so, there would be arenas in which agents would not even have to concern themselves with modest motive autonomy—indeed, the very arenas that are most pertinent to a discussion of unsavory seduction.

On the broad version of modest motive autonomy, what exculpates an agent's interfering with a target's efforts to manage her own motives at a given time is the adoption of a plan by that target allowing such interference. But entering a nightclub does not indicate that one has adopted such a plan. People come to nightclubs for all sorts of reasons other than to be unsavorily seduced, to accompany friends bent on seducing or being seduced, or to be around people, or to dance. The same is true of people attending speed-dating events. Some may be there to alleviate loneliness, or boredom, or just to appease a concerned and meddlesome parent. And this point is even more obviously applicable to other types of places where attempts at unsavory seduction may be relatively common: neighborhood bars, coffee shops, grocery stores, and the like. Thus, one cannot plausibly interpret a person's presence within an arena in which interference with others' efforts to rationally manage their own motives are common as indicating commitment to a plan allowing such interference.

But perhaps nightclubs and speed-dating events are like art auctions. Merely by entering an art auction one becomes bound by certain conventions, so that one bids by raising one's finger whether one plans to do so or not. Similarly, one might think, merely by walking into a nightclub or showing up at a speed-dating event, one becomes bound by a convention under which one forfeits the protection afforded by modest motive autonomy.

The conventions governing art auctions are fairly standard, and those administering art auctions take steps to publicize these conventions to potential participants. This matters, for it would be implausible to think that people who could not readily determine that they were entering a venue governed by special conventions would be bound by these conventions. And herein lies an important difference between art auctions and venues like nightclubs and speed-dating events. For under present conditions, entrants to a nightclub or a speed-dating event cannot readily determine that they are operating under a convention suspending modest motive autonomy. *Nightclub* encompasses a wide variety of venues that operate under a wide variety of conventions. And it is not as if such venues typically publicize conventions governing sexual pursuit to entrants, or even make provisions for inquiries about such conventions. The same observations hold, to at least some extent, of speed-dating events. Consequently, it is not plausible to think that nightclubs and speed-dating events resemble art auctions in the manner required to place entrants under a special set of conventions under which they forfeit the protections afforded by modest motive autonomy.

The Manipulation Account

Having argued that modest motive autonomy cannot be easily dismissed as either absurd or largely inapplicable within the realm of sexual pursuit, I turn to deploying it as part of an account of unsavory seduction's unsavoriness. As I have characterized it, unsavory seduction is both motive altering and rationality hampering. And as we noted previously, appeal to neither of these elements in isolation can explain unsavory seduction's unsavoriness. But if we interpret them as yoked so as to constitute a form of manipulation that violates modest motive autonomy, we can readily explain unsavory seduction's unsavoriness.

Consider the idea that unsavory seduction involves manipulation that is motive altering. Generally speaking, we can characterize manipulation of a person as an attempt to control or change that person in an artful manner so as to serve one's own purposes.[13] The manipulation involved in unsavory seduction converts initial sexual unwillingness to willingness to have sex based on sexual desire. A straightforward seducer might accomplish this by finding out as much as possible about a target's sexual proclivities, then artfully presenting himself or herself as possessing the very properties that tend to turn the target on. To do so is to manipulate the target's perceptions and beliefs so as to produce motivationally effective sexual desire for the seducer as an end product. But as the case of Jeffries and the waitress illustrates, other means of relevantly manipulating a target are possible. Via his "Speed Seduction" techniques, Jeffries detaches the waitress's motivationally charged feelings of sexual attraction from their proper historical objects, then reattaches these feelings to his own person. This is to manipulate another's motives so as to produce motivationally

---

13. See, for instance, the definition of *manipulate* at http://www.merriam-webster.com/dictionary/manipulate.

effective sexual desire for the seducer as a by-product. We can capture these observations by noting that unsavory seduction involves manipulation that is motive altering insofar as it seeks to generate motivationally effective sexual desire either as an end product or as a by-product of other motivational changes.

Now consider the idea that unsavory seduction involves manipulation that is rationality hampering. Here it might help to think again about the case of Jeffries and the waitress. Jeffries seeks to convert the waitress from indifference to sexual willingness by means of quasi-hypnotic techniques conjoined to crude behavioral conditioning. We can imagine less bizarre versions of this case in which, for instance, Jeffries seeks a conversion to sexual willingness by plying the waitress with enough alcohol to hinder her ability to think critically about his desirability, or by exhausting her to the same point by means of a sustained campaign of persuasion. In all of these versions of the case of Jeffries and the waitress, Jeffries artfully controls or changes the waitress in ways that hinder her capacity to choose to have the same, more, fewer, or differentially important motives based on her beliefs about the favorableness of her doing so. If effective, "Speed Seduction" techniques make exercise of this capacity impossible, while excessive alcohol consumption and psychological exhaustion make it more difficult to exercise than it otherwise would be. We can capture these observations by saying that unsavory seduction involves manipulation that is rationality hampering insofar as it involves controlling or changing another in a way that undermines her capacity to rationally manage her own motives.

One might think that this is an overly narrow understanding of *rationality hampering manipulation.* I would not so manipulate you were I to encourage you to attach much greater weight to considerations favoring changes in your motives than these considerations actually merit. Nor would I so manipulate you were I to induce you to change your motives by encouraging false beliefs in you. Such maneuvers hamper an agent's capacity to act according to good reasons, but this makes them *rationality hampering* in a sense that is too broad to be of help here. Appealing to the idea that I do something morally problematic to another any time that I induce her to retain or to change motives based on reasons that are not good yields an account of unsavory seduction's unsavoriness that falls seriously afoul of the second desideratum above.

Adopting the foregoing understandings of *motive altering* and *rationality hampering* manipulation, we have it that unsavory seduction involves manipulation that generates motivationally effective sexual desire in a target by means that make it more difficult or impossible for that target to make choices about retaining or changing her motives based on her beliefs about the favorableness of her various options. Such manipulation violates modest motive autonomy, one of the moral constraints that collectively govern how human beings ought to treat one another across various contexts. For this reason, unsavory seduction is unsavory. This is the *manipulation account* of unsavory seduction's unsavoriness.

Within the framework I have articulated, the plausibility of an account of unsavory seduction's unsavoriness depends on how fully it satisfies the three desiderata specified above. So to evaluate the manipulation account, let us consider whether and to what degree it satisfies each of these desiderata.

The First Desideratum

According to the first desideratum, a plausible account of unsavory seduction's unsavoriness should ascribe to it the right moral status, rendering it morally problematic rather than categorically immoral or innocuous. And it should do so by appealing only to moral commitments supported by reasons that most of us would not regard as eccentric or crazy.

On the manipulation account, unsavory seduction always violates a genuine moral constraint on human interaction. This moral constraint is not of overriding importance, and must be traded off against various other moral constraints in various contexts. Thus, on this account, unsavory seduction is not categorically immoral. But since unsavory seduction always violates a genuine moral constraint, it is not innocuous, either. It is, rather, morally problematic.

Of course, the first desideratum requires not just that an appeal to the manipulation account render unsavory seduction morally problematic, but that it do so by appeal to a rationally defensible moral commitment among members of my intended audience. There are several indications that this requirement is satisfied.

First, modest motive autonomy is a focus of agreement in normative ethical theory. J. S. Mill embraces something much like it from a broadly utilitarian perspective in *On Liberty*.[14] David Gauthier, one of the

---

14. See J. S. Mill, *On Liberty*, edited by A. Castell (New York: Appleton, 1947), 15–74.

best-known contemporary contractarians, mobilizes a version of modest motive autonomy in the closing chapters of *Morals by Agreement*.[15] And Christine Korsgaard offers something much like this normative constraint as part of her reconstruction of Kant's moral theory in *Creating the Kingdom of Ends*.[16] Classical utilitarianism, contractarianism, and neo-Kantianism are major rival normative ethical theories. That proponents of each accept versions of modest motive autonomy suggests that commitment to this principle is not eccentric or crazy.

Second, modest motive autonomy has the capacity to illuminate several difficult normative issues. Consideration of this principle has helped to shed light on whether and under what conditions certain professionals—for instance, physicians—ought to be forbidden to have sexual relations with their clients.[17] This principle has been mobilized to clarify the distinction between entrapment and legitimate arrest as well.[18] And I can imagine its helping to sort out some of the morally gray areas of parenting—for instance, the question of when it becomes morally problematic for parents to continue trying to inculcate preferred motives in their growing children.

Third, and most compellingly, modest motive autonomy enjoins respect for a capacity that many of us seem to value. We condemn past and present efforts to shape agents' motives in ways that involve undermining their capacity to rationally manage their own motives—efforts such as subliminal advertising and religious brainwashing. And we react with shock and dismay to the thoroughgoing, institutionalized devaluing of this capacity prominent in such notable dystopian visions as Margaret Atwood's *The Handmaid's Tale*, Aldous Huxley's *Brave New World*, and George Orwell's *1984*.[19] Given that many of us value the capacity for which

---

15. See David Gauthier, *Morals by Agreement* (New York: Oxford University Press, 1986), 330–55.

16. See Christine Korsgaard, *Creating the Kingdom of Ends* (New York: Cambridge University Press, 1996), 106–32.

17. See Council on Ethical and Judicial Affairs, American Medical Association, "Sexual Misconduct in the Practice of Medicine," *Journal of the American Medical Association* 266 (1991): 2741–45.

18. See Gerald Dworkin, *The Theory and Practice of Autonomy* (Cambridge: Cambridge University Press, 1988), 130–49.

19. See Margaret Atwood, *The Handmaid's Tale* (New York: Random House, 1986); Aldous Huxley, *Brave New World* (New York: Harper & Row, 1946); and George Orwell, *1984* (New York: Harcourt, Brace, 1949).

modest motive autonomy enjoins respect, and given that we have reason to foster respect for capacities that many of us value, it follows that we have reason to accept modest motive autonomy.[20]

Despite these considerations, one might yet harbor doubts about modest motive autonomy. After all, the phenomenon condemned by modest motive autonomy is a ubiquitous part of human life. We enter the world with a limited set of motives. Early on, features of our environment (including our families!) thrust additional motivational changes upon us without engaging any beliefs of ours about the favorableness of these changes. Later, when we are capable of having beliefs about the favorableness of having or retaining certain motives, we often find ourselves in situations where acting on such beliefs is difficult or impossible. Appealing to such observations, one might argue that modest motive autonomy enjoins us to respect a human capacity that is routinely bypassed by the workings of the world. If this is so, then commitment to this principle seems eccentric and rationally indefensible, not the sort of thing to which we can appeal while satisfying the first desideratum.

But that individuals' capacity to rationally manage their own motives is frequently undermined does not imply that we ought to resign ourselves to such undermining. Respecting modest motive autonomy is a measure that would help to prevent at least some nonrational thrustings of motivational changes onto other agents. By means of this measure, we can help reduce our odds of ending up with the ill consequences of agents having important decisions of their own driven by motives they have not had sufficient opportunity to evaluate and embrace. If we take the literature on identification seriously, these ill consequences can include alienation from one's own actions, and a consequent failure to integrate psychologically the various aspects of one's agency.[21]

Further, we think that there is a moral difference between a drowning that results from either nonhuman environmental causes or non-negligent

---

20. This reasoning is inspired by an argument mobilized by Ralph Wedgwood in defense of same-sex marriage. See Ralph Wedgwood, "The Fundamental Argument for Same-Sex Marriage," *Journal of Political Philosophy* 7 (1999): 225–42.

21. See, for instance, Harry G. Frankfurt, "Freedom of the Will and the Concept of a Person," in *The Importance of What We Care About: Philosophical Essays* (New York: Cambridge University Press, 1988), 21; or Harry G. Frankfurt, "The Faintest Passion," in *Necessity, Volition, and Love* (Cambridge: Cambridge University Press, 1999), 99–100; or Christine M. Korsgaard, *The Sources of Normativity* (Cambridge: Cambridge University Press, 1996), 90–130. Thanks to David Shoemaker for help with the Frankfurt citations.

accident and one that another planned, anticipated, or caused accidentally but negligently. Similarly, from a moral standpoint, we can distinguish between nonrational motivational change or stasis resulting from either environment or non-negligent accident and such change or stasis that is planned, anticipated, or caused accidentally but negligently by another. If the above observations about modest motive autonomy are correct, then cases of the latter sort evince a morally reproachable form of disrespect for a capacity valued widely within my intended audience. For these reasons, we can accept that the nonrational thrusting onto individuals of motivational changes or stasis is unavoidable and ubiquitous without having to regard a commitment to modest motive autonomy as eccentric and rationally indefensible.

Viewed cumulatively, the above considerations do not establish that rationality requires us to refrain from undermining others' capacity to manage their motives. But to show that the manipulation account satisfies the first desideratum, I need only show that accepting modest motive autonomy is supported by reasons of sufficient quality that most of us would not regard such acceptance as eccentric or crazy. And the above considerations are sufficient to discharge this burden.

The Second Desideratum

According to the second desideratum, a plausible account of unsavory seduction's unsavoriness should not be so broad in its implications as to condemn human activities widely judged morally innocuous. The key to satisfying this desideratum is to condemn unsavory seduction by appealing to sufficiently narrow moral considerations. It will not do, for instance, to condemn unsavory seduction by appeal to a prohibition on all activities that involve hampering a target's capacity to act according to beliefs about fact-based considerations supporting or opposing their various options. For such a principle would condemn, among other things, anesthetizing individuals in preparation for surgery. Nor would it do to condemn unsavory seduction by appeal to a prohibition on all activities that involve trying to change others' motives to suit one's own ends. Such a principle would condemn, among other things, virtually all public service messages.

Modest motive autonomy, of course, has a narrower scope than either of these principles. To explore whether this principle's scope is narrow enough for an appeal to it to satisfy the second desideratum, I shall consider an argument that an activity widely considered morally innocuous (the formation of mutual romantic love relationships) violates it. Then I will suggest how the reply I develop to this argument might be generalized.

Sarah Buss argues that there is an essential and intimate link between manipulation of the beloved and the formation of mutual romantic love relationships.[22] Such manipulation, according to Buss, enters the early stages of romantic love relationships in two places. First, manipulation is an integral part of expressing love to someone who may not yet reciprocate this attitude:

> At a minimum, we try to "be on our best behavior," to "hide our warts." Usually, we go further: we become atypically animated, or grave; we act so much more interested in his tales about his eccentric uncle with the talking parrot than we ever would have been before—or ever will be again.[23]

In the early stages of love, our primary challenge is to induce the beloved to "fall in love" with us. For most of us, straightforward rational argument to establish our suitability as an object of love is at best a risky strategy, so we resort to trying to manipulate the beloved into reciprocating our attitudes.

Second, claims Buss, early romantic love is usually too fragile to withstand complete straightforwardness. The aspiring lover cannot effectively court just by arguing that she loves and that her love ought to be returned. Thus, she must do something different to motivate the beloved to interact with her, else give up her romantic aspirations. Since straightforward rational argument will not do, she is pressed toward manipulating the beloved to interact with her in ways conducive to love flourishing.

But to manipulate others into feeling, wanting, and doing certain things is to interfere with the ability of those involved to manage their own motives. And one might think that doing so violates modest motive autonomy. Thus, if Buss were right about there being a very tight link between such manipulation and the formation of new love relationships, then modest motive autonomy would seem to condemn all, or nearly all, attempts to form such relationships. In this case, the manipulation account would fail to satisfy the second desideratum above.

---

22. See Sarah Buss, "Valuing Autonomy and Respecting Persons: Manipulation, Seduction, and the Basis of Moral Constraints." *Ethics* 115 (January 2005): 220–22.

23. See Buss, "Valuing Autonomy," 221.

As an initial reply to this objection, it is worth highlighting a point about the formation of love relationships that Buss's argument does not foreclose. Buss argues that most love relationships involve manipulation of feelings, wants, and actions in their earliest stages, leaving open the possibility that some might not. And this is an important possibility, especially in light of social scientific research suggesting that women tend to be rationally discriminating in their choices of both short- and long-term sexual partners.[24] Nothing precludes people from eschewing manipulation early in a relationship in favor of straightforward rational argument. If one had enough justified confidence in one's own merits, this might even be the most effective way to proceed. In any case, love can develop between parties who employ only straightforward rational argument, and modest motive autonomy certainly does not condemn what goes on in the early stages of such relationships.

But the class of such relationships might be vanishingly small, so it would be good not to have to lean too heavily on the above point. Fortunately, we need not do so. For modest motive autonomy is rather more modest than the above objection asserts. It condemns only attempts to induce motivational changes in others by means that make it more difficult or impossible to change motives based on beliefs about the favorableness of making these changes. It does not condemn attempts to induce motivational changes in others by means of efforts to alter others' beliefs about the favorableness of making these changes. Hiding warts, becoming atypically animated, and feigning interest in boring topics are all strategies that can and frequently do operate by affecting another's beliefs about the favorableness of coming to love the individual deploying these strategies. Indeed, if Buss is right that the manipulation involved in love's earlier stages usually consists of putting on an "act," then such manipulation can and frequently does respect modest motive autonomy.[25] For lovers' "acts" can and frequently do work by casting the "acting" lover as worthy of being loved, in the hopes of inducing beliefs in the intended audience that the "acting" lover possesses qualities that render coming to love her a favorable outcome. Thus, at least some of the motive manipulation asserted

24. For an overview of such research, see David M. Buss, *The Evolution of Desire: Strategies of Human Mating* (New York: Basic Books, 2003), 19–48. See also Geoffrey Miller, *The Mating Mind* (New York: Random House, 2000), 258–425.

25. See Buss, "Valuing Autonomy," 221.

by Buss to be tightly linked to the formation of new love relationships respects modest motive autonomy.

The upshot of these considerations is that even if we accept Sarah Buss's claims about manipulation and love, modest motive autonomy does not condemn all or virtually all attempts to form new romantic love relationships. Attempts to win a new lover by straightforward rational argument are consistent with modest motive autonomy, as are presumably more common attempts to win a new lover by manipulation that tends to induce motivational changes by altering beliefs about the favorableness of making these changes. Modest motive autonomy does condemn those attempts to win a new lover by manipulation that makes it more difficult or impossible for the individual involved to make motivational changes based on beliefs about the favorableness of doing so. But there is nothing absurd about the claim that some or even much of what is done in pursuit of romantic love is morally problematic, for romantic love has a checkered reputation. It would be absurd to claim that all or virtually all romantic love originates in morally problematic actions by would-be lovers. But as I have argued, modest motive autonomy does not imply the truth of this claim.

Another worry one might have is that modest motive autonomy is apt to condemn the rearing and education of children developed enough to reason for themselves on the same grounds it seemed apt to condemn the early stages of romantic love. Of course, the claim that rearing and educating such children always involves an element of wrongfulness seems absurd. But sometimes rearing and educating rationally competent children involves straightforward rational argument. Other times, it involves manipulation that tends to induce motivational changes by altering beliefs about the favorableness of making these changes. Neither such argument nor such manipulation falls afoul of modest motive autonomy. Thus, modest motive autonomy condemns as morally problematic only some of the rearing and education of rationally competent children, the subset in which such children are hindered in or blocked from rationally managing their own motives. This implication of modest motive autonomy is not absurd because, like romantic love, childrearing and pedagogy have their dark sides.

I suspect that this strategy of showing that activities that might seem to violate modest motive autonomy actually accord with it can be extended to redeem activities other than forming new love relationships and the rearing and education of rationally competent children. But there are endeavors that it clearly cannot be deployed to redeem, like subliminal advertising or the kind of hardcore brainwashing undergone by the character Alex in Anthony Burgess's *A Clockwork Orange*.[26] For reasons that should be apparent, modest motive autonomy condemns such endeavors wholesale. But this is not an absurd result either, for they are widely regarded as morally problematic.

Thus, an appeal to modest motive autonomy condemns unsavory seduction without similarly condemning activities like forming new love relationships and the rearing and education of rationally competent children. It does condemn subliminal advertising and hardcore brainwashing, but this is just what we should want and expect. Cumulatively, these considerations suggest that an appeal to modest motive autonomy can explain unsavory seduction's unsavoriness while satisfying the second desideratum.

The Third Desideratum

The third desideratum requires that a plausible account of unsavory seduction's unsavoriness be inclusive enough to condemn all unambiguous cases of unsavory seduction, all sexual pursuits in which conversion to sexual willingness is accomplished by what counts uncontroversially among us as a rationality bypassing alteration of a target's motives. The manipulation account has difficulty satisfying this desideratum, primarily because of the narrowness of its understandings of *motive altering* and *rationality hampering*. I developed these understandings by thinking about Jeffries's seduction of his waitress, but we are apt to regard as both motive altering and rationality bypassing at least some conversions to sexual willingness that are not well captured by this paradigm. To see this, consider a fictitious case.

Suppose that Pat desires Sam sexually, but has made a commitment not to have sex with anyone until after marriage. Pat's commitment is a rational response to Pat's belief that God ordains that sex is something that should only happen between husband and wife. Pat is intelligent, but has limited formal education and limited exposure to worldviews different from Pat's own. Sam is a sophist, someone well versed in the art of using rhetoric to shape the beliefs of others in ways that do not necessarily track

---

26. See Anthony Burgess, *A Clockwork Orange* (New York: W. W. Norton, 1986).

good reasons. Sam determines that the most effective means of converting Pat's initial sexual unwillingness to sexual willingness is to undermine
Pat's belief in the existence of God. Sam puts her best rhetorical efforts
into convincing Pat that Pat has reason to doubt the existence of God.
Sam's arguments are seriously logically flawed, but given Pat's limited
education, they are effective, and the two end up having sex.

Sam's manipulation of Pat is motive altering in the sense required
for unsavory seduction. By means of her (flawed) argumentation, Sam
brings Pat to act upon a motive upon which Pat would otherwise not have
acted: sexual desire for Sam. And there is a perfectly familiar sense in
which Sam's manipulation of Pat is rationality hampering. By means of her
(flawed) argumentation, Sam induces Pat to give up a practically significant religious belief for bad reasons: mistaken beliefs about the fact-based
considerations that Pat has for doing so. Thus, among members of my
intended audience, Sam's seduction of Pat is recognizably motive altering
and rationality hampering.

And yet, this seduction does not involve manipulation that falls afoul
of modest motive autonomy. This principle prohibits agents from engaging in manipulation that makes it more difficult, or even impossible, for
a target to change her motives based on beliefs about the favorableness of
making this change. But in arguing with Pat, Sam induces in Pat beliefs
that favor changing her motives. They are false and unwarranted beliefs,
but as I noted in discussing modest motive autonomy, this principle does
not prohibit agents from trying to alter one another's motives by inducing
in one another false or unwarranted beliefs. Thus, Sam and Pat provide us
with an unsavory seduction the unsavoriness of which is not illuminated
by the manipulation account.

Such cases are not difficult to multiply. Suppose that O, out of a complex mix of love, self-abasement, and dependency on her lover Rene,
agrees to spend some weeks at a chateau where she must accede to any
sexual demand put to her by any male resident as a condition of remaining there.[27] Suppose that during her time at the chateau, her sense of who
she is and why she matters becomes conjoined tightly to her submitting
to the sexual demands of those males with power over her, and that she
comes to eroticize such submission. Finally, suppose that some time after
her stay at the chateau, O encounters several men at a club with whom

---

27. The case is, of course, not mine. See Pauline Reage, *Story of O* (New York: Ballantine, 1965).

she is disinclined to have sex, at least until they leave the club and one of them flashes a ring at her indicating his association with the chateau. The memory of her sexual submissiveness at the chateau arouses her, and conjoined with her fear of losing all future access to the chateau and its residents, it suffices to convert her initial sexual unwillingness to sexual willingness.

There is a sense in which this seduction of O is motive altering, a sense made familiar by the work of any number of feminist theorists.[28] For the chateau is a patriarchal society writ small, and as a consequence of her experiences there, O comes to eroticize utter submission to the sexual desires of men. Only in the context of such an alteration of O's motives can we make sense of a flashing ring converting O's initial sexual unwillingness to sexual willingness. Thus, if we think of O's seduction upon leaving the club as extending back over her time at the chateau, as we must to make it psychologically plausible, it involves the alteration of some of O's motives. There is a familiar sense in which O's seduction is rationality hampering as well. Suppose we understand rationality to involve not just acting for reasons but also acting for genuine reasons. O's eroticization of sexual submission to men renders her unable to track genuine reasons in her encounters with denizens of the chateau, hampering her capacity to choose rationally. Thus, among my intended audience, the seduction of O is recognizably motive altering and rationality hampering.

But again, this seduction does not involve manipulation that falls afoul of modest motive autonomy. Arguably, the men at the chateau do induce a robust alteration in O's motives, for she leaves the chateau with a motive that she lacked when she entered, a recognizably sexual desire to submit herself sexually to chateau residents. But still, as the novella makes clear, O consents to every step in the acquisition of this motive based on her beliefs about what the resulting change in her motives is likely to entail. For this reason, O's acquisition of this motive does not fall afoul of modest motive autonomy, and her story provides us with another unsavory seduction the unsavoriness of which is not illuminated by the manipulation account.[29]

---

28. See, for instance, Catherine A. MacKinnon, *Feminism Unmodified* (Cambridge, MA: Harvard University Press, 1987), 46–62. Or see Andrea Dworkin, *Intercourse* (New York: Ballantine, 1987), 121–43.

29. It is worth noting the broader significance of this lacuna in the manipulation account. When a man in a patriarchal social order unsavorily seduces a woman, multiple serious wrongs are likely to have been committed. These include, but are not limited to, the unfair

Toward a Pluralistic Account

This failure to satisfy the third desideratum above is not unique to the manipulation account sketched above. A different sort of manipulation account might explain unsavory seduction's unsavoriness by appeal to the alleged wrongfulness of changing a target's motives so that they fall short of what the seducer regards as the relevant ideals governing what motives the target should have.[30] Such an account would have little trouble explaining the unsavoriness of Sam's seduction of Pat above. But it could not easily explain the unsavoriness of something like O's seduction, at least if perpetrated by misogynists of a certain stripe. And we can imagine a radical feminist account that explains unsavory seduction's unsavoriness by appeal to the seriously compromised quality of women's consent to sex under conditions of patriarchy. Such an account could readily explain the unsavoriness of O's seduction. But it would have difficulty explaining the unsavoriness of Sam's seduction of Pat in the case where Sam and Pat are both men.

So it seems that various competing accounts of unsavory seduction's unsavoriness suffer from the same drawback. They fail to satisfy the third desideratum because they are overly narrow, although they are overly narrow in different ways. This is consistent with there being one thing called unsavory seduction, the unsavoriness of which no one has yet managed to characterize in a sufficiently inclusive way. But it is also consistent with unsavory seduction being a class of phenomena loosely unified by their being seductions, motive altering, and rationality hampering, but with members of this class being different enough that their unsavoriness is best illuminated by appeal to multiple different accounts rather than to a single overarching account.

In prospect, such a pluralistic account looks quite promising. It can satisfy the first desideratum readily enough. We need only construct it from component accounts that, like the manipulation account, render unsavory

---

leveraging of women by means of the social, political, or economic status typically accorded to men, the discounting of women's needs and aims, and callousness in the face of women's heightened vulnerability in the aftermath of being seduced. Because of its narrowness, the manipulation account overlooks such elements, elements that cumulatively render the unsavory seduction of women by men within a patriarchal social order more wrongful than a practice like subliminal advertising. For this point, I am indebted to an anonymous referee for Oxford University Press.

30. Versions of this sort of manipulation account are championed in contributions to this volume by Anne Barnhill, Moti Gorin, and Claudia Mills.

seduction morally problematic by appealing only to commitments supported by reasons of sufficient quality that most of us would not regard them as eccentric or crazy. And if we construct a pluralistic account in the right way, then it can readily satisfy the second desideratum as well. The key is to construct it from component accounts that, like the manipulation account, are narrow enough to avoid condemning as morally problematic human activities widely judged morally innocuous. Further, unlike any of the above monistic accounts, a pluralistic account holds out the promise of satisfying the third desideratum, by virtue of its ability to appeal to multiple differing accounts of unsavory seduction's unsavoriness.[31]

In this way, our discussion of the successes and failures of the manipulation account ultimately points us toward an alternative, pluralistic account of unsavory seduction's unsavoriness. I suspect, for reasons that I have indicated, that a plausible such pluralistic account will analyze the unsavoriness of at least some unsavory seduction along the lines suggested by the manipulation account.[32] Whether and how the manipulation account can be successfully situated within a developed pluralistic account of unsavory seduction's unsavoriness remains to be seen.

---

31. If, as I am coming to believe, explaining variation in the seriousness of the wrongs involved in different unsavory seductions is a fourth desideratum of a plausible account of unsavory seduction, a pluralistic account has another advantage. On such an account, different unsavory seductions may involve different wrong-making elements, elements that can vary in their seriousness. And some unsavory seductions may involve multiple wrong-making elements, and thus be more seriously wrong than others because of the compounded wrongs that they involve.

32. I suspect as well that such an account will analyze the unsavoriness of other unsavory seductions along lines suggested by several other contributors to this volume. In this connection, I have in mind the sort of ideals-based accounts of wrongful manipulation mentioned in note 30, as well as the sort of "objective attitude" accounts of wrongful manipulation developed in different ways by Marcia Baron and Kate Manne.

9

The Implications of Ego Depletion for the Ethics and Politics of Manipulation

Michael Cholbi

"Free will does not mean one will, but many wills conflicting in one man."
—FLANNERY O' CONNOR, *Mystery and Manners: Occasional Prose*

THE STANDARD VIEW among philosophers is that manipulation aims to modify another person's choices by directly, but clandestinely, modifying a person's psychology. As Robert Noggle puts it, the victim of manipulation is "led astray" by the manipulator operating various psychological levers that impact the victim's beliefs, desires, or emotions.[1] Similarly, Claudia Mills observes that whereas coercion seeks to change an individual's choice situation by modifying the objective features of that situation, manipulation seeks to change an individual's choice situation by modifying her psychology.[2] So whereas the mugger coerces me when he tries to compel me to relinquish my wallet with the threat "your money or your life!," the psychiatrist manipulates me when she uses hypnosis to persuade me to give up my wallet. Likewise, Marcia Baron emphasizes the opacity of manipulation when she notes an important psychological asymmetry: manipulators cannot manipulate without intending to do so, but manipulation is no longer manipulation if its target is aware of being manipulated.[3] Manipulation is,

---

1. Robert Noggle, "Manipulative Actions: A Conceptual and Moral Analysis," *American Philosophical Quarterly* 33, no. 1 (January 1996): 44.

2. Claudia Mills, "Politics and Manipulation," *Social Theory and Practice* 21, no. 1 (Spring 1995).

3. Marcia Baron, "Manipulativeness," *Proceedings and Addresses of the American Philosophical Association* 77, no. 2 (November 2003): 39.

by necessity, *subtle*. This is why, for example, to utter 'I am attempting to manipulate you' is to engage in a performative contradiction. Like silence, mentioning manipulation destroys it. The intended effect of manipulation, as Baron notes, is to make it harder, if not effectively impossible, to choose other than as the manipulator desires that we choose, [4] so one way to reduce our susceptibility to manipulation is to become aware of it.

Much of recent social psychology research concludes that we are, unfortunately from an ethical perspective, much more susceptible to subtle—and seemingly irrational—influences on choice than we commonly recognize. For instance, we are creatures who tend to be more readily persuaded by someone who claims to share our birthday or our initials.[5] Worse still, we routinely overestimate our stoutness in being able to resist others' influence on us, thinking that while *other* people readily succumb to such manipulation, we ourselves are nearly immune.[6] Being manipulated is not only easier than we think, resisting it is harder than we think.

My purpose here is to investigate the ethical and political implications of one psychological phenomenon—known as *ego depletion*—that renders us susceptible to manipulation. On one commonsense picture, willpower and self-control are character traits that vary from person to person. But the strong-willed or self-controlled person has, as Aristotle remarked, achieved the "hardest victory" of all: the victory over the self and its desires. And once established, self-control is a resource that does not need replenishing. The strong-willed or self-controlled person chooses wisely and well, even as temptations or irrational influences concatenate.

The ego depletion hypothesis suggests that this commonsense picture is, in crucial respects, incorrect. While individuals vary in their ability to exercise self-control, self-control and willpower are resources that, within a given context, become depleted as they are exercised.[7] Having to exert self-control and willpower draws down the reservoir of these resources

---

4. Baron,"Manipulativeness," 42.

5. D. T. Miller, J. S. Downs, and D. A. Prentice, "Minimal Conditions for the Creation of a Unit Relationship: The Social Bond Between Birthdaymates," *European Journal of Social Psychology* 28 (1998).

6. W. P. Davidson, "The Third-Person Effect in Communication," *Public Opinion Quarterly* 47 (1983).

7. Mark Muraven and Roy F. Baumeister, "Self-regulation and Depletion of Limited Resources: Does Self-control Resemble a Muscle?" *Psychological Bulletin* 126 (2000); and Martin S. Hagger et al., "Ego Depletion and the Strength Model of Self-Control: A Meta-Analysis," *Psychological Bulletin* 136 (2010).

and makes subsequent such exercises more difficult. An appropriate metaphor, then, is that self-control and willpower are a muscle. Yes, some of us have stronger muscles than others, but all of us undergo muscle fatigue as we exercise.

Ego depletion's connection to manipulation is this: Ego depletion exerts a nonrational influence on our choice and conduct. Acting rationally can sometimes depend on the temporal order in which choices are made. However, ego depletion results in later choices being less governable by our powers of self-control and willpower than earlier choices. As our power to regulate our desires diminishes each time we must make conscious effort to keep those desires in check, our later desires exert outsized influence over our choices, sometimes to our detriment and in ways that we would not rationally endorse. The employee who must keep her anger in check as she is berated by a heavy-handed boss later gorges on ice cream. The recovering drug addict strains to stay away from the local drug markets, only to later end up arrested for soliciting prostitution. The shopper who must drive past luxury shops en route to purchase goods at a discount store later lets loose with a torrent of verbal abuse at her children. Presumably, these individuals would rationally regret the latter choices, choices for which ego depletion may well be essential to their explanation. Those with the ability to harness the power of ego depletion are thus well-positioned to manipulate others by creating choice environments temporally ordered so that ego depletion makes individual agents more likely to choose in ways the manipulator desires that they choose.

Because ego depletion makes us more susceptible to manipulation, a full account of the ethical and political significance of manipulation cannot overlook it. I suspect that the implications of ego depletion for manipulation are very broad, so my aim here is to outline one conceptual concern, one theoretical concern, and one practical or policy-based concern that arise from ego depletion. Conceptually, ego depletion suggests that although direct manipulation by others may be the paradigm of manipulation, manipulation can also occur through the instigation of absent others or merely through the fashioning of social environments that shape choice. On the theoretical side, ego depletion is an important example of exogenous practical irrationality and of diminished autonomy that is largely causally independent of character as it is understood in the Platonic-Aristotelian tradition. Finally, on a practical level, ego depletion needs to be a more central focus of theorists of justice, since it appears to be a significant contributor to poverty and other persistent injustices.

Seminal Experiments on Ego Depletion

The hypothesis that "prior exercise of volition" causes a "temporary reduction in the self's capacity or willingness to engage in volitional action (including controlling the environment, controlling the self, making choices, and initiating action)" has been confirmed in a wide variety of studies.[8]

In one classic study, led by Roy Baumeister, hungry subjects were placed in a room with a bowl of radishes and a bowl of freshly baked chocolate chip cookies. A portion of the subjects were instructed to eat radishes but no cookies, and another portion were instructed to eat cookies but no radishes. A third group of test subjects did not participate in this part of the experiment. After twenty minutes, all of the test subjects were asked to complete a geometrical drawing puzzle that, unbeknownst to them, was unsolvable. The subjects were told that they could try as many solutions to the puzzle as they wished and could work on the puzzle for up to 30 minutes, but they could also stop before solving it if they wished. Baumeister found that those instructed to eat radishes but not cookies not only reported greater frustration and desire to quit the puzzle task, they quit sooner than the other subject groups (after about eight minutes on average, compared to nearly nineteen minutes for those instructed to eat cookies) and attempted fewer solutions than the other subject groups (about 19 attempts on average, compared to about 34 attempts for those who ate cookies). Baumeister et al. conclude that these results are not explained by the claim that eating cookies improves mental performance when compared to eating radishes. Rather, the combined effect of eating radishes (an unpalatable food to many) and having to resist eating the cookies produced a "psychic cost" to the subjects, a cost that made them more inclined not to persist in solving the puzzle. "Self-regulation"—that is, the regulation of one's desires and actions—thus appears to draw on "some limited resource akin to strength or energy."[9]

Baumeister's team also conducted an experiment that involved the regulation of emotional response instead of choice. In this experiment, participants were asked to watch movies, either a humorous clip of Robin Williams or a scene from *Terms of Endearment* in which a woman

---

8. Roy F. Baumeister et al., "Ego Depletion: Is the Active Self a Limited Resource?" *Journal of Personality and Social Psychology* 74 (1998): 1253.

9. Baumeister et al., "Ego Depletion," 1256.

discusses dying from cancer. Subjects were instructed either to suppress their emotions while watching the clip or to let their emotions flow freely. The subjects were then asked to solve anagram puzzles, unscrambling a set of jumbled letters to make words. Regardless of whether subjects had watched the humorous clip or the tearjerker, those subjects instructed to suppress emotional expression solved nearly 50 percent fewer anagrams than those instructed to express their emotional responses.[10]

Other research supports the claim that ego depletion makes individuals more susceptible to particular persuasive tactics. Fennis, Janssen, and Vohs found that sales personnel achieved higher sales when they sequenced their pitches so that earlier pitches required more careful, information-intensive deliberation than later pitches.[11] For example, a salesperson trying to persuade a customer to upgrade a cell phone service plan might begin her pitch with a highly specific question, like "How much of your monthly bill pays for text messaging?" or "How many of your available calling minutes do you use every month?" These questions can then be followed up with queries of a more general kind, like "Do you really think your current plan gives you a good deal?" Fennis et al. found that such sequencing leads customers to consider their options less carefully, to generate fewer counterarguments to salespersons' assertions, and to rely upon simple heuristics in making their buying decisions.

Ego Depletion and Practical Reason

On its face, both the *explananda* and the *explanans* in these ego depletion experiments appear to form heterogeneous classes. Indeed, the phenomena in question are wide ranging. However, the common pattern is that individuals who must engage in effortful practical deliberation then find subsequent deliberation, particularly deliberation that involves inclinations that the individual is seeking to control, more effortful and challenging. In the radish/cookie experiment, those subjects who had to suppress their desires to eat cookies and substitute radishes then found it more difficult to continue with a frustrating task. They became less patient or industrious (i.e., more tempted to quit) when they attempted to solve the

---

10. Baumeister et al., "Ego Depletion," 1258-59.

11. B. M. Fennis, L. Janssen, and K. D. Vohs, "Acts of Benevolence: A Limited-Resource Account of Compliance with Charitable Requests," *Journal of Consumer Research* 35 (2009).

unsolvable geometry puzzle. In the experiment where participants had to suppress their emotional responses to the film clips, those participants were less dogged in solving the anagrams. The experiments concerning sales tactics required participants to deliberate with care until the point that their deliberative willpower wore down. The common thread in each experiment is that prior efforts to control desires or guide deliberation diminish subsequent ability to do likewise. Baumeister thus proposes that ego depletion is the result of an inability to regulate executive function and self-control.[12]

Ego depletion is likely to be a pervasive source of practical irrationality. For as ego depletion sets in, individuals' capacity to act in their own considered interests diminishes. More specifically, a feature of our desires and choices that is usually irrelevant to their rationality—the temporal order in which we confront those desires and choices—ends up playing a disproportionate role in how we navigate those desires and choices. Even if I am able to suppress my desire to direct an obscene gesture at the driver who cuts me off on the freeway on the way to work, I may be less able to suppress my desire to eat a fatty hamburger for lunch *because* I had to suppress my earlier desire not to gesture at the reckless driver. And even if I am able to suppress my desire for a hamburger, I may be less able to suppress my late-night desires to drink alcohol, watch pornography, or read Kant. (Well, maybe not that last one.) The concatenation of ego depleting events seems to put me less and less under the control of my own rational powers, such that I end up doing what (in a larger sense) I would prefer that I not do.

The ego depletion research emphasizes that individuals subject to this phenomenon devolve to choice strategies that simplify choice, usually to their detriment. The apparently compromised executive function of those undergoing ego depletion tends to lead individuals to make choices that favor immediate gains over long-term benefit; to avoid or duck decision, as a consequence of "decision fatigue"; to adopt a status quo bias in favor of familiar alternatives; to fixate upon a single factor (price or color of a product, for instance) above all else; or to devolve choice to an authority (a doctor or a salesperson, say).[13] These strategies seem designed to enable

---

12. Roy F. Baumeister, "Yielding to Temptation: Self-control Failure, Impulsive Purchasing, and Consumer Behavior," *Journal of Consumer Research* 28 (2002).

13. Burmeister et al., "Ego Depletion."

ego-depleted persons to streamline the process of choice by avoiding choice characterized by complexity, and while such strategies may sometimes produce rational choices, it is doubtful that their cumulative effect on rational choice is positive.

Two Forms of Manipulation

As noted at the outset, our standard model of manipulation understands it as a species of interaction wherein one person attempts to modify the attitudes or choices of another by clandestinely modifying the other's attitudes. Ego depletion eases others' ability to induce such modifications in us. Simple knowledge of the likelihood of another person being ego depleted places the actors on unequal rational footing. If A has reason to believe B is ego depleted—perhaps A is even responsible for B's ego depletion—then A holds a deliberative or persuasive advantage over B. Ego depletion gives manipulation one more entryway into our psychic economy. Because they are less able to withstand the unseen "pressure to acquiesce" exerted by manipulators,[14] individuals subject to ego depletion can more readily have their desires modified so that their actions end up benefitting others. As Thomas Hill has put it:

> Manipulation, broadly conceived, can perhaps be understood as intentionally causing or encouraging people to make the decisions one wants them to make by actively promoting their making the decisions in ways that rational persons would not want to make their decisions.[15]

Knowledge of the effects of ego depletion thus empowers would-be manipulators, enabling them to exploit the time order of choices in order to create a choice architecture that favors them and disempowers the rational agents they thereby manipulate.

Now, of course, it will often be the case that in situations of negotiation and the like, one party will have a deliberative advantage over the other. In most sales contexts, for example, salespersons have a significant advantage over the customer simply because they are far more knowledgeable

---

14. Baron, "Manipulativeness."

15. Thomas E. Hill, "Autonomy and Benevolent Lies," *Journal of Value Inquiry* 18 (1984): 251.

about the product. Such informational asymmetries can be remedied to some degree, but probably not completely eradicated, and to that extent, such asymmetries help to make manipulation possible. But from the standpoint of the ethics of manipulation, what makes ego depletion a particularly worrisome phenomenon is its pervasiveness and the ease with which it can be induced on the spot. Those with the ability to induce ego depletion in others, even lacking the explicit understanding that this is what they are doing, hold a decided advantage in non-cooperative deliberations. Even though they engage one another on rational terms, they do not engage one another with their full inherent capacities as rational agents, so that one party stands in a privileged position with respect to achieving her rational aims.

Ego depletion is thus a worrisome phenomenon in light of how manipulation is usually philosophically characterized. Yet ego depletion also challenges this picture of manipulation in one important respect. Our paradigm of manipulation is interactive—that is, we tend to think of manipulation as a state that A induces in B through A being present to, and engaged with, B in some communicative act. The manipulations made more probable by ego depletion, however, are not entirely interactive. For ego depletion can make individuals more susceptible to manipulation that occurs at many causal removes from the manipulators. Indeed, it is likely that most of the manipulation facilitated by ego depletion is what we might call *ambient* manipulation. Such manipulation occurs when an individual operates within a constructed environment designed to encourage her to make certain choices, even without those doing the encouraging being present. The modern supermarket, for example, is a deeply manipulative environment, despite there being no individual actually present to do the manipulating. The number of products at a typical U.S. supermarket has tripled in one generation and now numbers in the tens of thousands, including (typically) about 200 varieties of salad dressing, 300 varieties of cookies, and 40 varieties of toothpaste.[16] Furthermore, the supermarket is an environment that pedals the narcissism of small differences. Product choices are minutely differentiated: organic versus conventional produce; whole fruit versus prepped; low sodium and low fat; soda in 12-, 22-, or 64-ounce containers; and shampoo, conditioner,

---

16. Barry Schwartz, *The Paradox of Choice: Why More Is Less* (New York: Ecco/Harper Collins, 2003).

and shampoo *plus* conditioner. The opportunities for effortful deliberation, and hence for ego depletion, are staggering—and while I will not specu- late on what motivates the marketing tactics deployed by supermarkets, it hardly seems coincidental that sugary products and cigarettes are usually the last items available before checkout.

On its face, it might appear a stretch to call the supermarket a manipulative environment. After all, no person is present engaging in the overt verbal trickery, withholding of information, and so on that we associate with manipulation. On the contrary, the supermarket is an information-saturated environment, cluttered with pricing information, nutritional data, and recipe ideas. However, the supermarket, as a built environment, is designed to take advantage of ego depletion—to so bom- bard us with choice opportunities that our volitional control wears down. And who has not left the supermarket struck by the divergence between the healthfulness of the items on our shopping lists and the preponder- ance of junk foods in our carts?

The sociologist Barry Schwartz has proposed that the "official dogma" of Western industrial societies is that the more choice people have, the more freedom they have, and the more freedom people have, the higher their welfare or happiness. Schwartz contends that while providing peo- ple *some* measure of choice promotes freedom and happiness, modern industrial societies have passed the tipping point where additional choice actually diminishes freedom and happiness. Societies with boundless consumer choices raise our expectations for our choices, only to disap- point us; make acts of choice more taxing and energy-intensive, some- times even to the point of inducing volitional paralysis; and induce states of regret and second-guessing, as we imagine that since there are so many choices available to us, for each choice we make, there is some imagined alternative that would have been better. Schwartz goes so far as to sug- gest that this official dogma has contributed to the explosion of clinical depression.[17]

Schwartz is principally concerned with the impact that seemingly lim- itless choice options has on well-being. However, we ought be equally concerned with the impact that seemingly limitless choice has on our susceptibility to manipulation and on our autonomy more generally. Our choice-saturated societies are incubators for ego depletion. In a world with

17. Schwartz, *Paradox of Choice.*

over 300 cable television channels, several thousand cell phone calling plans, and multiple options as to where to school one's children, opportunities for choice are pervasive. But so too are opportunities for ego depletion and manipulation, either through direct interaction with others or via the ambient sorts of ego depletion I have been describing.

Autonomy and Character

A second worry about ego depletion concerns its consequences for attributions of autonomy. It is not obvious that manipulation is possible only among agents who are autonomous. Non-autonomous but still rational individuals could perhaps manipulate others, as well as being manipulatable themselves. However, I follow Kantians in holding that the connection between autonomous agency and rational agency is very tight, perhaps even analytic. That is, I am not quite sure how to make sense of the possibility of an agent who is self-governing but nonrational. To govern oneself is presumably to make choices that reflects the reasons one takes for making those choices, and so autonomy appears to presuppose some measure of rationality. Furthermore, what renders manipulation ethically suspect is that it bypasses or enfeebles our rationality.[18] Since ego depletion seems to make such bypassing or enfeebling much easier, it functions, at one remove, as a threat to our autonomy.

However, we must be careful in describing this threat. After all, ego-depleted individuals do seem morally responsible for their actions.[19] First, the ego depleted act *from reasons* when they make choices influenced by ego depletion. The ego depleted do not act against their better judgment in the moment, so to speak. Indeed, ego-depleted individuals may be doing precisely what they seek to do in such choice settings. And as Todd Long has argued,[20] the mere fact that a choice is made on the basis of manipulated information does not entail that we are not responsible

---

18. Noggle, "Manipulative Actions."

19. Neil Levy, "Addition, Responsibility, and Ego-Depletion," in *Addiction and Responsibility*, edited by J. Poland and G. Graham (Cambridge, MA: MIT Press, 2011), 104–105.

20. Todd Long, "Moderate Reasons-Responsiveness, Moral Responsibility, and Manipulation," in *Freedom and Determinism*, edited by Joseph Campbell, Michael O'Rourke, and David Shier (Cambridge, MA: MIT Press, 2004); and "Information Manipulation and Moral Responsibility," this volume.

for such choices. Second, those reasons in fact move them to act, so they do not suffer from weakness of will, compulsion, and the like. Hence, ego depletion does not inhibit our ability to rationally guide our conduct at the time we act.[21] In this regard, ego-depleted choices are (I will say) *weakly autonomous*, inasmuch as ego depletion still makes it possible for agents to act on reasons they recognize.

As I argued above, ego depletion facilitates manipulation because practical reasons that might otherwise be psychologically efficacious in individuals are not. Robert Noggle has observed that manipulation attempts to adjust others' internal psychological levers, but different acts of manipulation adjust different levers.[22] Manipulation can target others' beliefs, desires, or emotions. Understanding precisely which kind of lever is adjusted when manipulators exploit ego depletion requires further empirical study, as well as engagement with some complex and controversial questions in moral psychology. Indeed, a plausible account of how ego depletion enables manipulation could reference the manipulation of belief, of desire, or of emotion. In one regard, manipulation facilitated by ego depletion resembles the manipulation of emotions, since the manipulator takes advantages of ego depletion to make certain options appear more salient to her victim, much in the way that Noggle proposes that the manipulation of emotions shifts agents' attention or sense of relevance.[23] However, it seems most likely that ego depletion enables manipulation because it involves what Richard Holton has called "judgment shifts." In judgment shifts, agents who are faced with strong desires end up decoupling their judgments about what it is best for them to do from their desires. Holton proposes that this occurs when we are tempted to act against our better judgment,[24] but ego depletion appears to involve judgment shifts that are not catalyzed by the presence of some tempting alternative that moves us to act contrary to our best interests or reasons. Manipulation facilitated by ego depletion instead has the following form: A manipulates B into X-ing because B, being ego depleted, does X based on reason R_1, but would not have done X had she not been ego depleted, because other reasons R_2, R_3, and so on would have been sufficient to motivate her to

---

21. John Martin Fischer, *The Metaphysics of Free Will* (Oxford: Blackwell, 1994).

22. Noggle, "Manipulative Actions," 44–47.

23. Noggle, "Manipulative Actions," 46.

24. Richard Holton, *Willing, Wanting, Waiting* (Oxford: Oxford University Press, 2009).

do other than X. But B's doing X has B's full rational endorsement in the context of choice. As Neil Levy puts it:

> Since ego depletion induces judgment shift, the agent cannot reasonably be expected to take action of a kind that would prevent her from acting in accordance with her new judgment: After experiencing judgment shift, agents do not remind themselves of their values, or take other steps to test whether their (new) all-things-considered judgment coheres with their values, precisely because they *have* experienced judgment shift and are satisfied with their decision.[25]

Ego depletion thus enables the manipulation neither of beliefs nor of desires taken in isolation. Rather, ego depletion interferes with agents' executive function so as to produce desires that, in turn, bar agents from recognizing and acting upon their all-things-considered judgments.

Ego depletion thus makes a difference not to acting rationally as such but to whether we do what we most have reason to do. In this respect, ego depletion enables manipulation because it threatens what I will call *strong autonomy*: our capacity to appraise reasons for action and subsequently do what we take ourselves to most have reason to do. As Moti Gorin has proposed in this volume, victims of manipulation are wronged because manipulators induce attitudes in them that do not track reasons.[26] Manipulators are not concerned to influence those they manipulate so that they choose and act on the basis of reasons (or on the basis of the best reasons). The manipulator's efforts to change the manipulee's attitudes have a purely causal aim, to induce modifications to those attitudes that the manipulator desires, irrespective of whether the attitudes so induced reflect reasons the manipulee would otherwise endorse. Ego depletion thus provides those bent on manipulation with a causal tool with which to detach the attitudes of those they manipulate from their reasons.

The irrationality of ego-depleted choices, as I suggested earlier, stems largely from the ways in which it makes relevant the otherwise irrelevant temporal ordering of choices. Ego depletion is likely to result in patterns in which earlier choices are more likely to result in strongly autonomous

---

25. Levy, "Addiction, Responsibility, and Ego-Depletion," 106.

26. Moti Gorin, "Towards a Theory of Interpersonal Manipulations," this volume.

choices than later ego-depleted choices. More worrisome is that the later choices can undermine the effectiveness of the earlier choices, as a person who exercises volitional control in order to eat a healthy diet becomes ego depleted and succumbs to temptations later on. If, in the spirit of thinkers such as John Rawls, what we are concerned with is the shape of a person's life and her ongoing capacity to exercise her rationality in the pursuit of her conception of the good, then this pattern of strongly autonomous choices alternating with weakly autonomous choices should trouble us. This pattern underscores that the extent to which *a person* is autonomous cannot be evaluated merely episodically, in terms of her choices and actions taken in isolation. Rather, a person's autonomy must be appraised in terms of the interrelationships among her choices and actions.

Moreover, ego depletion accords well with—and in fact extends—the situationist trend in social psychology. Situationism claims that the human behavior is more heavily influenced by external or situational factors than by durable psychological traits or personality features. Setting matters more than character, say situationists. The well-known experiments in the situationist tradition (Milgram's obedience experiment, Zimbardo's imprisonment experiment, the various bystander experiments, Asch's group conformity experiments, etc.) suggest that situational factors exert significant influence on a wide range of behaviors, including altruism, willingness to defy authority, and so on. Ego depletion adds to this picture that strong autonomy itself is in important ways situationally influenced—that those whose environments place greater demands on their volitional capacities will be more likely to have their rationality manipulated and compromised. Characterological differences in self-control and the like are therefore less stark then they are presented in the Platonic-Aristotelian tradition in moral psychology. For even those with high levels of self-control are apparently susceptible to ego depletion that makes their choices less than fully rational. Furthermore, ego depletion suggests that interpersonal differences in self-control are likely to be narrower than *intra*personal differences in self-control—that is, differences in the effectiveness of self-control when subject to decision fatigue and when not subject to it. Thus, differences in manipulability probably are less personal and more situational.

This conclusion runs counter to much of the traditional philosophical literature on self-control and volitional capacities. For virtue theorists like Aristotle, differences in volitional capacities stem from differences in acquired character. Some individuals are fortunate enough to have been habituated to be temperate, courageous, and so on, and it is a mark of their having such virtues that their psychologies are harmonious in the sense that their values, desires, choices, and actions do not conflict. The temperate person, for example, not only seeks to be temperate and chooses temperate actions but also experiences pleasure at doing so. The phenomenon of ego depletion suggests that such harmony is rare or ephemeral. But more fundamentally, it implies that our vulnerability to manipulation may not reflect good character so much as good timing.

Poverty, Altruism, and Social Justice

Lastly, ego depletion helps to explain why the achievement of social justice and the alleviation of poverty have proven to be such intractable policy goals. In popular politics, postwar conservatism has tended to see poverty as a moral failing, stemming from family breakdown, lack of initiative, and so on. Liberalism has tended to attribute the resistance of poverty to lack of opportunity, poor education, and public policy failures. Broadly speaking, conservatives see poverty as effected by bad choices, whereas liberals see it as effected by bad environments.

Ego depletion suggest conservatives are correct in one respect, but liberals are correct in another: the *choice environments* in which the poor typically live are especially conducive to choices that maintain persistent poverty.

As noted above, modern consumer societies make available to us choices unprecedented in their number and complexity. Ego depletion, however, is not simply a function of the choices available to us. It is also a function of the resources with which we deliberate about the various options available to us. Those with fewer resources must exert greater willpower or self-control precisely because their lesser resources necessitate their deliberating about tradeoffs among a wider range of options. Consider a relatively ordinary decision: whether to replace a pair of shoes whose soles have cracked. For the well-to-do, such a decision may bring about ego depletion in the ways I outlined before: the buyer must choose among hundreds of styles. But the poor must not only confront this plethora of options. They must also confront tradeoffs that the wealthy do not: If I buy these shoes, will I have bus fare for the week?; Will I be able to pay for my parents' medications?; and so on. The wealthy can make these decisions based on preference alone. Yet for the poor, day-to-day life is more volitionally stressful due to their lesser resources.

Hence, in addition to all the other forms of scarcity faced by the poor, they face an environment in which willpower and self-control turn out to be scare as well. This scarcity is why many behavioral economists now hypothesize that ego depletion encourages behaviors that reinforce poverty. Conditions of scarcity have distinct psychological effects. Individuals with fewer economic resources have to make more choices, and more difficult choices, about how to deploy those resources. Harvard economist Sendhil Mullainathan[27] compares the situations of the rich and poor to that of two travelers packing for a future trip. The poor traveler has a small suitcase, the rich traveler a large suitcase. The rich traveler can pack all her essentials with space for discretionary items or for items acquired while traveling. The poor traveler cannot fit all her essential items in her smaller suitcase. The rich traveler will find packing an easier, less cognitively and emotionally demanding task. The open space in her suitcase is "bought" at a relatively cheap cost, since it would otherwise be filled with nonessential, discretionary items. Moreover, the rich traveler has much a greater margin for error than the poor traveler. If the poor traveler chooses badly, he will be missing some essential item. Hence, he must be a more vigilant and careful packer. Furthermore, Mullainathan suggests, the richer traveler will appear to others to be a more careful packer!

This metaphor seems to capture the volitional plight of the poor. Their relative lack of resources magnifies the significance of each choice, since each such choice is more likely to require substantive tradeoffs. The ego depletion hypothesis thus helps to explain the empirical finding that those in poverty are more likely to engage in self-defeating and seemingly irrational conduct, conduct that helps to keep them impoverished, because of the greater demands that poverty makes on their choice reservoir.

The economist Dean Spears has recently provided experimental corroboration for these conclusions.[28]Spears's team traveled to villages in India with varying levels of wealth.[29] A set of the participants were first

---

27. Sendhil Muallainathan and Eldar Shafir, *Scarcity: Why Having Too Little Means So Much* (New York: Times Books/Henry Holt, 2013), pp. 69–70.

28. Dean Spears, "Economic Decision-Making in Poverty Depletes Cognitive Control," Working paper #213, Princeton University Center for Economic Policy Studies, December 2010. http://www.princeton.edu/ceps/workingpapers/213spears.pdf.

29. That Spears conducted his research in rural India should alleviate worries that the findings about ego depletion enumerated here reflect the idiosyncratic attributes of WEIRD (Western, educated, industrialized, rich, and democratic) societies.

asked to squeeze a handgrip, with the amount of time spent squeezing the handgrip measured. They were then given the opportunity to buy a package of soap at significant discount from its retail price. Most deliberated for only a few seconds, and 42 percent opted to buy the soap. The experimenters then asked participants to squeeze the handgrip a second time, again measuring the grip time. Richer participants showed no significant differences between the first and second grip durations. However, the poorer participants were typically unable to grip as long the second go around. Spears concludes that poverty appears to make "economic decision-making more consuming of cognitive control for poorer people than for richer people."

It does not obviously follow from these findings that ego depletion and poverty will correlate in a linear way. One factor that has not yet been investigated in the ego depletion literature is the extent to which individuals see various options as 'live,' in William James's sense. In order, for instance, for choosing between two alternatives to result in ego depletion, an agent must see both options as live—that is, as genuine possibilities for her. Yet at certain very low levels of poverty, some alternatives may be sufficiently costly that agents rule them out *ab initio*, and it is only at higher levels of income that such alternatives seem sufficiently attainable that ego depletion can exert its effects. Furthermore, it may be that susceptibility to ego depletion does not diminish in a linear way as income or wealth grow, precisely because various alternatives that were previously not viewed as live become live with growth in income and wealth. My own suspicion is that modern, well-to-do societies may contain large swaths of individuals who are especially susceptible to ego depletion because they simultaneously occupy a stratum of income that enables them to see the acquisition of various consumer goods as live while being subjected to media that expose them to images of far greater wealth and to advertising for coveted consumer status symbols. Nevertheless, even if we lack a full understanding of the causal relationship between wealth and ego depletion, this does not empirically undermine the extant findings that identify a rough relationship between low levels of wealth and higher levels of susceptibility to ego depletion.

As mentioned earlier, ego-depleted choices appear to satisfy standard conditions for moral responsibility. Yet at the same time, they do not seem to be strongly autonomous, and (arguably) are not blameworthy. From a retributive perspective, those whose choices are shaped by ego depletion do not obviously deserve blame if the causal influence of ego depletion is great enough to render them incapable of choosing other than in an ego-depleted way. From a consequentialist perspective, that ego depletion is pervasive, difficult to avoid, and grounded in apparently universal attributes of human psychology suggests that blaming individuals for their ego-depleted choices would have few good consequences. Conservatives are thus correct about a proximate cause of poverty—that the poor too often make impulsive, self-defeating, or irrational choices—but liberals are correct about one of its background causes: poverty itself, with its power to deplete our volitional resources. Put in terms of manipulation, the poor suffer ambient manipulation to a greater degree than the well-to-do. Poverty is thus a source of poor self-control and a result of poor self-control. In this respect, Aristotle's belief that virtue requires various external goods should be seen in a new, and ironic, light. Temperance, at least, is easier for the rich, but not because they are any more virtuous than the poor.

Compounding this is the finding that exercising volitional control also appears to suppress altruistic tendencies. DeWall et al. subjected participants to a series of tasks.[30] In the first, subjects given a page of text were instructed to mark every occurrence of the letter *e*. In the second, subjects were again given a page of text. Some were again asked to mark every occurrence of *e*, but others were instructed to mark every *e* except if it was followed by a vowel or found in a word in which a vowel occurred two letters earlier. As expected, subjects assigned the more complex *e*-marking task worked more slowly. The researchers then asked both subject groups to read hypothetical scenarios in which they were asked to provide money or other help (donating money to a terminally ill child, giving directions to a lost person, lending someone a cell phone, etc). Those in the second group—those who had to mark the specific subset of *e*'s in the text—showed less willingness to help, a result the researchers attributed to the fact that the more complex text-marking task required them to work against the inclination established by the first task—that is, to mark every *e*. In other words, the second set of subjects were more ego depleted than the first and so demonstrated a lesser willingness to help others.

In a similar vein, Achtziger, Alós-Ferrer, and Wagner found that ego-depleted individuals become less cooperative.[31] They subjected participants

30. C. N. DeWall et al., "Depletion Make the Heart Grow Less Helpful: Helping as a Function of Self-Regulatory Energy and Genetic Relatedness," *Personality and Social Psychology Bulletin* 34 (2007).

31. Anja Achtziger, Carlos Alós-Ferrer, and Alexander Wagner, *Social Preferences and Self Control*, unpublished manuscript, 2010.

to the same text-marking task sequence and then asked participants to take part in the well-known "ultimatum game," in which two individuals determine how to divide a sum of money. The first player proposes a division and the second player can then accept or reject that offer. Ego-depleted individuals, it turns out, made lower offers than others, and were also more likely to reject low offers as unfair, even though, according to the game's rules, rejecting an offer means that neither player receives any money. Ego-depleted participants thus seemed more inclined to see others' offers as unfair even when they themselves would propose equivalent offers.

Taken together, these findings imply that ego depletion likely plays a role in the maintenance of poverty. The poor, because their environment places greater volitional demands on them, are more susceptible to manipulation. But the poor, again due to ego depletion, are less inclined to cooperate despite having more to gain from such cooperation. These tendencies likely reinforce one another, as individuals more susceptible to manipulation are exploited by others looking to manipulate rather than cooperate. Ego depletion, then, is likely to be a contributor to perceived moral pathologies within poor communities. Of course, I am not suggesting that the ego depletion, or any set of psychological factors considered in isolation, is wholly responsible for poverty and its persistence. Poverty is a complex condition due, no doubt, to a complex of causes, and neither I nor any other scholar investigating ego depletion is currently in a position to say how great ego depletion's contribution to poverty in fact is. Nevertheless, for policymakers, the ego depletion hypothesis implies social policies and conceptions of social justice, no matter how normatively attractive, are likely to flounder if they do not take ego depletion into account.

Conclusion

It is worth noting that ego depletion is not inevitable, for research has also found that a variety of factors appear to counteract it.[32] The consumption of glucose (except for those suffering from Type 2 diabetes), as well as laughter or other positive emotional experiences, seems to buttress or replenish volitional control.[33] Moreover, greater levels of self-awareness

---

32. Hagger et al., "Ego Depletion and the Strength Model."

33. D. M. Tice et al., "Restoring the Self: Positive Affect Helps Improve Self-regulation Following Ego Depletion," *Journal of Experimental Social Psychology* 43 (2007).

or self-monitoring help to overcome ego depletion. Activities that are self-affirming, such as recalling an incident in which one exhibited a trait one values, seem to enhance volitional control.[34] Furthermore, the *belief* that self-control is limited tends to be self-fulfilling, whereas those who affirm that their capacity to persevere or overcome exertion tend in fact to persevere in the face of ego depletion.[35] Individuals given the resources to monitor or track their efforts also appear less subject to ego depletion. For example, individuals who have a clock available to measure their performance on a task tend to become more aware of deterioration in their progress in performing the task and compensate with additional effort.[36]

Furthermore, our knowledge of ego depletion can be put to positive ethical use as well. For instance, consider addictive behavior.[37] The great majority of drug addicts are able to refrain from using their drug of choice for short windows of time. Indeed, one of the perplexities of addictive behavior is that addicts in the early withdrawal stage, when their physical dependence and desires are the greatest, nevertheless often manage to "get clean." It would be natural to expect that having weakened the bonds of physical dependence, addicts would then find it easier to forgo drugs. However, the contrary appears to be the case, a fact readily explained by ego depletion. The extraordinary resources needed to combat full-on addiction deplete addicts' willpower and self-control, making them *more* susceptible to their desires for drugs over the long term. Addiction wanes when addicts can break out of this pattern of persistent desire, typically by learning to avoid the situations, settings, or individuals they associate with drug use. Thus, ego depletion could be exploited for the benefit of addicts, by (for instance) imposing night curfews on those undergoing residential drug abuse rehabilitation to keep them away from drug markets.[38] Because ego depletion makes us more susceptible to manipulation, knowledge of its effects also makes us more susceptible to self-manipulation, a phenomenon we can leverage to our benefit.

---

34. B. J. Schmeichel and K. D. Vohs, "Self-affirmation and Self-control: Affirming Core Values Counteracts Ego Depletion," *Journal of Personality and Social Psychology* 96 (2009).

35. V. Job, C. S. Dweck, and G. M. Walton, "Ego Depletion—Is it All in Your Head? Implicit Theories About Willpower Affect Self-regulation," *Psychological Science* 21 (2010).

36. E. W. Wan and B. Sternthal, "Regulating the Effects of Depletion through Monitoring," *Personality and Social Pshcyology Bulletin* 34 (2008).

37. Neil Levy, "Addiction, Autonomy, and Ego-Depletion," *Bioethics* 20 (2006).

38. Levy, "Addiction, Responsibility, and Ego-Depletion."

But again, ego depletion is likely to be a permanent feature of late industrial society. No doubt early hominids suffered ego depletion. Desire, as philosophers as diverse as Plato, Kant, and Buddha pointed out, is a ubiquitous feature of the human condition, and the management of desire is a perennial theme in philosophy and in the self-help genre. As Amartya Sen observes, our "freedom of agency" can be "constrained by social, political, and economic circumstances."[39] The phenomenon of ego depletion is another instance of how our modern social environment saturated with choice is, paradoxically, an environment that makes us more readily manipulated, and as a consequence, less autonomous and less free.

---

39. Amartya Sen, *Development as Freedom* (New York: Alfred A. Knopf, 2000).

10

Non-Machiavellian Manipulation and the Opacity of Motive

Kate Manne

WHEN WE THINK about manipulation, and what it is to be manipulative, it's natural to focus initially on some pretty unsympathetic characters. One of Robert Noggle's leading examples is Iago, who is essentially pure evil.[1] Sarah Buss begins with the effete seducer, Johannes, of Kierkegaard's invention.[2] Marcia Baron starts with Ayn Rand; Anne Barnhill with Dick Cheney.[3] Moti Gorin had the example of a used car salesman.[4] And I myself was initially drawn to thinking about Isabelle of *Dangerous Liaisons*, and the cutesy—but to my mind, creepy—Amelie of *Amelie*, who is a well-meaning but ultimately misguided meddler in the arc of people's lives.[5] These characters are all out of the ordinary in more ways than one,

---

1. Robert Noggle, "Manipulative Actions: A Conceptual and Moral Analysis," *American Philosophical Quarterly* 33, no. 1 (1996): 43.

2. Sarah Buss, "Valuing Autonomy and Respecting Persons: Manipulation, Seduction, and the Basis of Moral Constraints," *Ethics* 13, no. 3 (January 2005): 201–10.

3. Marcia Baron, "Manipulativeness," *Proceedings and Addresses of the American Philosophical Association* 77, no. 2 (November 2003): 37; Anne Barnhill, "What Is Manipulation?" this volume.

4. In the workshop version of his paper for this volume, the example was subsequently dropped, I believe.

5. In my original draft paper for this volume, entitled "Leaving Well Enough Alone," (ms) which I subsequently came to largely disagree with and ultimately discard. Thanks to Christian Coons and Michael Weber for allowing me to do this, and for encouraging me to write this paper by way of an alternative contribution—and for patiently waiting on the results. Thanks also to audiences at the BGSU Applied Ethics and Public Policy Workshop in March 2012, and to Marcia Baron for subsequent fruitful correspondence. Baron's contribution to this volume was also a big part of what prompted me to explore the relationship between manipulation and intention here, as will become clear later on.

of course. But part of it is that manipulating others is either a way of life for them, or at least seems to be something they have disturbingly few scruples about.

However, as each of the above authors either explicitly acknowledges, or at least seems to suggest via their choice of other examples, manipulation is very much an everyday occurrence too. And most people's manipulative tendencies are fortunately more local. Noggle talks about someone's sulking in order to get his own way about having Chinese food yet again.[6] Buss discusses the manipulative nature of many ordinary seduction techniques.[7] Baron talks about manipulating your children into behaving decently in a restaurant or on an airplane.[8] Barnhill has the example of baking cookies in order to make your house smell enticing to potential buyers.[9] And Gorin has the example of complimenting your boss on some genuine accomplishment of hers, in order to try to improve your standing in her eyes.[10] Some of these behaviors may not be ideal, perhaps, but they are morally small fry. And they are hardly out of the ordinary.

I suspect that manipulation is also pretty common in the context of many close—and seemingly otherwise good—relationships. Members of the same family often behave quite manipulatively towards each other, for example, even if they have little tendency to be manipulative in general. And most of us should cop to the fact that we ourselves can be a bit manipulative from time to time, at least towards particular others with whom we have a complex history. Nor is manipulation always a one-way street, in terms of social power. There can be manipulative dynamics, where both parties to the relationship try to manipulate the other, or one person effectively invites the other to pull their strings, so to speak. It can be convenient to be able to rely on someone else to finagle you into doing what

---

6. Noggle, "Manipulative Actions," 46–47. Noggle also explicitly observes in opening that "a large portion of the wrongs that people commonly do to one another—especially to friends and loved ones—are forms of manipulation. Even ordinarily moral people who seldom violate rights to life, liberty, or property—people who would not assault, abduct, or steal from one another—often engage in manipulation," 43.

7. Buss, "Valuing Autonomy and Respecting Persons," 220–21.

8. Baron, "Manipulativeness," 45. Moreover, in her contribution to this volume, Baron explicitly proposes to focus primarily on cases of manipulative behavior which are not the morally most egregious—i.e., where there is room for debate about its moral status; see her essay, "The *Mens Rea* and Moral Status of Manipulation," this volume.

9. Barnhill, "What is Manipulation?," this volume.

10. Moti Gorin, "Towards a Theory of Interpersonal Manipulation," this volume.

you really, in your heart of hearts, wanted to do all along. Manipulation of this kind may still be untoward, but it's not at bottom unwelcome. Indeed, quite the contrary.[11]

We might wonder whether common or garden-variety manipulation of these various different kinds can be understood as merely being much milder variants of the sort of behavior that Iago exhibits, when he deceives Othello into thinking that Desdemona is being unfaithful to him, which subsequently drives Othello mad. I suspect and am going to argue that there are important differences, which should subsequently make us cautious about the risk of over-generalizing from more extreme cases, with all their moral co-morbidities. In particular, I am not convinced that ordinary manipulative behavior is always conscious or intentional, even in a weak sense of what such a conscious manipulative intention might be held to be. For, I think that people's motives in behaving manipulatively are often quite opaque to them. This suggestion runs counter to certain going accounts of manipulation, such as Noggle's, as we'll see. And it would also have tricky—and interesting—moral implications, which I'll go on to explore as well.

But as well as the main intended upshot of this essay, I also have an ulterior—although not opaque—motive. For, I am generally inclined to think that many ordinary moral failings and foibles can be traced to divisions and opacities within the self. For example, we often tell ourselves not to do something, or at least that we ought not do it. But we keep doing it anyway, not so much because of weakness of will but, rather, because our will was never mobilized in the first place. That is, the original moral judgment was not insincere so much as hollow, in being disassociated from our sense of self, or at least our sense of agency. This is one common form of moral self-division.[12] And we may also sincerely avow one thing,

---

11. This goes against my own suggestions in "Leaving Well Enough Alone." (ms) In particular, I subsequently came to think that the relationship between successful manipulation and overriding the manipulated party's will is significantly more complicated than I had been allowing. Cf. Allen Wood, who emphasizes the subversion of the manipulated party's freedom in his contribution to this volume, "Coercion, Manipulation, Exploitation."

12. Elsewhere, I say more about the phenomenon of moral dissociation, and connect it with P. F. Strawson's idea that one can adopt the objective attitude towards oneself as well as others. I suggest that such possibilities make it plausible to temper motivational or judgment internalism, but that it need not be abandoned; see my "Tempered Internalism and the Participatory Stance," in *Motivational Internalism*, edited by Gunnar Björnsson, Caj Strandberg, Ragnar Francén Olinder, John Eriksson, and Fredrik Björklund (New York: Oxford University Press, forthcoming).

but find ourselves thinking another—or keep seeing the world in a way incompatible with our avowal.[13] Either of which discrepancies we may be unable to admit to, or even so much as recognize, at least without some prodding. Similarly, I think we sometimes tell ourselves that we're doing one thing, or acting in a certain spirit, when in reality what we're doing or feeling is nothing of the sort. This last possibility is what this essay will in large part be about. That is, I'll be interested in the ways in which our own motives in acting can be opaque or unclear to us. Or so it strikes me as natural to describe the cases that follow.

But a word of terminological caution is in order before we continue. The notion of an opaque motive is meant to be suggestive here, but it is ultimately merely stipulative. It will function throughout as a kind of neutral placeholder for whatever mental-cum-explanatory states do the relevant theoretical work in the examples adduced below.[14] Questions about whether or not these sorts of behavioral dispositions could really be *intentions*—of an unconscious or subconscious kind, say—or whether they should be understood as a distinct kind of motive will of course be controversial.[15] As will questions about the nature and ubiquity of *unconscious* motivations. And these are not controversies which I would be able to do justice to in the present context. So I will concentrate in what follows on the examples themselves and on some of their moral contours. I will not be taking a stand on how the psychological phenomena therein should ultimately be theorized—which, as I see it, would depend on a whole host

---

13. I think that cases of implicit bias are plausibly often like this.

14. I borrow this useful general strategy from Mark Schroeder; see his *Slaves of the Passions* (New York: Oxford University Press, 2007), 9. Not that my choice of terminology is risk-free, admittedly. In particular, some Kantians would naturally want to reserve a more specialized job description for the notion of a motive. Thanks to Marcia Baron for useful discussion of the possible distinctions one might draw here between motives, goals, and intentions (and also see below).

15. Cf. G. E. M. Anscombe's distinction between intentions and motives, the latter of which is held to be a broader category than the former. Although I'm not attempting to follow her usage here, she does hold that declarations about one's own motives in acting may be sincere but false. And motives are said to "interpret" a person's actions (§12). Whereas Anscombe claimed, notoriously, that acting intentionally involves a kind of spontaneous knowledge or awareness of what one is doing. In particular, she claims that denying one's awareness of what one is doing, or declaring merely observational knowledge thereof, is to "refuse application" to the sort of 'Why-question' whose applicability is a mark of genuinely intentional actions. She goes on to discuss the "curious intermediary" answer to this question, "I don't know why I did it" or "I found myself doing it," which culminates in the suggestion that these actions may be *voluntary* without being intentional (§16). G. E. M. Anscombe, *Intention* (Oxford: Basil Blackwell, 1957).

of delicate issues within both moral psychology and the philosophy of action.[16]

I

Let me make a start, then, by telling you a story. Joan is a woman in her late sixties, who now lives alone. Her partner of many decades died a few years ago, and they never had any children. She has a few friends who live locally, but she is generally pretty isolated. So Joan is, as one might expect, rather lonely. Although, being a proud person, she'd be loath to ever admit it.

But Joan does find herself wondering, increasingly resentfully, why her younger brother and his two teenage children don't come to visit her more often. They live only one state over, a mere four-hour drive away. And they don't even call. Not that it really matters, Joan would be quick to add—she is perfectly all right on her own. It is just that she is a little shocked that her only remaining relatives have barely paid her the time of day, ever since the funeral. Which they left early, she could not help but notice. Or so she might remark in conversation, or think darkly to herself.

Still, Joan is determined to keep up what she might describe as *her* side of the bargain, when it comes to preserving good family relations. In particular, she has come to make a point of sending each of her relatives an expensive and carefully chosen birthday gift, whenever their birthday rolls around. Although she can little afford to make such extravagant purchases, given her modest pension, she keeps doing so regardless. She tells herself that she is being thoughtful and generous, and showing the proper family spirit—*somebody* has to make an effort to keep up the connection. Or again, so she might say, if only to herself.

I doubt that it will come as a surprise when I tell you that, at this point, Joan's gifts are effectively functioning as a rebuke to the relatives she feels hurt and wronged by. Her gifts are effectively *designed*—to use another suggestive expression—to make them all feel guilty for not paying her more attention. Her gifts have become pointed. And Joan is depicting herself here as the morally injured party, who is neglected and misunderstood, as

---

16. For two particularly insightful discussions of unconscious motives and their relation to reasons for action, see Nomy Arpaly, *Unprincipled Virtue: An Inquiry into Moral Agency* (Oxford: Oxford University Press, 2003); and J. David Velleman, *The Possibility of Practical Reason* (New York: Oxford University Press, 2000).

well as virtuous and long-suffering. She is playing the part, in other words, of a self-appointed martyr.

But nor will it come as a surprise, I'd hazard, if I told you that these truths are the furthest thing from Joan's mind in acting as she does. It would simply never occur to her that she is trying to lay a guilt trip on her relatives—and she might have a hard time so much as admitting that she is inwardly resentful.[17] We can even imagine her stumbling across and reading an article about passive aggressive gift-giving. She shakes her head over this behavior, evincing disapproval, without thinking to connect it to what she has been doing. Or maybe she goes through the mental motions of examining her own conscience, but quickly dismisses the possibility that she does anything at all like this. And if the charge was made to her by her relatives, or even a neutral third party, she would be incredibly defensive and genuinely surprised. She is just making an effort to be a good sister and aunt, she'd protest. What else can she do, since her relatives are evidently far too busy to visit her more regularly? And she is no longer capable of driving so far to see them. Or so she might declare, and genuinely believe (whether or not this is true independently of what may now have effectively become a kind of self-fulfilling prophecy).

I hope that the story I've just told will seem psychologically plausible, perhaps even familiar, to you. Passive-aggressive gift-giving is a common enough tendency. And, just to be clear, I don't mean to be moralizing here. For one thing, I think that most of us have probably caught ourselves doing things of this general nature from time to time as well. And I also feel a fair amount of sympathy for Joan, although it of course doesn't follow that what she's doing is unobjectionable. How to think about her behavior morally remains less than clear to me, as I'll eventually explain. But first, we should ask: what exactly is she doing?

---

17. I am aware of how gendered this example might seem. But altering the gender of the key character here—as I was initially inclined to do—doesn't feel natural to me. These sorts of scripts *are* often gendered. (A similar script for men might be learned helplessness, where certain basic household chores are simply not done, or else are done so poorly, that others, usually women, end up taking over.) And if women are traditionally relied upon to buy the birthday gifts in a family, then it is not all that surprising that this would become a natural social outlet for aggression. Other forms of passive aggressive gift-giving include buying the recipient slightly the wrong thing—or completely the wrong thing—in addition to leaving the price tag on (especially if the item was clearly rescued from the discount bin). Some people also describe in great detail the much better present that they very nearly got you, but for some reason didn't. And there is also the trick of giving a nice gift to some people, and a mean or peculiar gift to others, on the same occasion. Which is awkward for everyone.

II

In particular, we should ask: Are Joan's actions manipulative? I take it to be very natural to describe them in this way.[18] We can readily imagine Joan's relatives reaching for this word when they try to characterize their unease or even anger with her behavior. And if there was a debate between her brother and his children (say) about whether or not the charge is fair, my own intuitions would tend to side with the prosecution, given the case as described so far.

But there is a potential ambiguity about what it means to behave manipulatively which is worth bringing out here. It might mean *being* manipulative as a person, insofar as you act in this way—even if you are not a manipulative person generally. But the thought is that the more you do this sort of thing, or at least are inclined to do it, the more manipulative of a person you are or become. On the other hand, behaving manipulatively might mean merely that your *action* is manipulative, whether or not you are *being* manipulative in acting in this way. For, it is natural to say that some actions are designed to achieve such-and-such, even if this isn't the agent's design or intention in so acting. That is, it seems to me that an action can sometimes be truly described as having a certain purpose, or having a certain success condition, even if we would at least hesitate to ascribe such a purpose or intention to the agent in performing it. These actions might be said to have something of a life of their own, then.[19]

One reason this might happen is sheer force of habit. Suppose that I have been trying for a long time to get you to like me. But I've gradually become discouraged and less enamored with this idea—or simply with you. I thus no longer intend to try to win you over. But my actions have not quite kept pace with my recent change of heart. So I keep behaving in a friendly (or even slightly obsequious) manner, more or less out of habit, even though I no longer really want to get you to like me or to make a

---

18. Or, alternatively, to describe them as *attempts* to be manipulative, if one is taking 'X behaved manipulatively towards Y' to imply success in this endeavor—as I myself am not here.

19. See Velleman for a similar distinction, which undergirds the claim that "it was my resentment speaking, not I," after I have gone off at a friend when I wasn't consciously intending to. But he argues that I can still be held responsible for my outburst, insofar as I am responsible for keeping myself under control; Velleman, *The Possibility of Practical Reason*, 126–27. Cf. Arpaly, who discusses and disputes the adequacy of this general suggestion; Arpaly, *Unprincipled Virtue*, 6–7.

friend of you. My actions thus seem designed to achieve a certain outcome which I the agent no longer want. They are merely the behavioral residue of a now defunct intention.

But, even if such a distinction can be made out satisfactorily, it's not obvious that Joan's behavior should be understood along these lines. We can imagine Joan's relatives being quite angry with her, and their anger seeming justified (depending on how the story was filled in in more detail—of which more later). In which case, we might be hesitant to commit ourselves to saying that it is merely Joan's *actions* that are manipulative rather than that *Joan* is behaving manipulatively in acting as she does. And this is despite the fact that Joan is not supposed to be (consciously) aware of what she's doing in the morally relevant sense. Nor could she easily *become* consciously aware of this, in the sense in which we can summon up a standing belief that is not currently present to consciousness. Which raises the interesting question of whether, and in what way, manipulative behavior might be thought to require intent. And would Joan's case (if it is thought to be psychologically plausible, and to be a plausible case of manipulation) obviate this requirement?

Not necessarily. For, as Marcia Baron points out (this volume), the claim that manipulative behavior requires intent permits of several importantly different readings. The strongest possible version of this claim would be that manipulative actions must always be done with the conscious *de dicto* intention of manipulating the target into doing, thinking, or feeling some fairly specific thing. That is, there must be a conscious intention to be manipulative as such, or under that very description. I take it that few theorists would buy a claim quite this strong. One can presumably be a manipulative person without having the concept feature prominently in one's mental lexicon. Children of a young age can be serial offenders when it comes to manipulation. And even adults do not usually manipulate their victims with a Machiavellian declaration of manipulative intent.

But Robert Noggle has endorsed a slightly weaker claim in the vicinity, to the effect that manipulative actions must always be done with a conscious *de dicto* intention to do something which is at least conceptually close to being manipulation, or perhaps even constitutes the correct conceptual analysis thereof. Noggle suggests that it would be counterintuitive to suppose that manipulative actions can be performed unknowingly.[20]

---

20. Noggle doesn't say much to explain why he thinks this. But he does suggest in passing that "it makes little sense to prohibit someone from acting manipulatively if she is unable to

And he subsequently moves to characterize manipulative actions in terms of the associated intention, such that an act counts as manipulative if and only if the agent intends to lead the target *astray*—that is, away from what the agent takes to be the ideal thing for the target to do, think, or feel.[21]

I think that Noggle's account of manipulation runs into several problems, not least of which is that manipulative people often seem to me to be trying to push their targets into doing, thinking, or feeling precisely what the manipulative person thinks they should. Joan's case plausibly illustrates this. She behaves manipulatively towards her relatives in order to get them to feel as guilty about their behavior towards her as she at least implicitly thinks they should.[22] It might be argued that she takes their envisaged guilt to be the right emotional state for them to be in, but on the basis of the wrong reasons. I'm not convinced that this is so though, since Joan's gifts are meant to serve as a pointed *reminder* (as well as adding to the stock) of what she might take to be exemplary reasons for her relatives to feel guilty about not paying her more attention. Each dollar she spends on them is essentially an investment in augmenting her sense of moral injury, and so *ought* to make them feel guiltier and guiltier, by her own lights. What a generous person she is! And how selfless, how lonely. They ought to be ashamed of themselves. They *still* haven't called, despite her always being so nice. This also serves to highlight another reason why Noggle's account – according to which manipulative actions have to be done from a "certain kind of insincere, conniving intention"[23] – seems likely to be too narrow, as well as overly rationalistic. People like Joan cannot afford to go around consciously

---

tell when she is doing so"; "Manipulative Actions," 48. I am not sure that this is true: I can "prohibit"—or, at least, strongly discourage—someone from behaving insensitively, even though they will *ipso facto* be unaware that they are behaving insensitively when they are indeed doing so. For another thing, it becomes very difficult on Noggle's account to tell whether one person has manipulated another (since they have to "look into their own hearts" to see whether they were intending to lead their target astray; "Manipulative Actions," 51). So a straightforward prohibition turns out to be off the table anyway.

21. Noggle, "Manipulative Actions," 48. It also seems clear from his discussion that he does not mean to allow that unconscious intentions (the possibility of which are not mentioned) might suffice to play this role.

22. Moreover, it's not clear to me that unremittingly narcissistic manipulators will typically have any real conception of how their targets would ideally be, independently of what they would prefer for them to be like. However, see Barnhill, "What Is Manipulation," this volume, for a more sympathetic take on Noggle's account of manipulation, along with several proposed amendments to it.

23. Noggle, "Manipulative Actions," 48.

getting the knives out. It would spoil the whole plot, in which they have cast themselves as victims.

In the present volume, Baron offers a helpful discussion of the *mens rea* of manipulation. Having introduced the question of whether manipulation requires intent, she suggests that an affirmative answer will generally hold when this claim is cashed out in a nuanced way. Baron explicitly rejects the above claim that an agent who behaves manipulatively towards another must have an intention to manipulate her target under that description—that is, what I am calling a manipulative intention *de dicto*. But this leaves open the possibility that she must have an intention to perform some action which is in fact manipulative, which I will call a manipulative intention *de re*. Baron initially considers in this vein the possibility that manipulative actions require the intention of leading the other to do something, via means which would in fact be manipulative. This requirement could hold whether or not the person thinks of these actions as *being* manipulative, or even as being attempts to lead the target *astray*, à la Noggle. But Baron goes on to suggest that even this requirement is likely to be too strong. For, agents behaving manipulatively may merely be *reckless* in pursuit of the goal of getting their target to do something. The idea is that manipulative actions can stem merely from "a determination to bring about a particular result and a willingness to be very pushy or somewhat deceptive to reach that result."[24] So agents need not intend to take the manipulative means to the relevant end here.

But maybe agents nonetheless have to be determined to bring about a particular result, or to pursue the relevant end, the achievement of which is a suitable *actus reus* to make for a manipulative action. And Baron does want to hang onto a claim in this vicinity—namely, that manipulation will at least generally involve an intention to get the other to do something (or to think or feel something, as I take it she would also want to allow).[25] Joan's case would be compatible with this requirement under the assumption that there are genuine intentions which are at least to some extent unconscious, with Joan's motive being one such.[26] For, Joan does not consciously intend

---

24. Marcia Baron, "The *Mens Rea*," this volume, p. 15.

25. See Baron, "Manipulativeness," 45.

26. This is a possibility which Baron and I are both at least friendly to (although as I noted in opening, I want to leave room for theorists to hold that intentions themselves have to be conscious, and that cases like Joan's involve unconscious motives of a somewhat different kind). Whereas Baron wants to explicitly allow for the possibility that intentions can be unconscious; see "Manipulativeness," 51, n.9. Thanks to Marcia for extremely helpful

to make her relatives feel guilty—which is the description under which her action might count as being manipulative. To be clear, Joan's actions are certainly done with a conscious intention under other descriptions. For example, she consciously intends to buy her relatives extravagant gifts for their birthdays. But shopping for a gift on Amazon does not a manipulative action make—that is, it does not in itself constitute a suitable *actus reus* here. So the end which Joan is consciously pursuing in acting as she does is not suitably manipulative. And the end which *is* suitably manipulative—namely, making her relatives feel guilty—is not something which she's conscious of in acting as she does.[27]

One might now naturally wonder whether this unconscious intention or otherwise opaque motive (however one wants to think about it, exactly) must at least be *available* to Joan's consciousness, in order for her actions to count as being manipulative. Or to count as being blameworthy, which may amount to much the same thing, if one is taking manipulation to be a moralized or thick concept.[28] I'll circle back to such questions a bit later on.

But whatever the case, I think that we can lack control over our own manipulative behavior in still deeper ways. For, as well as behaving manipulatively despite not consciously intending to, I think that people can behave manipulatively despite consciously intending *not* to. Or so the following example is intended to suggest.

III

"My whole life I've been a fraud. I'm not exaggerating. Pretty much all I've ever done all the time is try to create a certain impression of me in other people. Mostly to be liked or admired." So begins David Foster Wallace's story, "Good Old Neon."[29] The protagonist, Neal, talks about his motive

---

discussions about her views here, which I had originally misunderstood, having overlooked this important caveat.

27. Although, without having a suitably manipulative end (albeit possibly unconscious), it seems plausible to think that her actions would not count as being manipulative, although they might still leave her relatives *feeling* as if they had been treated manipulatively. I am therefore sympathetic to the upshot of Baron's nice discussion, "The *Mens Rea*," this volume, of the difference on this score between being manipulative and being intimidating, along with the difference between manipulating versus insulting someone.

28. See, e.g., Baron and Wood, both this volume, for discussions of this issue, on which I needn't commit myself one way or the other here.

29. David Foster Wallace. "Good Old Neon," in *Oblivion: Stories* (New York: Little, Brown, 2004), 141.

"deep down" in getting good grades in school and doing well in sports as having been merely to have the transcript and the varsity letters to show for it. He wants to do well simply in order to impress people, and he doesn't feel much of anything when he does get what he wants. All there is is the fear that he won't be able to get it again. Even his first sexual encounter is mired in self-consciousness and subsequent self-disgust. "Now I'm the guy that Mead let get to second with her," he thinks in the heat of the moment. He kicks himself afterwards that this was his primary thought, and that he subsequently never really felt "the soft aliveness or whatever of her breast."[30] The girl in question failed to make much of an impression generally. "I couldn't see anything except who I might be in her eyes."[31]

Neal tries many different things in an effort to stop being or at least feeling like a fraud, all throughout his twenties. These include "EST, riding a ten-speed to Nova Scotia and back, hypnosis, cocaine, sacro-cervical chiropractic, joining a charismatic church, jogging, pro bono work for the Ad Council, meditation classes, the Masons, analysis, the Landmark Forum, the Course in Miracles, a right-brain drawing workshop, celibacy, collecting and restoring vintage Corvettes, and trying to sleep with a different girl every night for two straight months."[32] Finally, Neal signs up for some intensive psychotherapy.

But Neal runs into the usual problem which besets people who are, or at least think they are, more intelligent than their therapists. He immediately sets out to create a certain impression of himself in Dr. Gustafson, to "lead him around by the nose." "And yet I wanted help and really was there to try to get help," Neal reports.[33] After six months, he finally tells his therapist about feeling like a fraud and feeling alienated from himself. ("I had to use this uptown word of course, but it was still the truth".)[34] He even admits that he has been trying to manipulate him all along. Dr. Gustafson smiles (knowingly?) and says: "If I understand you right, you're saying that you're basically a calculating, manipulative person who always says what you think will get somebody to approve of you or form some impression of you which you think you want." Neal reluctantly agrees that this is

---

30. Foster Wallace, "Good Old Neon," 141.

31. Foster Wallace, "Good Old Neon," 142.

32. Foster Wallace, "Good Old Neon," 142–43.

33. Foster Wallace, "Good Old Neon," 143.

34. Foster Wallace, "Good Old Neon," 144.

accurate, if "a little simplistic."[35] He confesses that "this fraudulent, calculating part of my brain [is] firing away all the time, as if I were constantly
playing chess with everybody and figuring out that if I wanted them to
move a certain way I had to move in such a way as to induce them to move
that way."[36] It's as good a description of an unremittingly manipulative
outlook as any that I've heard.

To Neal's bitter disappointment, Dr. Gustafson goes on say exactly the
sort of thing that Neal would have expected him to say all along—namely
that, in sincerely confessing to always being a fraudulent and manipulative person, he has at last said something sincere, thereby proving that he
can do it—that he really is capable of behaving non-manipulatively. But,
as Neal is quick to observe, the conclusion does not follow. A true confession can still be fraudulent and manipulative if the aim is not to expose
yourself or reveal a piece of who you are, but merely to be *seen* to expose
yourself or reveal a piece of who you are—such that the truth of what you
reveal is more or less incidental.[37] That Dr. Gustafson does not cotton onto
this possibility "was depressing, much the way that discovering somebody
is easy to manipulate is depressing."[38] Neal has been hoping that someone will be able to see through his act. At this point in the story, he gives
up on trying to get help. He instead tells his therapist that the therapy is
really helping—partly out of pity for him, partly out of boredom—mean-
while planning to kill himself. His "exhausting and solipsistic" mindset
has become too much for him to bear.[39]

To cut a long story short, Neal does kill himself. (I'm not ruining the
plot; you find this out at the beginning.) As he's preparing to do so, he
watches himself writing a final letter to his sister, Fern, who is the one
person he seems to care about. And yet:

> I won't pretend it was fully authentic or genuine.... A part of me was
> still calculating, performing—and this was part of the ceremonial

---

35. Foster Wallace, "Good Old Neon," 145.

36. Foster Wallace, "Good Old Neon," 145–46.

37. Neal also talks about the "paradox," which he thought of during a mathematical logic
class in college, that the more you become aware of being a fraud, the harder you will try
to appear authentic to others, and the more fraudulent you become—and become aware of
being; Foster Wallace, "Good Old Neon," 147.

38. Foster Wallace, "Good Old Neon," 155.

39. Foster Wallace, "Good Old Neon," 155.

quality of that last afternoon. Even as I wrote my note to Fern, for instance, expressing sentiments and regrets that were real, a part of me was noticing what a fine and sincere note it was, and anticipating the effect on Fern of this or that heartfelt phrase, while yet another part was observing the whole scene of a man in a dress shirt and no tie sitting at his breakfast nook writing a heartfelt note on his last afternoon alive, the blondwood table's surface trembling with sunlight and the man's hand steady and face both haunted by regret and ennobled by resolve, this part of me sort of hovering above and just to the left of myself, evaluating the scene, and thinking what a fine and genuine-seeming performance in a drama it would make if only we all had not already been subject to countless scenes just like it in dramas ever since we first saw a movie or read a book, which somehow entailed that real scenes like the one of my suicide note were now compelling and genuine only to their participants, and to anyone else would come off as banal and even somewhat cheesy or maudlin, which is somewhat paradoxical when you consider—as I did, sitting there at the breakfast nook—that the reason scenes like this will seem stale or manipulative to an audience is that we've already seen so many of them in dramas, and yet the reason we've seen so many of them in dramas is that the scenes really are dramatic and compelling and let people communicate very deep, complicated emotional realities that are almost impossible to articulate in any other way, and at the same time still another facet or part of me realizing that from this perspective my own basic problem was that at an early age I'd somehow chosen to cast my lot with my life's drama's supposed audience instead of with the drama itself, and that I even now was watching and gauging my supposed performance's quality and probable effects, and thus was in the final analysis the very same manipulative fraud writing the note to Fern that I had been throughout the life that had brought me to this climactic scene.[40]

The curtain falls; we all applaud; and the house lights go up.[41]

40. Foster Wallace, "Good Old Neon," 175–76.

41. Although there are interesting questions about the extent to which Neal might be a distinctively modern character, who owes his neuroses more to the ubiquity of television than the performativity of life in general (as the last passage clearly hints at; and this was also a preoccupation of Foster Wallace's more generally). The story also messes around with the

Neal's case suggests that not only can people behave manipulatively while not consciously intending to—as Joan's case was meant to illustrate—but people can even behave manipulatively despite consciously intending not to. For we can watch ourselves act, as if from the perspective of a third party. And we can watch ourselves watching ourselves—that is, be conscious of that self-consciousness—and so on without limit. It may wind up being unclear who we're acting, or performing, for. And, even when we feel ourselves to be the most spontaneous, to be the most ourselves, we may suspect ourselves of merely playing the part of someone who is *not* playing the part.[42] Such can be our predicament as both self-conscious and social creatures—which is to say, as the only animals who can perform for our own benefit, and stand back and watch the show, as both actor and audience.

IV

Is Joan to blame for her manipulative behavior? Is Neal responsible for being the way he is? I don't have anything definitive to offer by way of answers here. Let me just canvass a few reasons why I am in two minds about such questions.

First we should consider the obvious complications. Joan is not aware (or is not consciously aware, if one can hear a difference here) that she's behaving manipulatively, we're supposing. But she may or may not be able to figure this out by reflecting on her own behavior, or perhaps by being called to account as to what she's doing and why. One previously mentioned possibility is that Joan in fact couldn't become aware of her manipulative tendencies without their being extinguished in the process.

---

reader in a way that would be fun but for certain obvious and sad parallels between fiction and reality. But we are clearly meant to wonder: What is Neal attempting to get us to think of him here? Or is this really his one true confession? Plus there's an eerie twist at the end— which I won't spoil for you. Thanks to Adam Kelly for suggesting I read the story in the first place, and for an interesting subsequent discussion about the nature of secular confessions.

42. Similarly with displays of emotions which are sometimes beyond one's conscious control—but, crucially, not always. (Or one may at least have conscious control over getting into a position where you know you might really lose it.) For example, one may seriously ask oneself, after having burst out crying in front of someone and still in the midst of tears: Why am I actually crying? Am I crying because I am upset, or (at least partly) because I want to show you how upset I am? Cf. Velleman's example of crying as an authentic display, in playing the part of oneself; J. David Velleman, *How We Get Along* (Cambridge: Cambridge University Press, 2009), 15.

Suppose that Joan is a relatively and/or self-consciously conscientious person, who knows very well that manipulation is generally wrong, and also has a robust sense of what such behavior generally includes. Then it might be that her becoming aware of her opaque motive of making her relatives feel guilty by sending them expensive birthday gifts would render it more or less impossible for her to continue down this road—at least if we were to hold fixed her moral personality. For it would destroy her sense of herself as the martyr in this story. This would plausibly matter when it comes to assigning blame here. For, while we might be critical of Joan's tendency towards martyrdom, or her capacity for blindness as to what she's really doing, it would at least be nice to know that she wouldn't do this consciously. That is, she wouldn't set out to do things which would make her relatives feel guilty. This might make her all the more dogmatic though in insisting that she has no such ulterior motive in acting as she does. How could she even be suspected of this? For, she might insist, she is not a manipulative sort of person. And, as far as she's aware, she isn't— given that she is effectively inclined to look the other way while she does manipulative things.[43]

On the other hand, Neal is all too well aware of what he's doing, obviously. But he doesn't seem to be able to change his manipulative ways. It is virtually compulsive behavior: "I just couldn't seem to stop," he says.[44] And if 'ought' implies 'can'... well, you see where this is going. But it should also be recorded that Neal's relationships with others sound morally none too pretty. He recalls of his former lover, Beverly: "She said she'd never felt the gaze of someone so penetrating, discerning, and yet totally empty of care, like she was a puzzle or problem I was figuring out. She said it was thanks to me that she'd discovered the difference between being penetrated and really known versus penetrated and just violated." Yikes.

Beverly's indictment of Neal also brings out a potentially important difference between him and Joan. Whereas Neal sees people in a calculating, objectifying way—especially according to his former lover—Joan very well may not. People like Joan do not necessarily behave manipulatively

---

43. This sort of reasoning can also occur in second and third-person cases—often with pernicious results. He isn't the type to do that; so therefore, he didn't. Cognitive dissonance is thereby avoided. We see this pattern of reasoning being deployed to ironic effect by Antony in *Julius Caesar*: "But Brutus says he was ambitious; and Brutus is an honorable man." By *modus tollens*...Thanks to Daniel Manne for pointing out this sort of inference to me, and connecting it with the play.

44. Foster Wallace, "Good Old Neon," 143.

out of a sense of entitlement or contempt for other people, let alone a Machiavellian sense that these others are puppets or pawns in their own schemes.[45] In some ways, it is the opposite. For, people like Joan behave manipulatively as the result of feeling that they have lost control, or that they have been written off themselves. They are trying to regain some power from a position of felt powerlessness, in admittedly unseemly ways. And this is not to say that Joan envisages her relatives in a morally healthy way, of course. One is tempted to say that there is a kind of object permanence that is missing here, at the level of their personhood. They pop into and out of existence for Joan insofar as they figure in *her* life—that is, as injurious to her, having little by way of their own acknowledged independent reality. But it may be difficult for Joan to recover her sense of their reality when they very seldom visit. It's not personal, we might say to Joan, but in a way that is the problem. And there is also the simple point that people like Joan behave manipulatively because of real emotional vulnerabilities and unmet psychic needs of theirs (of which more later on). In which case, we might be inclined to try to acknowledge the reality of the sin without placing much blame on the sinner.

There is another reason for being hesitant to blame Joan for what she's doing. Suppose, as is easy enough to imagine, that her manipulative tendencies are more or less isolated to her passive aggressive gift-giving. Now, why might this be the case? Plausibly, the uncertain social meaning of giving someone a gift helps to create and sustain such motivational ambiguities. For, giving someone a gift is quite a bit more complicated than merely causing them to have some new object in their life.[46] It *says* something to the other person about their value or prospective value to you. In this case, it says "You mean so much to me." But whether this is an

---

45. Cf. Buss, who says that an agent who behaves in an excessively controlling fashion is treating his target as "a character in his plot, rather than as someone with whom he shares the world, someone whose plot interacts with his own in ways he has not himself plotted"; Buss, "Valuing Autonomy and Respecting Persons," 229. Joan does not seem quite like this though, on grounds I'll go on to suggest. But I do think that this is an insightful characterization of how some manipulative people, like Neal, tend to view and treat others. I see Neal as a non-Machiavellian character not because of how he thinks about others, but because of how he thinks about how he thinks about others—namely, with self-loathing and a real desire to change, albeit primarily for his own sake.

46. This point was first brought to my attention by a wonderful talk by Barbara Herman that I heard, entitled (as I recall) "Doing Too Much," in which she cited gift-giving as an example of a social practice in which doing too much (i.e., going 'over the top') can be just as problematic as doing too little.

overture or an unspoken rebuke can sometimes be hard to discern. And sometimes a gift really is just a gift, of course. All this gives Joan what is often and suggestively called 'plausible deniability.' That is, she can credibly go on telling not only others but also herself that she's doing one thing (i.e., being generous) while actually doing another (i.e., being manipulative). The ambiguous nature of gift-giving helps her keep up the charade.

Still, as I suggested earlier, it would nevertheless make sense if Joan's relatives were becoming increasingly irritated with her manipulative behavior. And we can make their irritation, even anger, seem quite reasonable by telling *their* side of the story, which has gone untold so far. For, while it is true that they live but a four-hour drive from Joan, they have very little money and even less by way of time. And crucially, they don't drive. In reality, going to visit Joan is an eight-hour ordeal involving a taxi, a train, and two long bus rides. This is not the real reason, though, why they don't visit her more often—although this may be what they tell each other and even themselves. But the truth is that Joan has never been an easy person to get along with. She is prickly and unpredictable, and wants people to go visit her but then tires of their company quickly. She has gone to little effort when they've visited her in the past. She is also liable to make little hurtful comments, to slip in snide remarks, about what they're doing with their lives—and what is it that they're wearing? It is quite a flattering outfit, since they've put on a little weight. A backhanded compliment if ever there was one.

Against such a backdrop, it would at least make psychological sense that Joan's gifts have gradually come to provoke exasperation and even anger in her relatives. For, they have cottoned onto what she's trying to do, even though Joan herself has not. Perhaps they have even asked her nicely not to spend so much money, since they cannot hope to reciprocate. They are annoyed that she's ignored them. And, more deeply, they wish that Joan would just come out and ask that they see each other more regularly, if that is really what she wants. And it isn't clear that it is. More likely, she is ambivalent—lonely but also hostile, and keener on having visitors in theory than in practice.

So the resentment here is mutual. And this attitude might seem not only understandable but also entirely reasonable on the part of Joan's relatives. This is good evidence, I take it, that what she is doing is somewhat blameworthy. Maybe we were just hesitant to assign blame to her because she is a rather pathetic figure. Who might nonetheless be to blame for acting as she does.

This possibility is bolstered by the observation that many theorists think that there is no general barrier to the moral assessment of actions which are done without a suitable *de dicto* moral motive. Consider Huck Finn-type cases, which have recently been widely discussed in the literature on moral worth or virtue (the flipside of the current coin). Huck Finn believes that he ought to turn Jim over to the slave-hunters, but ends up dissembling to protect him, much to his own surprise. Huck is subsequently disgusted by his own putatively immoral behavior, in failing to help return Jim to his "rightful owner."[47] But Huck nevertheless seems to deserve some moral praise for protecting Jim, given that he appears to act out of good if inchoate moral instincts.[48] Admittedly, the case does not have quite the same structure as Joan's case. For, Joan thinks that she is doing one thing (i.e., being generous) when she is actually doing another (i.e., being manipulative); whereas Huck intends to do one thing and winds up doing just the opposite. Still, one might think that if we can praise people for doing things which they don't consciously set out to do, then there is no general problem with assigning blame on such bases either.

One might also think that Joan can be blamed for failing to do something which she *does* have conscious control over—namely, scrutinizing her own motives in acting as she does. That is, we might hold that people are responsible for undertaking a certain inner activity—that is, some sort of process of self-examination—on a semi-regular basis. In which case, Joan's failure to recognize what she's up to might be the result of something like moral negligence, and subsequent self-deception, which can be criticized accordingly. Similarly, we might criticize her for not being more attuned to her relatives' perspectives, and focusing mainly or exclusively on how they are treating *her*. The thought being that her resentment would quickly dissipate, and her manipulative behavior would wane, if she was more sensitive and imaginative about what is going on in their

---

47. Mark Twain, *The Adventures of Huckleberry Finn* (New York: Vintage Classics, 2010), 103.

48. For some interesting recent discussions, see, e.g., Julia Driver, *Uneasy Virtue* (Cambridge: Cambridge University Press, 2001); Arpaly, *Unprincipled Virtue;* and Julia Markovits, "Acting for the Right Reasons," *Philosophical Review* 119, no. 2 (2010): 201–42. The case was originally introduced to the literature by Jonathan Bennett, in "The Conscience of Huckleberry Finn," *Philosophy* 49, no. 188 (1974): 123–34. I offer my own take on the case in my "On Being Social in Metaethics," in *Oxford Studies in Metaethics, Vol. 8*, edited by Russ Shafer-Landau (Oxford: Oxford University Press, 2013), 50–73.

lives. Her brother might be going through a nasty divorce at the moment. And the kids might be busy with school and their college applications. Not to mention that it would represent a sixteen-hour round trip for them.

But there are reasons to hesitate to add the duty to engage in such self-examination to the list of other duties we might plausibly be thought to have. For it's just not clear that the undifferentiated activity of self-examination will get us very far here. "Know thyself" is almost as general a piece of advice as the mandate "Be good," and it seems little more useful. We may be just as likely to end up rationalizing our own behavior, or reinforcing our own sense of victimhood, as we are to end up admitting that we are behaving rather badly. We may also wind up rationalizing away our own attempts at rationalization. But it does seem wise in general to at least make an effort to be conscious of our own desires and fantasies, and mindful of the ways in which our actions might be clumsy attempts to play them out. We can readily imagine, for example, that Joan fantasizes about her relatives coming to feel guilty about the way they have neglected her. At the more extreme end of things, she might find herself vividly imagining them being wracked with guilt at her funeral—if they bother to show up, that is, she thinks with real self-pity. But she never makes the connection between this maudlin fantasy of hers (and make no mistake, it is a fantasy, despite its grim content) and the reaction she tacitly supposes they might have upon opening her gifts—namely, abject guilt. The suggested lesson is this, then: we should be careful what we wish for, and the ways in which our actions might constitute attempts at wish fulfillment.[49]

Reflection of this kind is still quite hard to do, though, especially just on one's own. It is surely no accident that Neal sought therapy, and perhaps even that we can picture Joan most easily as being socially rather isolated. For, our opaque motives and hidden agendas will often come out more readily in conversation with others. Sometimes the sheer act of explaining ourselves to another person helps us to better understand, or

---

49. Iris Murdoch is particularly lucid on the moral liability that one's self-serving fantasies represent, and went so far as to claim that "the chief enemy of excellence in morality (and also in art) is personal fantasy: the tissue of self-aggrandizing and consoling wishes and dreams, which prevents one from seeing what is there outside one." Iris Murdoch, *The Sovereignty of Good* (London: Routledge & Kegan Paul, 1970), 59. She also explains that what seems "true and important" to her in Freudian theory is that the psyche is "an egocentric system of quasi-mechanical energy, largely determined by its own individual history, whose natural attachments are sexual, ambiguous, and hard for the subject to understand or control. Introspection reveals only the deep tissue of ambivalent motive, and fantasy is a stronger force than reason," 51.

forces us to face up to, what we are actually doing. And some people will also be able to bring certain patterns of behavior to our attention, or call us out regarding a suspicious amount of dovetailing between our unspoken desires and the likely results of our behavior. Provided that our unspoken desires aren't too hard to glean, of course—which oftentimes they won't be, at least to a person who knows us well.

But nor should we overstate the potential corrective influence of others here. On the contrary, some people seem to seek out others who can be relied upon to chip away at their conscience, or their sense of obligation, thereby relieving "the moral burden" (to borrow Michael Stocker's phrase). A wonderful scene at the beginning of *Sense and Sensibility* helps to bring this out. Mr. John Dashwood initially proposes to take three thousand pounds of his own fortune, and give it to his father's widow and her daughters, his half-sisters. Mrs. John Dashwood does not approve of this plan, though, and is determined to talk him out of it. And Mr. Dashwood surely has an inkling of this going into the discussion, given the alacrity with which he seizes on each of his wife's proffered counter-claims and spurious objections—all the while maintaining an air of utmost conscientiousness. Their exchange begins like this:

> "It was my father's last request to me," replied her husband, "that I should assist his widow and daughters."
>
> "He did not know what he was talking of, I dare say; ten to one but he was light-headed at the time. Had he been in his right senses, he could not have thought of such a thing as begging you to give away half your fortune from your own child."
>
> "He did not stipulate for any particular sum, my dear Fanny; he only requested me, in general terms, to assist them, and make their situation more comfortable than it was in his power to do. Perhaps it would have been as well if he had left it wholly to myself. He could hardly suppose I should neglect them. But as he required the promise, I could not do less than give it; at least I thought so at the time. The promise, therefore, was given, and must be performed. Something must be done for them whenever they leave Norland and settle in a new home."[50]

---

50. Jane Austen. *Sense and Sensibility* (New York: Dover, 1996), originally published in 1811.

"Well, then, *let* something be done for them; but *that* something need not be three thousand pounds. Consider," she added, "that when the money is once parted with, it never can return. Your sisters will marry, and it will be gone forever. If, indeed, it could be restored to our poor little boy–"

"Why, to be sure," said her husband, very gravely, "that would make great difference. The time may come when Harry will regret that so large a sum was parted with. If he should have a numerous family, for instance, it would be a very convenient addition."

"To be sure it would."

"Perhaps, then, it would be better for all parties, if the sum were diminished one half. Five hundred pounds would be a prodigious increase to their fortunes!"

"Oh! Beyond anything great! What brother on earth would do half so much for his sisters, even if *really* his sisters! And as it is— only half blood!—But you have such a generous spirit!"[51]

You can see where this is going. Eventually Mrs. Dashwood talks Mr. Dashwood out of giving his relatives so much as a penny. Between them they decide that the destitute widow is perfectly comfortable as she is—if anything, the obligation is the other way around. She should be giving *them* money, since she is practically rolling in it. In the film version, it is also hinted that being any richer would be detrimental to their characters.

This scene brings out a further complication when it comes to manipulative motives and the assignment of moral blame. Namely, sometimes the motive behind a manipulative action is not merely the agent's own. Mr. and Mrs. Dashwood are about as selfish as each other, but Mrs. Dashwood is clearly the more cutthroat of the pair. And Mr. Dashwood seems to solicit or at least welcome her in her ruthlessness to absolve him of his scruples. They are easily dispatched with – or, rather, redirected. Here, as elsewhere, other people can enable us to let ourselves go, morally. And not just morally. Who here has not upon occasion allowed our dining companion to convince us to order a dessert to share, or at least to have a taste of theirs? ("Well, if you're going to twist my arm...") And then proceeded to polish it off.

---

51. Austen, *Sense and Sensibility*, 5.

V

Manipulative actions have naturally been connected, as we've been see-ing throughout, to a tendency to be conniving and calculating, and to objectify other people.[52] They have also been identified as one end of a spectrum which runs from manipulation to *bona fide* coercion.[53] And in many ways this is right, of course. But I think there are other connections which deserve emphasis here as well, and which somewhat complicate the moral landscape, in practice and in theory. I've suggested in particu-lar that there are common psychological connections between manipula-tion and vulnerability and the sense of being powerless. For example, manipulative behavior is often a cry for attention—attention that may genuinely be owed to the person crying out for it. And it is also one end of a continuum which runs from manipulation to the mere anxiety to please, or to win the approval of others, by altering one's usual mode of self-presentation.

There might be a temptation to summarily declare that people should be more honest or authentic, rather than resorting to such underhanded tactics in order to get their due or to appear in the best light. And there is obviously something residually unattractive about manipulative behavior and manipulative people generally.[54] Yet we can readily imagine that Joan simply has too much to lose by admitting to her relatives—or even to her-self—that she is inwardly very lonely, that she needs more human contact. We might imagine that, as she knows, her requests or even pleas would have very little effect on them. For, while her relatives are not callous, they are also rather selfish, and they have their own lives to lead. And admitting that you need something and may not be able to get it can be emotionally

---

52. See, e.g., Noggle, "Manipulative Actions"; Buss, "Valuing Autonomy and Respecting Persons"; and Baron, "The *Mens Rea*," this volume.

53. See Wood, "Coercion, Manipulation, Exploitation," this volume.

54. So I don't take myself to be disagreeing with Baron here, when she says that, although manipulative actions are sometimes warranted, "being a manipulative person is never a good thing" in itself; Baron, "Manipulativeness," 37. I suspect that it's more a question of emphasis—where here, I am looking to emphasize the degree to which being manipula-tive can at least be understandable, as a psychological matter. Baron has room to allow this though. Indeed, she herself notes in closing that "reliance on such [manipulative] tech-niques may be due to powerlessness, and may be a reaction to being viewed as less than fully rational. For such people—for many children, and in the past and all too often in the present, women—perhaps the only means of persuading the other is to badger, beg, cajole, flatter, or lie," 50.

pretty devastating. It can also be humiliating to ask without receiving. So Joan acts out instead, much as a child might.

Neal is admittedly a much less sympathetic character than Joan. Even so, he might be thought to evince an extreme version of a rather natural tendency. Most of us care quite a bit—perhaps more than we would care to admit—about what others think of us. And there is a fine line between trying to show others our good sides, or live up to their expectations, versus putting on a show or trying to control what they think of us in a manipulative manner. And it isn't always clear to us which it is we're doing. Am I saying what I think, or saying what you want to hear, which I also happen to think? Do I in fact think this? Or am I just used to saying it, primarily for your benefit?

And is it always illicit to edit ourselves for others? Surely not—and as I'd presume almost everyone would acknowledge.[55] Yet we may underestimate the extent to which even being relatively unguarded and disinclined to put on a performance may be something of a luxury. People with little power often have to be quite careful, even crafty, about the image of themselves they're projecting into the world. People with unfamiliar faces in an environment may need to wear a mask in it, to be more or less expressionless, or to wear a little smile.[56] And sometimes one does not merely withhold one's thoughts and feelings, or refrain from behaving in the ways that one would ordinarily tend to. One positively embellishes or affects a certain attitude, in order to create a certain impression of oneself. Moreover, very different personae may need to be adopted in order to put one's best foot forward under different sorts of circumstances. Being two-faced generally gets a bad rap, of course. But people with multiple identities may need multiple faces, and to cultivate the ability to switch seamlessly between them.

Your face can also freeze in an expression slanted towards the world you inhabit with the most energy. To mention an example uncomfortably close to home: one may find oneself attempting to play the part of the sort of woman who philosophers generally find congenial, or at least

---

55. As Baron also notes in her contribution to this volume, even Kant was surprisingly tolerant of polite dissembling in order to facilitate smoother social interactions; Baron, "The *Mens Rea*," this volume, 115–16.

56. Although it should also be admitted that inscrutability can infuriate people. Women in particular are often required to be legible, interpretable, or as I have often heard it put, 'open.' So, sometimes, you can't win.

acceptable, upon entering the field. Forget the 'one,' actually; let's talk about me. It has not escaped my attention that my voice has dropped a few registers, that my prosody is more measured now. I wear glasses; I didn't used to. I am embarrassed to admit that my original Australian accent has gotten a bit weaker, notwithstanding my desire to keep it. Or do I actually want this? Am I in fact guilty of unconscious cultural cringe? More likely, I have unconsciously picked up on and unwittingly come to mimic the manner of the North American philosophers I primarily interact with and who I in some sense want to emulate.[57] I am particularly anxious to maintain a certain tone of voice, and a certain demeanor generally, during Q&A sessions—which teem with undercurrents of power, both toxic and exciting. A complicated mixture of assertiveness and relaxedness feels like the thing to aim for, regardless of how relaxed or unrelaxed I might feel (a distinction which becomes increasingly hard to make out, since feelings follow actions). Subsequent conversations have suggested to me that some people have come away believing that I am much more confident than I am. And quite likely this has worked to my advantage, for the most part. I admit, I don't agonize over it. I am not going to try to change—or at least, not anytime soon. And I wouldn't go so far as to call my behavior manipulative, albeit inadvertently so. But then again, who knows? Not me, quite possibly.

---

57. That some people are chameleons when it comes to picking up other accents apparently has a neurological basis. Or so I have been told. My (Australian) family and (American) spouse rightly poke gentle fun at me for being eager to point this out though, as I am admittedly wont to do. And as I have indeed just done.

Bibliography

Achtziger, Anja, Carlos Alós-Ferrer, and Alexander Wagner. *Social Preferences and Self Control*. Unpublished manuscript, 2010. http://ssrn.com/abstract=1869148.

Aleichem, Sholem. "Today's Children." In *Tevye the Dairyman and The Railroad Stories*, translated by Hillel Halkin. New York: Schocken, 1987.

Anderson, Scott. "Coercion." *Stanford Encyclopedia of Philosophy*, edited by Edward N. Zalta. http://plato.stanford.edu/archives/win2011/entries/coercion/.

Andre, Judith. "Power, Oppression and Gender." *Social Theory and Practice* 11, no. 1 (1985): 107–22.

Anscombe, G. E. M. *Intention*. Oxford: Basil Blackwell, 1957.

Aristotle. *Nicomachean Ethics*. In *A New Aristotle Reader*, edited by L. L. Ackrill. Princeton: Princeton University Press, 1987.

Aristotle. *The Rhetoric and Poetics of Aristotle*. New York: McGraw-Hill, 1984.

Arpaly, Nomy. *Unprincipled Virtue: An Inquiry into Moral Agency*. Oxford: Oxford University Press, 2003.

Atwood, Margaret. *The Handmaid's Tale*. New York: Random House, 1986.

Austen, Jane. *Sense and Sensibility*. New York: Dover, 1996.

Baron, Marcia. "Manipulativeness." *Proceedings and Addresses of the American Philosophical Association* 77, no. 2 (November 2003): 37–54.

Baumeister, Roy F. "Yielding to Temptation: Self-control Failure, Impulsive Purchasing, and Consumer Behavior." *Journal of Consumer Research* 28 (2002): 670–76.

Baumeister, Roy F., Ellen Bratslavsky, Mark Muraven, and Dianne M Tice. "Ego Depletion: Is the Active Self a Limited Resource?" *Journal of Personality and Social Psychology* 74 (1998):1252–65.

Beauchamp, Tom, and J. Childress. *Principle of Biomedical Ethics*, 6th ed. Oxford: Oxford University Press, 2008.

Benn, Stanley I. *A Theory of Freedom*. Cambridge: Cambridge University Press, 1988.

Bennett, Jonathan. "The Conscience of Huckleberry Finn," *Philosophy* 49, no. 188 (1974): 123–34.

Blumenthal-Barby, J. S. "Between Reason and Coercion: Ethically Permissible Influence in Health Care and Health Policy Contexts." *Kennedy Institute of Ethics Journal* 22, no 4. (2012): 345–66.

Blumenthal-Barby, Jennifer, and Hadley Burroughs, "Seeking Better Health Care Outcomes: The Ethics of Using the Nudge." *American Journal of Bioethics* 12, no. 2. (2012): 1–10.

Broyles, Sheri J. "Subliminal Advertising and the Perpetual Popularity of Playing to People's Paranoia." *Journal of Consumer Affairs* 40 (2006): 392–406.

Burgess, Anthony. *A Clockwork Orange.* New York: W. W. Norton, 1986.

Buss, David M. *The Evolution of Desire: Strategies of Human Mating,* rev. ed. New York: Basic Books, 2003.

Buss, Sarah. "Valuing Autonomy and Respecting Persons: Manipulation, Seduction, and the Basis of Moral Constraints." *Ethics* 115 (January 2005): 195–235.

Butler, Judith. *Gender Trouble: Feminism and the Subversion of Identity.* New York: Routledge, 1990.

Cave, Eric M. "Unsavory Sexual Seduction." *Ethical Theory and Moral Practice* 12 (2009): 235–45.

Cave, Eric M. "What's Wrong with Motive Manipulation?" *Ethical Theory and Moral Practice* 10, no. 2 (December 2007): 129–44.

Christman, John. "Autonomy and Personal History." *Canadian Journal of Philosophy* 21, no. 1 (1991): 1–24.

Christman, John. "The Historical Conception of Autonomy." In *The Politics of Persons: Individual Autonomy and Socio-Historical Selves,* 133–63. New York: Cambridge University Press, 2009.

Cohen, Stewart. "Justification and Truth." *Philosophical Studies* 46 (1984): 279–96.

Coons, Christian, and Michael Weber. *Paternalism: Theory and Practice.* New York: Cambridge University Press, 2013.

Copp, David. "Defending the Principle of Alternate Possibilities: Blameworthiness and Moral Responsibility." *Nous* 31, no. 4 (1997): 441–56.

Council on Ethical and Judicial Affairs, American Medical Association. "Sexual Misconduct in the Practice of Medicine." *Journal of the American Medical Association* 266 (1991): 2741–45.

Dancy, Jonathan. *Ethics Without Principles.* New York: Oxford University Press, 2006.

Davidson, W. P. "The Third-Person Effect in Communication." *Public Opinion Quarterly* 47 (1983): 1–15.

DeWall, C. N., R. F. Baumeister, M. T. Gailliot, and J. K. Maner. "Depletion Makes the Heart Grow Less Helpful: Helping as a Function of Self-Regulatory Energy and Genetic Relatedness." *Personality and Social Psychology Bulletin* 34 (2007): 1653–62.

Driver, Julia. *Uneasy Virtue.* Cambridge: Cambridge University Press, 2001.

Dworkin, Andrea. *Intercourse.* New York: Ballantine, 1987.

Dworkin, Gerald. *The Theory and Practice of Autonomy*. Cambridge: Cambridge University Press, 1988.

Faden, Ruth R., and Tom L. Beauchamp, with Nancy M. P. King. *A History and Theory of Informed Consent*. New York: Oxford University Press, 1986.

Fahmy, Melissa Seymour. "Love, Respect, and Interfering with Others." *Pacific Philosophical Quarterly* 92, no. 2 (June 2011): 174–92.

Feinberg, Joel. *Doing and Deserving*. Princeton: Princeton University Press, 1970.

Feinberg, Joel. *The Moral Limits of the Criminal Law, Volume 3: Harm to Self*. New York: Oxford University Press, 1986.

Fennis, B. M., L. Janssen, and K. D. Vohs. "Acts of Benevolence: A Limited-Resource Account of Compliance with Charitable Requests." *Journal of Consumer Research* 35 (2009): 906–24.

Fichte, J. G. *Foundations of Natural Right* [1796]. Edited by F. Neuhouser, translated by Michael Baur. Cambridge: Cambridge University Press, 2000.

Fischer, John Martin. "The Cards That Are Dealt You." *Journal of Ethics* 10 (2006): 107–29.

Fischer, John Martin. "Manipulation and Guidance Control: A Reply to Long." In *Action, Ethics, and Responsibility*, edited by Joseph Campbell, Michael O'Rourke, and Harry Silverstein. 175–86. Cambridge, MA: MIT Press, 2010.

Fischer, John Martin. *The Metaphysics of Free Will*. Oxford: Blackwell, 1994.

Fischer, John Martin, and Mark Ravizza. *Responsibility and Control*. Cambridge: Cambridge University Press, 1998.

Foster Wallace, David. "Good Old Neon." In *Oblivion: Stories*, 141–81. New York: Little, Brown, 2004.

Frankfurt, Harry. "Alternate Possibilities and Moral Responsibility." *Journal of Philosophy* 66, no. 23 (1969): 829–39.

Frankfurt, Harry. "The Faintest Passion." In *Necessity, Volition, and Love*. 95–107. Cambridge: Cambridge University Press, 1999.

Frankfurt, Harry. "Frankfurt-Style Compatibilism: Reply to John Martin Fischer." In *Contours of Agency: Essays on Themes from Harry Frankfurt*, edited by Sarah Buss and Lee Overton, 1–31. Cambridge, MA: MIT Press, 2002.

Frankfurt, Harry. "Freedom of the Will and the Concept of a Person." *Journal of Philosophy* 68, no. 1 (January 1971): 5–20.

Frankfurt, Harry. "Freedom of the Will and the Concept of a Person." In *The Importance of What We Care About: Philosophical Essays*, 11–25. New York: Cambridge University Press, 1988.

Franklin, Christopher Evan. "Plausibility, Manipulation, and Fischer and Ravizza." *Southern Journal of Philosophy* 44, no. 2 (2006): 173–92.

Gauthier, David Gauthier. *Morals by Agreement*. New York: Oxford University Press, 1986.

Glover, Jonathan. *Responsibility*. New York: Humanities, 1970.

Goodin, Robert. *Manipulatory Politics*. New Haven: Yale University Press, 1980.

Gorin, Moti. "Do Manipulators Always Threaten Rationality?" *American Philosophical Quarterly*, 51, no. 1 (January 2014).

Greenspan, Patricia. "The Problem with Manipulation." *American Philosophical Quarterly* 40, no. 2 (April 2003): 155–64.

Grice, H. P. "Logic and Conversation." In *Studies in the Way of Words*, 22–40. Cambridge, MA: Harvard University Press, 1989.

Grizzly Man. Film directed by Werner Herzog, 2005.

Hagger, Martin S., Chantelle Wood, Chris Stiff, and Nikos L. D. Chatzisarantis. "Ego Depletion and the Strength Model of Self-Control: A Meta-Analysis." *Psychological Bulletin* 136 (2010): 495–525.

Hausman, D. M., and B. Welch. "Debate: To Nudge or Not to Nudge." *Journal of Political Philosophy* 18 (2010): 123–36.

Hegel, G. W. F. *Elements of the Philosophy of Right*. Edited by A. Wood, translated by H. B. Nisbet. Cambridge: Cambridge University Press, 1991.

Henriques, Diana. "Madoff Scheme Kept Rippling Outward, Across Borders." *New York Times*, December 19, 2008. http://www.nytimes.com/2008/12/20/business/20madoff.html?pagewanted=all.

Hill, Thomas E. "Autonomy and Benevolent Lies." *Journal of Value Inquiry* 18 (1984): 251–67.

Holton, Richard. *Willing, Wanting, Waiting*. Oxford: Oxford University Press, 2009.

Hume, David. *Enquiry Concerning the Principles of Morals* [1777]. In *Enquiries Concerning Human Understanding and Concerning the Principles of Morals*, 3rd ed., edited by L. A. Selby-Bigge, with notes by P. H. Nidditch. Oxford: Clarendon Press, 1975.

Huxley, Aldous. *Brave New World*. New York: Harper & Row, 1946.

Job, V., C. S. Dweck, and G. M. Walton. "Ego Depletion—Is it All in Your Head? Implicit Theories About Willpower Affect Self-regulation." *Psychological Science* 21 (2010): 1686–93.

Isikoff, Michael. "'We Could Have Done This the Right Way': How Ali Soufan, FBI Agent, Got Abu Zubaydah to Talk without Torture." *Newsweek*, April 25, 2009.

Kant, Immanuel. *Groundwork for the Metaphysics of Morals* [1785]. Translated by Allen Wood. New Haven: Yale University Press, 2002.

Kant, Immanuel. *The Metaphysics of Morals*, In *Practical Philosophy* [1798]. Edited by and translated by Mary J. Gregor. Cambridge: Cambridge University Press, 1996.

Korsgaard, Christine. *Creating the Kingdom of Ends*. New York: Cambridge University Press, 1996.

Korsgaaard, Christine. *The Sources of Normativity*. Cambridge: Cambridge University Press, 1996.

Krugman, Paul. "The Chinese Disconnect." *New York Times*, October 22, 2009. http://www.nytimes.com/2009/10/23/opinion/23krugman.html?_r=1&hp.

Levy, Neil. "Addiction, Autonomy, and Ego-Depletion." *Bioethics* 20 (2006): 16–20.

Levy, Neil. "Addiction, Responsibility, and Ego-Depletion." In *Addiction and Responsibility*, edited by J. Poland and G. Graham, 89–111. Cambridge, MA: MIT Press, 2011.

Levy, Neil. *Hard Luck: How Luck Undermines Free Will and Moral Responsibility.* New York: Oxford University Press, 2011.

Locke, John. *An Essay Concerning Human Understanding.* Edited by Peter H. Nidditch. Oxford: Clarendon Press, 1979.

Locke, John. *Two Treatises of Government* [1689]. In *The Works of John Locke, A New Edition, Corrected.* London: Thomas Tegg, 1823.

Long, Todd R. "Moderate Reasons-Responsiveness, Moral Responsibility, and Manipulation." In *Freedom and Determinism*, edited by Joseph Campbell, Michael O'Rourke, and David Shier, 151–72. Cambridge, MA: MIT Press, 2004.

Mack, Eric. "In Defense of Blackmail." *Philosophical Studies* 41 (1982): 273–84.

MacKinnon, Catherine A. *Feminism Unmodified.* Cambridge, MA: Harvard University Press, 1987.

Manne, Kate. "On Being Social in Metaethics." In *Oxford Studies in Metaethics, Vol. 8*, edited by Russ Shafer-Landau, 50–73. Oxford: Oxford University Press, 2013.

Manne, Kate. "Tempered Internalism and the Participatory Stance." In *Motivational Internalism*, edited by Gunnar Björnsson, Caj Strandberg, Ragnar Francén Olinder, John Eriksson, and Fredrik Björklund. New York: Oxford University Press.

Markovits, Julia. "Acting for the Right Reasons." *Philosophical Review* 119, no.2 (2010): 201–42.

Marx, Karl. *Capital.* Translated by B. Fowkes and D. Fernbach. New York: Vintage, 1977–81.

Marx, Karl. *Marx Engels Collected Works.* New York: International Publishers, 1975.

Mayer, Jane. *The Dark Side: Inside the Story of How the War on Terror Turned Into a War on American Ideals.* New York: Doubleday, 2008.

McGinn, Colin. *Mindfucking: A Critique of Mental Manipulation.* Durham, UK: Acumen, 2008.

Mele, Alfred. *Autonomous Agents: From Self-Control to Autonomy.* New York: Oxford University Press, 2001.

Milgram, Stanley. *Obedience to Authority: An Experimental View.* New York: Harper & Row, 1974.

Mill, J. S. *On Liberty.* Edited by A. Castell. New York: Appleton, 1947.

Miller, D. T., J. S. Downs, and D. A. Prentice. "Minimal Conditions for the Creation of a Unit Relationship: The Social Bond Between Birthdaymates." *European Journal of Social Psychology* 28 (1998): 475–81.

Miller, Geoffrey. *The Mating Mind.* New York: Random House, 2000.

Mills, Claudia. "Goodness as Weapon." *Journal of Philosophy* 92 (1995): 485–99.

Mills, Claudia. "Politics and Manipulation." *Social Theory and Practice* 21, no. 1 (Spring 1995): 99–130.

Morris, Herbert. *On Guilt and Innocence*. Berkeley: University of California Press, 1976.

Muraven, Mark, and Roy F. Baumeister. "Self-regulation and Depletion of Limited Resources: Does Self-control Resemble a Muscle?" *Psychological Bulletin* 126 (2000): 247–59.

Murdoch, Iris. *The Sovereignty of Good*. London: Routledge & Kegan Paul, 1970.

Nagel, Thomas. "Concealment and Exposure." *Philosophy and Public Affairs* 27, no.1 (1998): 3–30.

Nahmias, Eddy. "Review of Freedom and Determinism." *Notre Dame Philosophical Reviews*, June 11, 2005. http://ndpr.nd.edu/review.cfm?id=2841.

Noggle, Robert. "Manipulative Actions: A Conceptual and Moral Analysis." *American Philosophical Quarterly* 33, no. 1 (January 1996): 43–55.

Nozick, Robert. "Coercion." In *Philosophy, Science, and Method: Essays in Honor of Ernest Nagel*, edited by Sidney Morgenbesser, Patrick Suppes, and Morton White, 440–72. New York: St. Martin's, 1969.

The Oath. Film directed by Laura Poitras, 2010.

O'Connor, Flannery. *Mystery and Manners: Occasional Prose*. New York: Farrar, Straus, and Giroux, 1970.

O'Connor, Timothy. *Persons and Causes*. New York: Oxford University Press, 2000.

Ormerod, David. *Smith and Hogan Criminal Law*, 13th ed. New York: Oxford University Press, 2011.

Orwell, George. *1984*. New York: Harcourt, Brace, 1949.

Parfit, Derek. *On What Matters*, vol. 1. Oxford: Oxford University Press, 2011.

Parfit, Derek. "Rationality and Reasons." In *Exploring Practical Philosophy: From Action to Values*, edited by Dan Egonsson, Jonas Josefsson, Bjorn Petersson, and Toni Ronnow-Rasmussen, 17–39. Aldershot: Ashgate, 2001.

Pavonne, Louisa. "Ten Tips for a Seller's Open House," April 1, 2007. http://voices.yahoo.com/ten-tips-sellers-open-house-262866.html.

Pereboom, Derk. *Living Without Free Will*. Cambridge: Cambridge University Press, 2001.

Pettit, Philip. *Republicanism: A Theory of Freedom and Government*. Oxford: Oxford University Press, 1997.

Piro, George. Interview with Scott Pelley. *60 Minutes*. CBS, January 27, 2008. http://www.cbsnews.com/video/watch/?id=3756675n.

Pratkanis, A. R. "The Cargo-Cult Science of Subliminal Persuasion." *Skeptical Inquirer* 16 (1992): 260–72.

Rawls, John. *A Theory of Justice*. Cambridge, MA: Harvard University Press, 1971.

Reage, Pauline. *Story of O*. New York: Ballantine, 1965.

Ross, W. D. *The Right and The Good*. New York: Oxford University Press, 1930.

Rousseau, Jean-Jacques. *The Social Contract and Other Later Political Writings* [1762]. Edited and translated by V. Gourevitch. Cambridge: Cambridge University Press, 1997.

Rovane, Carol. *The Bounds of Agency: An Essay in Revisionary Metaphysics.* Princeton: Princeton University Press, 1998.

Rudinow, Joel. "Manipulation." *Ethics* 88, no. 4 (July 1978): 338–47.

Russell, Bertrand. "Freedom in Society." *Harper's Magazine,* April 1926.

Sabini, John, and Maury Silver. "Lack of Character? Situationism Critiqued," *Ethics* 115 (2005): 535–62.

Saltz, Rachel. "Let's Film These Poor People; Maybke We'll Get Rich." *New York Times,* May 22, 2012, C3.

Satz, Debra. *Why Some Things Should Not Be For Sale.* Oxford: Oxford University Press, 2010.

Scanlon, Thomas. *What We Owe to Each Other.* Cambridge, MA: Belknap, 1998.

Schelling, Thomas. *The Strategy of Conflict.* Cambridge, MA: Harvard University Press, 1980.

Schmeichel, B. J., and K. D. Vohs. "Self-affirmation and Self-control: Affirming Core Values Counteracts Ego Depletion." *Journal of Personality and Social Psychology* 96 (2009): 770–82.

Schroeder, Mark. *Slaves of the Passions.* New York: Oxford University Press, 2007.

Schwartz, Barry. *The Paradox of Choice: Why More Is Less.* New York: Ecco/HarperCollins, 2003.

Sen, Amartya. *Development as Freedom.* New York: Alfred A. Knopf, 2000.

Skinner, Quentin. "The Republican Idea of Political Liberty." In *Machiavelli and Republicanism,* edited by Gisela Bock et al., 293–309. Cambridge: Cambridge University Press, 1990.

Spears, Dean. "Economic Decision-Making in Poverty Depletes Cognitive Control." Working paper #213, Princeton University, Center for Economic Policy Studies, December 2010. http://www.princeton.edu/ceps/workingpapers/213spears.pdf.

Steadman, James. "Moral Responsibility and Motivational Mechanisms." *Ethical Theory and Moral Practice* 15 (2012): 473–92.

Stern, Lawrence. "Freedom, Blame, and Moral Community." *Journal of Philosophy* 71 (1974): 72–84.

Stiff, Chris, and Nikos L. D. Chatzisarantis. "Ego Depletion and the Strength Model of Self-Control: A Meta-Analysis." *Psychological Bulletin* 136 (2010): 495–525.

Strawson, P. F. "Freedom and Resentment." In *Studies in the Philosophy of Thought and Action,* edited by P. F. Strawson.71–96 New York: Oxford University Press, 1968.

Strawson, P. F. "Tempered Internalism and the Participatory Stance." In *Motivational Internalism,* edited by Gunnar Björnsson, Caj Strandberg, Ragnar Francén Olinder, John Eriksson, and Fredrik Björklund. New York: Oxford University Press.

Sunstein, Cass R., and Richard Thaler. "Libertarian Paternalism is Not an Oxymoron." *University of Chicago Law Review* 70 (2003): 1159–1202.

Sussman, David. "What's Wrong with Torture?" *Philosophy and Public Affairs* 33, no. 1 (2005): 1–33.

Talk to Her. Film directed by Pedro Almódovar, 2002.

Taylor, James Stacey. *Practical Autonomy and Bioethics*. New York: Routledge, 2009.

Thaler, Richard, and Cass Sunstein. *Nudge: Improving Decisions About Health, Wealth, and Happiness*. New York: Penguin, 2008.

Theus, Kathryn T. "Subliminal Advertising and the Psychology of Processing Unconscious Stimuli: A Review of Research." *Psychology and Marketing* 11 (1994): 271–90.

Tice, D. M., R. F. Baumeister, D. Shmueli, and M. Muraven. "Restoring the Self: Positive Affect Helps Improve Self-regulation Following Ego Depletion." *Journal of Experimental Social Psychology* 43 (2007): 379–84.

Todd, Patrick. "Manipulation," In *The International Encyclopedia of Ethics*, edited by H. LaFollette, 3139–45. Oxford: Blackwell, 2013.

Twain, Mark. *The Adventures of Huckleberry Finn*. New York: Vintage Classics, 2010.

Velleman, J. David. *How We Get Along*. Cambridge: Cambridge University Press, 2009.

Velleman, J. David. *The Possibility of Practical Reason*. New York: Oxford University Press, 2000.

Vermeule, Blakey. *Why Do We Care about Literary Characters?* Baltimore: Johns Hopkins University Press, 2009.

Wallace, Jay, *Responsibility and the Moral Sentiments*. Cambridge, MA: Harvard University Press, 1994.

Wan, E. W., and B. Sternthal. "Regulating the Effects of Depletion through Monitoring." *Personality and Social Psychology Bulletin* 34 (2008): 32–46.

Ware, Alan. "The Concept of Manipulation: Its Relation to Democracy and Power." *British Journal of Political Science* 11 (1981): 163–81.

Wedgwood, Ralph. "The Fundamental Argument for Same-Sex Marriage." *Journal of Political Philosophy* 7 (1999): 225–42.

Wertheimer, Alan. *Exploitation*. Princeton: Princeton University Press, 1999.

What Went Wrong: Torture and the Office of Legal Counsel in the Bush Administration: Hearing Before the Senate Committee on the Judiciary Subcommittee on Administrative Oversight and the Courts, 11th Cong. 2009. http://www.judiciary.senate.gov/hearings/hearing.cfm?id=e655f9e2809e5476862f735da14945e6.

Wood, Allen. "Exploitation," *Social Philosophy and Policy* 12 (1995): 136–58.

Wood, Allen. "Exploitation." In *Exploitation*, edited by Kai Nielsen and Robert Ware, 1–25. New York: Humanities, 1997.

Wood, Allen. *Kantian Ethics*. New York: Cambridge University Press, 2008.

Wood, Allen. *Karl Marx*, 2nd expanded ed. London: Taylor and Francis, 2004.

Wryobeck, John, and Yiwei Chen. "Using Priming Techniques to Facilitate Health Behaviours." *Clinical Psychologist* 7, no.2 (October 2003): 105–108.

Zimmerman, Michael. *An Essay on Moral Responsibility*. Totowa, NJ: Rowman and Littlefield, 1988.

Zimmerman, Michael. "Taking Luck Seriously." *Journal of Philosophy* 99 (2002): 553–76.

Zwolinski, Matt. "The Ethics of Price Gouging." *Business Ethics Quarterly* 18 (2008): 347–78.

Index